jon r. luini
allen e. whitman

STREAMING AUDIO: THE FEZGUYS' GUIDE

New Riders

201 West 103rd St. • Indianapolis, Indiana, 46290
An Imprint of Pearson Education
Boston • Indianapolis • London • Munich • New York • San Francisco

Streaming Audio: The FezGuys' Guide

International Standard Book Number: 0-7357-1280-8

Library of Congress Catalog Card Number: *2001-099283*

06 05 04 03 02   7 6 5 4 3 2 1

Interpretation of the printing code: The rightmost double-digit number is the year of the book's printing; the rightmost single-digit number is the number of the book's printing. For example, the printing code 02-1 shows that the first printing of the book occurred in 2002.

Printed in the United States of America

Trademarks

Warning and Disclaimer

Publisher
David Dwyer

Associate Publisher
Stephanie Wall

Executive Editor
Jeff Schultz

Production Manager
Gina Kanouse

Acquisitions Editor
Kate Small

Development Editor
Damon Jordan

Technical Editor
David Warner

Product Marketing Manager
Kathy Malmloff

Publicity Manager
Susan Nixon

Project Editor
Todd Zellers

Copy Editor
Karen Gill

Indexer
Lisa Stumpf

Manufacturing Coordinator
Jim Conway

Book Designer
Suzanne Pettypiece

Cover Designer
Aren Howell

Proofreader
Sossity Smith

Composition
Gloria Schurick

Contents at a Glance

Table of Contents

About the Authors

Jon R. Luini has been in the trenches of streaming audio since the beginning. Involved in the first-ever live music concert broadcast (way back in 1994), Jon saw the Internet bubble inflate and explode (dodging numerous big money buyouts and attacks by hungry lawyers) as a founder of IUMA and MediaCast (the first Internet broadcast production company) and co-creator of *Addicted To Noise* (the first online music magazine). Jon runs an Internet and music consulting and technology company, Chime Interactive, plays in a band, and resides with his wife and expanding cat near Santa Cruz, California.

Allen E. Whitman likes anything that has a practical use. A lifetime musician and sometime journalist, Allen currently lives in Northern California's East Bay (pig-Latin for "Beast") region.

Jon and Allen have been providing Internet audio enlightenment as the FezGuys since 1996. Their writings have been featured in *Tape Op*, *EQ Magazine*, *Gig Magazine*, *Webmonkey*, *Pro Sound News*, *Replication News*, and *Revolution*. The FezGuys have been moderators, panelists, and interviewers at various industry events, including Streaming Media West, Webnoize Conference, Webzine, Macworld Expo, South By Southwest (SxSW) Interactive, North By Northwest (NxNW), NAB (National Association of Broadcasters), and the SF Expo for the Musician.

Visit them at www.fezguys.com. Harass them at fezguys@fezguys.com.

They welcome your comments, however bizarre.

Dedication

Jon: For all the talented people and great ideas that never made it, my lievert Sheila, and Motor who kept us company through it all.

Allen: For Sophie and the blossoming of common sense everywhere.

Acknowledgments

Business thanks (in alphabetical order):

A special thanks to Wild Bill Goldsmith (KPIG), Rusty Hodge (SomaFM), and Joe Satriani and Mick Brigden for their assistance in making the case studies possible.

Thank you to the following folks who ensured that we had the latest stuff: Keri Walker, Jeremy Buschine, Carol Hernandez, and Nicole Scott with Apple; Christine Berkley at Bias Inc.; Tony Santos and Nicole Scott from Edelman; Greg Ogonowski at Orban; Carmen Klotz at QDesign; Frank Casanova at QuickTime; Steve Foldvari and Louise Cote at Sonic Foundry; Kari Bulkley and Bruce Herbert at Sorenson Media; Caroline Dorsey at Telos; Bob Reardon at Waves.

General thanks (in no particular order):

Sheila Schat, Linda & Jim Luini, The Spanier clan, Ange Meyer (dOOd where's my car?), Jon Fox, Cory Smith, Eric Davis, Elan Papa, Jeff Patterson, Heidi De Vries, The Gorski Effect, Cindy Lawes, Betsy Winder, Allen E. Whitman III, Frankie Thorington, Ted and Joann Savarese, The Saunders Dude Ranch, Tom Makris, Hector LaTorre, Erik Bjorling, Richard Smith, Gwen Hammer, House o' Zoka, Jim Smith, Tony Savona, Bill Colitre, Jeff Mulholland, The Leet Family, Jamie Lemoine, James Ray, Michel Hoche-Mong, The Stand Out Selector, and, of course, Kate Small, Damon Jordan, Todd Zellers, and the rest of the patient editorial staff at New Riders (good thing you people have a sense of humor).

Tell Us What You Think

As the reader of this book, you are the most important critic and commentator. We value your opinion and want to know what we're doing right, what we could do better, what areas you'd like to see us publish in, and any other words of wisdom you're willing to pass our way.

As the Associate Publisher for New Riders Publishing, I welcome your comments. You can fax, email, or write me directly to let me know what you did or didn't like about this book—as well as what we can do to make our books stronger.

Please note that I cannot help you with technical problems related to the topic of this book, and that due to the high volume of mail I receive, I might not be able to reply to every message.

When you write, please be sure to include this book's title and author as well as your name and phone or fax number. I will carefully review your comments and share them with the author and editors who worked on the book.

Fax: 317-581-4663

E-mail: stephanie.wall@newriders.com

Mail: Stephanie Wall
         Associate Publisher
         New Riders Publishing
         201 West 103rd Street
         Indianapolis, IN 46290 USA

Introduction

What Is This Book?

In this book, you'll find everything you need to know about getting started, using, and mastering the basics of streaming audio. Maybe you suddenly find yourself with the responsibility of upgrading your company's entire online presence. Or you have an overwhelming desire to provide streaming music through your band's Web site. You might want to include the chortling glurbles of your infant grandchild (alongside the 500 photographs) on a family Web site. At any level of responsibility and urgency, you will find useful, real-world, step-by-step explanations empowering you to create streaming audio in just a couple of hours.

Assumptions About the Reader

You should already have a basic knowledge about operating a stereo system and a computer. For example, you should already know that *stereo* means two channels of sound. It is also assumed that you can get around on your computer comfortably: opening, using, and closing files, folders, and applications. It is further assumed that you know how to download and install applications from the Internet and already have a Web site, however simple. The next step is merely connecting those two common devices. It is really that simple.

Because Windows-based operating systems are currently the most prevalent desktop environment, and because Macintosh-based operating systems are heavily favored by the professional music community, this book focuses on these two operating systems. Users who are working within Unix or other operating systems who are conversant enough with Mac and Windows platforms can also make use of the information in this book.

Although this book contains software applications purchased from companies, it is also possible to get perfectly satisfactory results using shareware or freeware applications. A list of these and other applications can be found in the Appendix, "Tools and Resources."

This book uses a fair smattering of audio and computer tech jargon, but nothing too obscure. If you see an unfamiliar term, check the Glossary.

What This Book Will Give You

This book will give you the ability to take whatever sound, song, speech, or noise you fancy and place that sound, song, speech, or noise online, in a variety of formats, wherever you see fit. It also provides online resources to further your abilities.

What This Book Will Not Give You

- Information on downloading music online
- Resources for creating a Web site.
- Information on file sharing or peer-to-peer networks (P2P)
- A record contract
- Considerate neighbors
- Good digestion
- A mastery of the English language
- Hives

PART I

What It Is and What You Need

Part I: What It Is and What You Need

Streaming audio is a very technical process and there's some basic knowledge to cover first. A good understanding of these ground floor concepts will be the foundation for your comfortable understanding of this rapidly evolving medium. The chapters in Part I will introduce and define the necessary hardware and software tools and technologies. Very likely, you have much of it already, in the same room, waiting to be hooked up. Much of the software can be downloaded (if not already included when you purchased your computer) and used affordably—in some cases even free of charge. By the end of this Part, you'll have your system configured and your digital audio ready to be encoded into a choice of streaming audio formats.

CHAPTER 1

Introduction to Streaming Audio

Most people shake their heads in bewilderment at the mention of "streaming audio." The audio part's all right, they may think, but they're not so sure about the "streaming" bit.

Throughout recorded history humanity has made music. Once a person hears a good song, it's a safe bet that they wouldn't mind hearing it again. Composers and performers are asked for an encore, Thomas Edison invents a technology and tools to capture songs and take them anywhere. This portability rapidly evolves with the phonograph record, the airwaves, the cassette tape, the compact disc, and only recently to computers. It's only natural that someone would create a system to transfer songs between computers linked to the Internet. Streaming audio is that system.

What Is Streaming Audio?

Streaming audio is similar to traditional radio broadcasting except that the Internet is used to send and receive audio instead of using the airwaves. Just like turning on the radio, streaming audio is listened to in real time. This is much more convenient than the two-step process of listening to an audio file after a (frequently time-consuming) download is complete.

Several components are involved in listening to streaming audio. It starts with a connection to the Internet (via dial-up modem, DSL/ISDN, LAN, and so on) and a Web browser such as Netscape or Internet Explorer. Using the browser on a home computer, the user visits a Web site that offers audio of some kind or another. It may be music, or spoken word...anything that makes noise. When clicking on a link to that content, a player application starts playing automatically.

What really happens here is that the player application connects to a streaming server and requests the chosen streaming audio content. The streaming server takes the streaming audio from either a static preprocessed file or a continuous live feed (such as an ongoing Internet "radio" station) and begins sending the audio over the Internet connection to the user. After a brief buffering process, the audio is played through the user's speakers as it is received. (Buffering is performed to avoid excessive dropouts, and is similar to the feature on most portable CD players that prevents dropouts from jarring vibrations.)

As shown in Figure 1.1, streaming audio is delivered to the user's computer over an Internet connection, typically a telephone or cable line. The technology that makes streaming audio work is primarily about squeezing the original audio file down to as small a size as possible and still reach the user in some semblance of sonic legibility. Standard dialup telephone modems can only handle a limited amount of information—that's why streaming audio, to the ears of careful listeners, is often defined by its limitations. Most streaming audio does not sound like the original audio file. It has been compressed (squashed) and had portions of its original frequency spectrum removed. But remember: We're not talking about audiophile-quality sound here. We're talking about usefulness. Streaming audio is an extremely useful technology. By the time you are finished with this book, you should be able to see that for yourself.

FIGURE 1.1

Audio pathway from live-encoding station through the Internet, to server through the Internet, and to home PC and player/speakers.

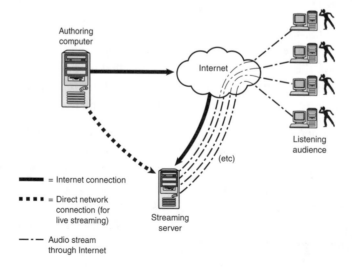

What Is the Difference Between Download and Streaming?

Unlike downloaded audio, streaming audio is heard as it is delivered to the user. When downloading audio content from the Internet at slower modem speeds, it's often necessary to wait as long as 30 minutes or more to hear one three-minute song. The familiar analogy for streaming audio is that it's like turning on your radio: You hear it immediately, in real-time. On the other hand, downloadable audio is like going to a store, buying a CD, and listening to it only after you have returned home.

A (Very) Brief History

Streaming audio is still a very young technology. Consider that the home computer has only been around a few years longer than the CD format. In terms of what the next few years has in store, you wouldn't be too far-out to consider the current state of streaming audio as the technical equivalent of vacuum tubes. A brief chronology follows:

- **Prior to 1991**—The Sun-AU format (also called Ulaw) is the downloadable audio standard. It's small (8 bit), available in mono only, and sounds like a really bad telephone connection. A handful of people have excruciatingly slow dial-up connections (2400 baud).

- **1993**—AIFF and WAV formats become commonly used for downloadable audio. The formats can sound great when not super-compressed, but files are too large and take too long to download. The average home dial-up rate increases to 14.4k baud and the World Wide Web arrives in our collective consciousness.

- **1994**—A digital media compression scheme called MPEG (for Motion Picture Experts Group) piggybacks the Web's dramatic increase in use. The scalable audio portion of MPEG technology offers much smaller files, which enables much faster download times and better sound quality. Individuals and corporations make players and encoders to support online audio's growing popularity.

- **1995**—Streaming audio enters the scene. High profile companies such as Progressive Networks (later to be renamed RealNetworks) with their RealAudio product and Xing Technologies' Streamworks product make the streaming audio easily available to all, although still at poor quality. Web users no longer have to wait for an audio file to download before listening.

- **1996**—RealNetworks and Xing begin to continually trot out new versions of their software. Macromedia's Shockwave Audio is released, allowing MPEG 1, Layer III (MP3) technology to be embedded into Web pages. The big players, including Microsoft and Apple, recognize the value of this rapidly expanding market. Everyone works feverishly to stay ahead of the pack, hoping to become the one standard for streaming audio. Smaller companies are buried or gobbled up in the increasingly aggressive fight for market share. Within months, millions of people are online. Launched later in the year, Liquid Audio, a distribution system, includes superior quality audio based on Dolby Labs AC3 technology. The hype about Internet audio peaks, and major corporations throw big money into securing market share.

- **1997**—RealNetworks expands its focus to include video. Microsoft launches NetShow (soon to become Windows Media).

- **1998**—The popular use of the MP3 format shakes the roots of the music business. Users begin to have access to fast connectivity via DSL and cable-modems, allowing for streaming of ever-higher quality audio. Internet radio arrives.

- **1999**—MP3's popularity and low price make it the most popular downloadable audio format. MP3 also offers some competition in the streaming audio arena. Portable MP3 players, such as the Rio, become available. Streaming audio formats that survive the first five years— RealMedia, Windows Media, and QuickTime—launch more aggressive marketing campaigns. Nullsoft, creators of the popular Windows-based MP3 player, Winamp, launches SHOUTcast, a simple and stable MP3-based streaming audio system.

- **2000–2001**—Web sites such as `www.live365.com` offer to handle individuals' streaming for free and large streaming service providers Akamai, Digital Island, and Speedera expand their services for corporate clients. The Internet hype bubble bursts but, thankfully, innovation continues.

Streaming Audio Uses

Streaming audio has become commonplace for a variety of commercial and non-commercial uses. From traditional (streaming a terrestrial FM radio station) to esoteric (streaming audio files of the sound of gamma rays hitting Earth's atmosphere), the technology has inspired millions of people to make their own online audio statement. A quick list of uses includes the examples mentioned previously, as well as private family Web sites, music or band promotion, public sector information, corporate marketing, emergency services dispatch, language and pronunciation tutorials, and live concerts. You can even listen to conversations with Tibetan llamas recorded in stone huts at high altitude. There's no limit to what the fertile mind can do.

Formats

In the context of this book, a *format* is the technology used to encode and stream audio over the Internet. The four major formats include MP3, Windows Media, RealMedia, and QuickTime, although other lesser known formats also exist. Anyone with suitable audio know-how, programming skill, and time can create a streaming audio format, and many have.

NOTE

A list of lesser-known formats such as Ogg Vorbis, Beatnik, Clipstream, and more is included in Chapter 12, "Advanced Authoring Techniques."

Why Different Formats Are Available

The reason that multiple formats exist is equal parts corporate struggle for dominance and the creativity and curiosity of software programmers (different people trying to solve the same problem in different ways). Although several streaming audio formats exist, this book focuses on the most commonly used formats: RealNetworks' RealMedia, Microsoft's Windows Media, Apple's QuickTime, and SHOUTcast's MP3 offering. A brief overview is given for the less common, but worthy open-source standard format Ogg Vorbis.

NOTE

Each format contains one or more *codecs*, a specific software tool used to compress and decode any kind of media, including audio. Some codecs overlap between formats. For example, all formats that are covered in this book support the MP3 codec. It can be confusing, but MP3 is technically only a codec, not a format.

How Do Formats Differ, and How Are They Similar?

Although all formats provide the same basic functionality, each has its pros and cons. All the formats support the MP3 codec, but some also have their own higher-quality, proprietary codec. All formats can be integrated with other technologies, such as Flash, DHTML, and JavaScript, as well as embedded into more elaborate presentations. Each format works better with some technologies than with others, so it is best to research each independently with your individual presentation requirements in mind.

RealNetworks' RealMedia streaming audio format has been around the longest, and streaming media is the company's backbone. Long experience and a fairly reliable product line on a variety of operating system platforms are offset by a high price tag relative to other formats. This is especially true if you run your own server. You will need to pay a license fee based on your maximum projected concurrent (simultaneous) user load. RealNetworks does provide free entry-level versions of their tools and servers to get you hooked. The RealMedia format includes its own optimized audio codec (just like Windows Media and QuickTime) that offers the same quality audio as MP3 in a smaller file.

Microsoft's Windows Media got a late start in the streaming audio game. However, because statisticians report that 90% of all computers use the Windows operating system (and Windows Media components are included on all new Windows-based PCs), it's been a cakewalk for Microsoft to quickly develop a huge number of Windows Media-enabled users. That makes it an easy sell for content providers to use the Windows Media format. Because Windows Media is a small part of a large company, crucial survival profitability from their streaming media tools isn't necessary. On the upside, Microsoft doesn't charge for the software. On the downside, because the server product is used to drive sales of the Windows OS, it's only available for Windows NT/2000. A Macintosh-compatible player is available, as well as limited support for Macintosh users wishing to author in the Windows Media format. The Windows Media format also includes a proprietary audio codec that, like RealNetworks and QuickTime, provides more efficient compression than MP3. (That is, it offers the same quality in less space, or better quality in the same space.)

QuickTime, Apple's proprietary digital media management technology, has been around longer than RealAudio; however, only in recent years has a full, streaming audio component been added. Partially because of Apple's history as primarily a desktop and content-creation platform (as opposed to being a server solution), it's been harder for Apple to get support from within the streaming industry. Strong historical ties to the creative community have helped compensate for this, along with a reinvigorated product line. Like Windows Media, QuickTime doesn't charge per-user server license fees. Entry-level encoding tools cost around $30. QuickTime's audio codec of choice is licensed from Canadian industry partner QDesign, which, yet again, provides better quality compression than MP3, with the same audio quality in less space, or better quality in the same space.

MP3 (MPEG 1, Layer III) is actually an open standard codec and not specifically a streaming audio format. MP3's wild popularity has resulted in it being included in many different Internet audio-delivery products, both for download and, in recent years, streaming. For the purposes of this book, Nullsoft's Winamp and SHOUTcast system will be used for MP3 streaming format examples. Licensing for the MP3 codec is controlled by Fraunhofer-Gesellschaft. Information on how to write your own encoder or player using the MP3 codec is available for a modest price, but including it in your software requires a licensing agreement with the Fraunhofer folks. The thoughtful crew at Nullsoft has taken care of all of the licensing issues and offers its software for free. Thus, no additional licensing fees are involved for each concurrent streaming user.

See Chapter 2, "Preparing Yourself," to decide which format works best for your individual needs.

Standards: Proprietary Versus Public

It's important to be aware of certain basic differences between streaming audio formats and their family of tools, products, and software. Some products are built on open systems and standards, such as MP3, allowing for any software author to add features and usefulness, in which case, all users benefit. Other products are built around proprietary formats, such as Windows Media, RealMedia, and QuickTime, and are designed to maintain the intellectual property value of the company, ensuring profit and longevity. Obviously, in times of market growth, there's considerable corporate investment toward proprietary system innovation. Conversely, during times of cutbacks, corporate proprietary advances tend to stop. But progress is always being made in the open-standard community. Everyone benefits because nobody has to toe a corporate bottom-line. Interestingly, the more popular that open-standards are, the more the corporate community participates in them. That means less control by a single corporation over streaming audio distribution channels. Who wants to suddenly find they can't afford to stream their music because the one company that provides the service has decided to double its price? It's an old story.

NOTE

Whenever possible, supporting open standards is encouraged. The use of open standards actively helps the industry as a whole by supporting common sense, real-world development of useful tools.

Authoring

Authoring, for the purposes of this book, is the process of choosing your audio content and digitizing, encoding, and delivering that content (in any variety of streaming formats) to your streaming server for delivery to your audience. In the authoring process, you'll use a number of different tools. This book will walk you through the processes with Step-by-Step tutorials. Though dictionaries haven't caught up with this new common usage, using the word "author" as a verb is sort of catchy.

Live Versus On-Demand

You can choose from two different authoring scenarios. The first scenario is "live," where real-time streaming audio is sent from the author's computer to a streaming server computer for redistribution to multiple listeners. The second scenario is "on-demand," where streaming audio files are authored and then uploaded to a streaming server computer for redistribution to multiple listeners. Live streams require an encoding application that talks directly to the streaming server. This process is susceptible to interruptions because more live network paths are involved, resulting in more points of possible failure. Because of this, live streaming is typically only performed when another alternative doesn't exist, such as a live concert broadcast or a radio simulcast.

When creating on-demand streams, authors can take advantage of third-party software tools that export to the desired streaming audio format. Third-party tools for on-demand authoring also offer advanced processes such as "set it and forget it" batch encoding for multiple audio files to multiple formats.

Server Stream Distribution

Server stream distribution is the process of delivering your audio content to your listeners. Without a server to take your audio programming and send it to listeners for you, you would need to make a connection from the authoring computer to each listener. Server stream distribution is also much easier and more efficient than e-mailing the content as an attachment to each person who wants to listen to it.

Unicast Versus Multicast

Streaming servers deliver audio to listeners in two primary ways. The first method, unicast, involves each listener receiving his own copy of the audio stream, like two cups connected by a string. A streaming server in unicast with 100 listeners would have a complex web of 100 cups and strings. In unicast, each listener requires as much bandwidth as the stream to which they are listening. This means that 100 users listening to your 24Kbps audio stream requires 2.4Mbps of bandwidth. (For more details about bandwidth, see Chapter 2.)

The other delivery method, multicast, involves multiple users on a network sharing the same bandwidth. This is the same as a traditional terrestrial radio station sending out signals into the airwaves just once and everyone within range tuning in to whatever is playing at that moment. On-demand content is typically not delivered via multicast because it's rare that multiple users will click on the same on-demand link at the same time. However, multicast holds the future of live streaming because it's a more efficient delivery method and can save enormously on bandwidth costs. Multicast also spreads bandwidth costs across many networks instead of focusing them all at one location. This makes it possible to avoid interruptions by obtaining programming from a different network path if problems exist. Of course, some people don't like the idea of having to pay for someone else's bandwidth, and this is one of the many issues to be resolved before multicast becomes the standard.

Unicast is still the standard streaming delivery model. For this reason, it will be used for the examples in this book.

Progressive (or HTTP) Versus Real-time Streaming

Real-time streaming occurs when a two-way conversation exists between the streaming audio player on the listener's computer and the streaming server. Advanced technologies take advantage of this two-way conversation to provide features such as "seeking" to a different location, switching to a lower-bandwidth stream (in case of interruptions), or deciding that a larger buffer is required. Some users behind firewalls can have problems streaming content from a realtime streaming server.

Progressive streaming (also called *progressive download* or *HTTP streaming*) occurs when a player application plays the audio as it receives a stream without being able to change the stream after it has begun.

Comparing the two technologies, imagine that you ordered food in a restaurant and then decided to have your dessert served before your main course. Real-time streaming could handle your request, but progressive streaming will make you wait until everything else has been served.

Progressive streaming is worth using because it can be done through any Web server (hence its other HTTP name). Audio streams delivered through a Web server avoid most firewall problems because typical firewall configurations allow web traffic.

Because real-time is the most common and feature-full type of streaming, this book uses it for most of its examples.

Summary

Now you've a got a handle on what streaming audio is and a basic understanding of how it works. It's time to plug this information into the next chapter and put it to work!

CHAPTER 2

Preparing Yourself

Encoding Computer and Audio Hardware Requirements

A few pieces of hardware are necessary to stream audio. Within your computer, certain specifications must be met, such as disk space, processor speed, and RAM. You also need a handful of necessary external objects, such as cabling and speakers. Having a home stereo system of some kind or another—placed close to the computer—is useful, too.

Disk Space

Digital audio, especially raw (uncompressed) stereo audio, takes up a lot of space on a computer's hard drive. A sound file of raw audio requires about 5MB of disk space per channel per minute. Therefore, a three-minute stereo song file is about 30MB. An entire album of three-minute songs requires somewhere in the neighborhood of 500–650MB of disk space, depending on how many songs are on the album. You get the picture. Since you're dealing with using a lot of disk space, it's important to know how much free disk space is available on your authoring computer.

With the price of disk space dropping faster then a Chicago Cubs' fly ball, it's feasible to acquire a hard drive large enough to have at least 1GB of disk space free at all times. In a perfect world, a minimum of 2GB of available disk space is recommended for your computer's hard drive. Calculate that figure after all of the applications and the operating system are installed.

Disk space on a hard drive can be thought of using the "if you build it, they will come" theory of physical space. More lanes on a freeway do not a quicker commute make. They mean more cars on the freeway at that exact moment.

A larger hard drive won't help you get your work done any faster, but you'll be able to have more things going on at once. And it's not like you won't use the additional space. Something always comes along to fill it up (see "Backup Storage" later in this chapter).

Processor Speed

Computers get faster clock speeds practically every day. Faster is good in the realm of streaming audio. A faster computer can handle more tasks simultaneously. It also means a smaller chance of getting bogged down or crashing as the machine manipulates big audio files. Nonetheless, older, "slower" machines can do the job, but encoding will take longer.

For Windows/PC users, a clock speed of 500MHz minimum is recommended. It's possible to get by on 300MHz, but you'll be catching up on your reading while waiting for audio to process. As of this writing, almost every new, off-the-shelf computer has a processor running at 1GHz clock-speed or higher.

For Mac users, a PowerPC era (or newer) machine is required. Machines using the G4 processor running at 450MHz or above are recommended.

RAM

As with processor speed and disk space, higher numbers are better. For either Mac or Windows platforms, a minimum of 128MB of RAM is preferred, although it's possible to squeak by on 64MB. New computers typically ship with 256MB of RAM installed. Extra RAM is available for as little as $35 for additional chunks of 256MB. If you're going to do a lot of audio processing, you'll definitely benefit from installing as much RAM as the computer can accommodate. Committed users frequently have 512MB to a full gigabyte of RAM.

To measure how much RAM is currently installed on your computer, perform the following simple steps:

On a Macintosh:

1. Click anywhere on the desktop, or select Finder as your current application.

2. Select About This Computer from under the Apple Menu icon at the top left of your screen.

3. Read the number after Built-In Memory in the pop-up window.

If you are using Windows:

1. Click the Start button at the lower-left corner of your screen.

2. Go to Settings and then Control Panel.

3. Within the Control Panel window, click System and read the number on the bottom line of the General area of the system pop-up window.

Audio Card

Most Macs process audio right out of the box through RCA or $\frac{1}{8}$" mini plug inputs. Some iMac and iBook hardware does not include audio inputs, so a Universal Serial Bus (USB) audio *frob* is required. This external device converts regular audio—for example, from your stereo—into the USB inter-face so that computers can process it.

Windows/PC systems generally come bundled with audio capability, but it's wise to peek around at the backside of your machine to make sure. Examining the box is easier than getting the manufacturer on the phone. Look for a single $\frac{1}{8}$" mini plug or dual RCA audio input/output plugs. If your computer doesn't have audio input/output capability, you need to install an after-market audio card. Pick up a SoundBlaster (or a *clone*) card from your local store or Web site.

NOTE

If you have an older computer and have been thinking about upgrading, now might be a good time. Finding an audio card for a machine that is five or more years old is probably more trouble than it's worth. Fully usable, new Windows computer systems—without video monitor—are currently available for as low as $600.

CD-ROM Drive

Any modern computer sold within the past five years typically comes with a CD-ROM drive installed. A CD-ROM drive is essential for bringing audio in from a compact disc. If you don't have a CD-ROM drive in your com-puter, it's a straightforward task to hook up your home stereo CD player—which is also, technically, a CD-ROM drive, except that it reads audio only, not data—to your computer's audio inputs.

If you're going to purchase a new computer, consider getting a CD-RW. CD-RW stands for Compact Disc-Read and Write. These are also known as CD burners. The price is slightly higher, but having and using a CD burner just might change your musical life.

Like the CD-ROM, a CD-RW can read audio or data CDs but, unlike the CD-ROM, it can also create, or burn, CDs, with audio or other file formats. Using blank CDs—easily purchased just about anywhere—you can use CD burners for backing up applications and crucial data, moving files off of your hard drive to make space for other work, or even creating the ultimate party mix CD for your next hoe-down. CD-RW burning speeds are constantly increasing and, yet again, it's good to get the fastest burner available.

Backup Storage

Make sure important files are backed up in case of disaster. Unfortunately, crashes and data loss happen more often than the computer industry would like to admit. Think of backups as insurance. Most professionals back up their work on a daily basis. The backup operation eventually becomes second nature and is always a good idea. Here, system speed can make a big difference.

Transferring copies of your work to an external hard drive or removable storage media (Jaz or Zip disks, for example), burning work-in-progress files onto a CD using a CD-RW drive or the older, tried-and-true computer-tape systems (such as DAT or cassette) are all serviceable. Given all options, either using an external hard drive or burning to a CD is recommended.

Sound Source

The sounds that you will be streaming over a network have to come from somewhere, and typically it's the CD-ROM drive or your home stereo. Extra Credit users might have mixers and more complex systems (see Chapter 11, "Advanced Audio Optimization"). In the most basic example, though, making the pieces of the entire system talk to each other is simply a matter of connecting the source of the sound to your computer's audio inputs. The source might be a CD, cassette, phonograph, radio, television, or even a live microphone. Of course, you could use existing digital files gleaned from the Internet and saved on your desktop. Answering machines have been used as well, too much general amusement. The possibilities are endless.

Cabling and Audio Routing

Almost every home stereo consumer electronic device comes with a set of RCA cables. Most sound cards come with ⅛" stereo mini plugs for input and output. You'll recognize ⅛" plugs from the headphone and line outputs of portable CD or MP3 players. Refer to Figure 2.1 to see the difference between the two types of cable plugs.

FIGURE 2.1

RCA cables and ⅛" stereo mini plugs are the industry standard for computer audio input and output.

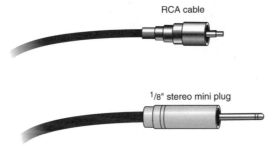

RCA cable

⅛" stereo mini plug

Cabling is necessary when connecting to and from each type and size of external audio source. Advanced users will investigate higher-quality cabling options such as XLR breakout boxes and pricey, but nice professional grade cable. The difference in audio quality between a ⅛" mini jack and stereo RCA cable is negligible.

NOTE

Some computers' ⅛" mic inputs are mono and should only be used if the computer's sound card has no line-level input.

All of the tools must be hooked together in the physical world so that they can do their thing in the digital world. After everything is set up, the cabling might look like plastic spaghetti that's fallen behind the desk, but the principle is basic. Simply route your audio source to your computer (see Figure 2.2).

FIGURE 2.2

A simple cabling diagram connecting your home stereo to your home computer.

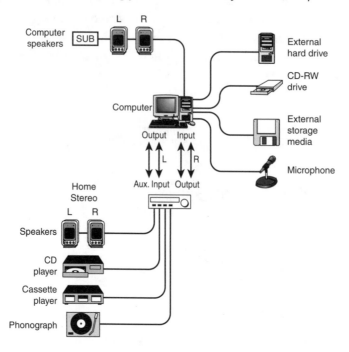

Monitor System

Monitor is a fancy word describing what you use to listen to your audio—it's your speakers, really. Your monitor could be little portable headphones for $5 or big, heavy, wooden speaker boxes costing thousands of dollars apiece. Your home stereo speakers will do fine. By the way, speakers are the most important element in your audio food chain, and this is an appropriate place to spend a little money. Depending on how careful a listener you are and how important audio quality is to you, a decent pair of speakers (that's right, a pair—stereo is where it's at!) is key for being able to hear what's going on. In addition, having quality speakers makes it easy to hear important frequency differences when performing advanced audio optimizations.

Many brands and models of self-powered speakers are specifically designed to be directly connected to a computer's audio output. These can be remarkably inexpensive and of good quality. A small system that includes a *subwoofer* is recommended. It shouldn't be necessary to spend more than $40 for a good computer speaker system.

Encoding Computer Software Requirements

There are a number of pieces of software to fit into the streaming audio puzzle. Below is a list of the basic tools you'll need.

Operating Systems: Windows and Macintosh

The operating system (OS) is the platform upon which all of your applications rest. Streaming audio software tools and applications are upgraded so rapidly that it's helpful to have the most recent and stable version of your OS as possible. For Windows users, it's advisable to have Windows 98 or newer. For Macintosh users, OS 9.1 or newer is recommended.

Streaming Audio Players

A player is a computer software application for playing back your streaming (or downloaded) audio files. Because you're learning several streaming formats, several players are necessary. Windows Media, RealMedia, and QuickTime all require their own players to stream files encoded using these formats. MP3 files, because manufacturers recognize MP3's popularity and because MP3 is not a proprietary format, can be streamed through any of the previously mentioned players, as well as a host of free or shareware players available online. Even though these freeware and shareware players are small, free, and simple to install, you can still purchase any number of other third-party players. These third-party players often take up a lot of memory, feature all manner of groovy visual effects to go along with your music, and cost as much as a tank of gas. This book uses Winamp, a popular and free download from www.winamp.com, as a basic MP3 streaming player for Windows. For the Macintosh MP3 streaming player, the book will use iTunes, which can be found at www.apple.com/itunes.

A list of players can be found in the Appendix, "Tools and Resources."

Rippers and Encoders

A *ripper* is a software application that pulls, or *rips*, a song from the CD in your computer's CD-ROM drive onto your computer as an uncompressed, raw audio file (WAV for Windows and AIFF for Macintosh).

An *encoder* is a format-specific software application that squeezes, or *encodes*, the raw audio file on your computer to a tiny size, making it ready for uploading to your streaming server.

Software tools are available that perform both tasks of ripping and encoding. Appropriately enough, they're called ripper/encoders. The examples in this book separate these two steps, so ripper/encoders won't be covered in depth.

A list of other rippers, encoders, and ripper/encoders can be found in the Appendix.

Waveform Editors

Almost like having a recording studio in a computer, waveform editing allows users to manipulate audio files in complex and necessary ways, at the click of a mouse. Volume level adjustments, fades, normalizing, and equalization, among other things, become easy to do. For Windows users, this book uses SoundForge 5.0 (www.sonicfoundry.com). For Macintosh users, Peak 2.6 LE (www.bias-inc.com) is the tool of choice.

A list of other waveform editors can be found in the Appendix.

Finding the Format That Fits

Each format has advantages and drawbacks. (See Chapter 1, "Introduction to Streaming Audio," for more information.) These factors include cost, ease-of-use, reliability, scalability (how many different ways you can encode), and the way they can work with other technologies. If you want to reach as many people as possible, consider providing multiple formats. In this way, listeners can choose what works best for them.

Operating System Performance

Anyone who has struggled with making Internet applications work properly knows that some formats perform better on certain operating systems than others. This is particularly noticeable for platforms created by the big players who also create operating systems. Microsoft's Windows Media provides the best experience for Windows users, whereas Apple's QuickTime is measurably more stable on MacOS. OS-independent formats RealMedia and MP3 used to favor Windows because of Microsoft market share dominance. With Apple's Phoenix-like rise from the ashes, RealMedia and MP3 performance on both operating systems has pretty much evened out. With increased consumer demand for Macintosh versions of the tools, companies have dedicated more resources to programming them efficiently on the Macintosh.

Users who plan to run their own streaming server using existing computers need to know on which operating system each streaming server can run. Many high-end users use a version of Unix (typically Linux, FreeBSD, or Solaris). See Table 2.1.

TABLE 2.1   Streaming Server Operating System Availability by Format

Format	Windows NT/2000	Windows 98/ME	Unix	Macintosh
Windows Media	yes	no	no	no
SHOUTcast	yes	yes	yes	no
RealMedia	yes	yes	yes	no
QuickTime	yes	no	yes	yes

Cost: Licenses, Hardware, and Bandwidth

The costs associated with running a streaming server are broken down into a few key areas: hardware, bandwidth, and licensing. Bandwidth and hardware remain the same regardless of the format. Hardware costs include the price of server computers, routers, and cable (see the section called "Server Computer and Audio Hardware Requirements," later in this chapter). Bandwidth costs are directly related to how many listeners tune in. Refer to "Server Stream Distribution" in Chapter 1 for a further discussion of bandwidth costs.

As noted in Chapter 1, server stream licensing is different for each format. Table 2.2 illustrates which formats require payment for software, which require additional fees based on how many concurrent users you want to support, and which provide basic-level free versions.

TABLE 2.2   Streaming Server Fees by Format

Format	Free Version Available	Full Version Costs	Per-User Fees
Windows Media	yes	no	no
SHOUTcast	yes	no	no
RealMedia	yes (25 users)	yes	yes
QuickTime	yes	no	no

Most organizations outsource their streaming server needs to other companies that specialize in this area. These companies wrap hardware, bandwidth, system administration, and licensing fees together for you. If you're streaming to a small number of listeners (up to 25 concurrent listeners), you can avoid fees in all formats. If you are serving a middle-sized streaming audience (up to 200 concurrent listeners) and intend to run your own server, you will do well to avoid formats that charge a per-user license. It might be better to outsource streaming server needs at this level.

Complexity and Flexibility

The common basic audio stream consists simply of a link on a Web page that opens the correct player, allowing the user to listen to the author's content. Authors might want to provide a more compelling experience by including video content, playlists, digital rights management (DRM), synchronization with other media, or other forms of interactivity. Your specific needs play a critical role in which format you choose. Windows Media and RealMedia have done extensive work to provide digital rights management, for example. If you plan to provide any of these somewhat more complex interactive add-ons to your streaming audio, spend time researching each format. Some formats have strengths and reliability in different areas. It's also not uncommon that the engineer who is making it all happen might be more comfortable with one particular format than another.

Server Computer and Audio Hardware Requirements

The following sections offer basic hardware requirements for setting up your own streaming server, as opposed to leasing from a third party. Note: A streaming server must support every one of your listeners. Its requirements shift radically based on a constantly fluctuating amount of concurrent users. The examples in this book use a machine that needs to unicast a 56k stream to 100 concurrent users.

Disk Space

Your streaming server will need enough disk space to not only store all of your streaming media, but also to store logfiles documenting users (so that you can run reports on that data) and the operating system. Logfiles on a heavy-use streaming server can quickly take up gigabytes of disk space. Streaming servers should start with at least a 40GB hard drive. More high-end users will want to consider hundreds of gigabytes of disk space and even optimized disk systems such as the fast SCSI RAID configurations.

Processor Speed

Since server computers need to be very flexible to deal with widely varying processing demands it's best to have as fast a clock-speed as you can get. Macintosh and Windows recommendations are below.

For Windows/PC (or Linux/FreeBSD UNIX) users, a clock speed of 1GHz minimum is recommended.

For Mac users, a PowerMac G4 running at 850MHz or above is recommended.

RAM

For streaming media server computers, at least 1GB of RAM is recommended. It's possible to get by on less, but with pricing where it is these days, why bother risking running out of memory?

Network Card

You'll want to make sure you have a 100Mbps-network card to give yourself enough networking headroom. Due to TCP/IP networking protocols, 10Mbps cards can start to have problems with collisions and retransmission far below the theoretical 10Mbps maximum.

Backup Storage

As always, back up your vital data. Backing up gigabytes of data can be time-consuming work, so choose a method that's quick, local, and portable (so you can remove the data backup to another location in case of fire, earthquake, or other disaster). Digital linear tape (DLT) is a good solution for server backups, but having extra disk drives dedicated for backups is often a cheaper (and quicker to recover from) solution.

Serving from Your Encoding Computer

If you plan to use the same computer to serve and encode, remember to account for the hardware requirements that both duties involve. It's unwise to choose this configuration if you are serving any more than 25 users because it doubles the chance of problems. What might only be a temporary resource glitch on an encoding computer could turn into a fatal error when shared with a streaming server. However, serving from your encoding computer to low numbers of concurrent users still doesn't guarantee seamless operation. If you do choose to encode and stream from the same computer, one way to increase the reliability of your stream is to use a dedicated box just for that purpose.

Network Bandwidth Requirements

A big part of streaming audio is about transferring encoded streams across networks. Transferring a single stream from your authoring computer to a server computer on the other side of the room requires a small amount of bandwidth. Transferring many files or live streams to servers at a remote location and providing for heavy streaming traffic can require enormous government-level amounts of bandwidth. Here's a general assessment of bandwidth needs for streaming audio.

Authoring

Authoring streaming audio requires a certain amount of network connectivity (bandwidth) between you (the author), a streaming server, and your listeners.

The bandwidth that is necessary between the encoding computer and your streaming server is based on whether you're using a live or on-demand encoding scenario. For on-demand encoding, any connection will suffice. Author scheduling requirements are the only important factor in uploading content. Authors can leave a transfer running all night over a dial-up modem connection or do it all in 10 minutes over a broadband DSL line. Although the former scenario might make you drink yak-butter tea and wear burlap, either speed still gets the job done.

When authoring within the live scenario, sufficient bandwidth must exist between the author's encoding computer and the streaming server to enable the stream to be delivered in real-time. Advanced users set up dedicated connections, such as ISDN lines, as insurance to lessen the chance of a stream's delivery being affected by Internet connectivity bottlenecks. A live stream's smooth delivery is also assisted by keeping some headroom within your connectivity.

Always factor in a little space for network overhead, emergency troubleshooting, or possible line problems. If you know you have 128k available (as with ISDN lines), don't send more than an 80k or 100k stream over it. When using a residential DSL connection to send a live stream to a server, encode your audio at bit rates as low as possible to minimize the chance of interruption. The average route from the author's computer to the listener's computer involves about 10 other computers scattered throughout the Internet. (It's not uncommon to go through 20 or even 30.) Each computer you go through is another place you have absolutely zero personal control over the connection's stability. Remember, if your live encoding stream is interrupted, it affects every person who is listening.

Streaming Server

Unicast streaming means that a separate copy of each audio stream is sent to every concurrent listener. This also explains why the largest bandwidth requirements are between the streaming server and listeners. If 100 people are listening to a single 56Kbps stream at the same time, it's necessary to provide for 100 users at 56Kbps each. This amounts to 5600Kbps, or 5.4Mbps. As you can see, a popular stream being accessed by many people at the same time can quickly require substantial bandwidth at the server.

Although you've heard it already, it bears repeating: When choosing a format, it's vital to estimate how many people you need to stream to concurrently.

The more users to which a streaming server delivers content, the more resources (Internet connectivity and computer processing power) that are required. These resource requirements quickly become more pronounced when you improve the quality of your content by encoding at higher bit rates. Obviously, streaming a song to two people simultaneously doesn't require as powerful a server and as much bandwidth as streaming an Emmylou Harris concert live to 10,000 people. You might be able to stream the former from a residential DSL connection, but you can't do the latter without a rack of computers and many megabits of bandwidth.

When determining how many concurrent users you want to support, remember to allow extra headroom for other related traffic. For example, if you're using the same network connection for serving Web traffic, calculate in those requirements as well. If you plan on running a streaming server from a home connection, also include whatever bandwidth you might need for browsing the Web, sending and receiving e-mail, and so on. Finally, always check with the ISP that is hosting your server to get bandwidth cost estimates. Take a look at Table 2.3 to get a feel for how much bandwidth is required for your projected audience.

TABLE 2.3   Streaming Server Bandwidth Needs by Audience Size

Stream Bit Rate	# Concurrent Listeners	Bandwidth Required
24Kbps	1	24Kbps
	10	240Kbps
	100	2.3Mbps
	1000	23Mbps
56K	1	56Kbps
	10	560Kbps
	100	5.4Mbps
	1000	54Mbps
128K	1	128Kbps
	10	1.2Mbps
	100	12Mbps
	1000	125Mbps

About Your Audio Source

It's always preferable to use the absolute best-sounding source material when creating audio files for streaming. The nasty hissing and distortion heard on old cassette tapes only becomes worse through the process of encoding. For the purposes of clarity, try to bring your audio into the computer from a digital source (CD, DAT, minidisc, or digital video, for example). Still, perfectly serviceable streaming audio files can be crafted using analog sources (such as Hi-8, VHS, phonograph record, or clean cassette). For live streaming, be mindful of the Gain Chain to assist you in achieving the highest possible audio quality (see "The Gain Chain" in the next section).

Audio Optimization

Since the sound quality of streaming audio is so often defined by its limitations it's helpful to do a little modifying to the overall tone and shape of your source audio. Don't worry, the process is pretty straightforward and, once you've tried it the first time, you'll realize it's actually kind of fun. You're changing the way your source audio sounds and you'll find you can do some odd things. Maybe you won't actually end up saving your source audio in those odd and interesting ways, but it's nice to know you can do it, just the same. Below are a couple of tools and techniques to get you started.

The Gain Chain

From the first time a sound source is recorded, and with each succeeding generation, the overall quality of your audio is defined by the gain setting. The gain is simply the volume at which the sound source is recorded onto the recording medium (tape, minidisc, DAT, and so on). Too high a gain setting creates unwanted distortion. Too low a gain setting requires the listener to turn up the volume so high that the inherent distortion of that recording medium (usually below the threshold of hearing at normal volume levels) becomes plainly audible. Both scenarios are bad juju. The key is to set the volume level as high as it will go within any given recording medium without distorting. Trust your ears here. If it sounds good, it usually is.

Fading

The human ear and brain are typically not too keen on sounds that begin and end abruptly. If you are creating short audio streams from a longer piece of sound, fade in the beginning of the segment and fade out the end. Experiment with fast and slow fades to see which makes more sense for that particular piece of audio. Your waveform editor is the application to perform these simple functions. It is also helpful to place one or two seconds of silence at the beginning of your streaming audio file. Before your online listener actually hears a sound, they'll often experience a brief awkward pause while the server accessed by their computer gets its act together. This is called *buffering*.

NOTE

It's a good idea to add an extra second or two of silence at the end of the song as well. Sometimes formats lose the last second or two of your streaming audio file.

Compression

Compression (standard *lossless* audio compression) is a gentle massaging or sculpting of sound to smooth out the difference between loud and soft sections. Compression is useful for preparing audio files for encoding. Streaming formats, after being piped through online networks, tend to sound better if the pre-encoded source audio is all about the same volume. A waveform editor is the tool to use here. Audio gurus spend lifetimes understanding the nuances of perfect compression. But this is only streaming audio, so don't stress it. Most waveform editors provide a few basic settings. Try a little bit of compression on your audio file, prior to the encoding process. Let your ears be your guide.

NOTE

Encoding and decoding an audio file for the streaming process is also a form of compression, called *lossy* compression. In lossy compression, elements of the sound are permanently thrown away to save space.

EQ

Speaking of streaming audio's ability to deliver decent sound, did we mention carving up the sound frequency spectrum? Format codecs are able to squish large raw audio files down to a tiny size by removing parts of the audio that are seen as redundant. Using your waveform editor, perform the following basic EQ changes to your source audio to help them be better sounding streaming audio files, especially when encoding at low (below 56Kbps) and medium (up to 96Kbps) bit rates.

If you do plan to encode at low to medium bit rates, especially when using the live encoding scenario, remove the lowdown lows (39Hz and below). Your audio file won't need them where it's going. While you're at it, toss out the high-end highs (18kHz and above), too. When encoding for streams below 56Kbps, experiment with boosting mid frequencies (around 2.5kHz) to compensate for the frequencies you threw away. The overall sound quality of low bit rate encoded spoken word files especially benefit from this treatment.

All this sonic manipulation won't sound very good when compared to the original source recording, but it'll translate a lot better through the encoding process as a sonically legible file. The encoder (when encoding at low bit rates) removes these frequencies anyway. Performing these EQ changes prior to the encoding process frees the computer to spend more time doing a good job encoding the frequencies that matter. You won't have to adjust much unless you're actually removing certain frequency ranges. A little boost or cut of certain frequencies goes a long way.

On-Demand Audio: Getting Your Source into Digital Format

In the following two examples, you'll rip a song from a CD to a digital (uncompressed) audio file on your computer desktop.

STEP-BY-STEP: Ripping from a CD to a Digital File Using Audiograbber v1.80

1. Insert an audio CD into the CD-ROM drive of your Windows computer.

2. Run the Audiograbber program and select Settings, MP3 Settings (see Figure 2.3).

FIGURE 2.3

Grab To: Wav file selected in Audiograbber's "MP3 Settings."

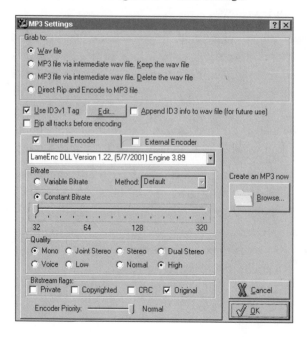

3. In the Grab To area of the dialog box, select Wav File. This setting tells Audiograbber to make the ripped file into a WAV format file.

4. Go to Settings, General Settings and choose the directory location for your folder of WAV audio files.

5. Click OK.

6. Make sure only the tracks you want to rip are checked in the Track List dialog box. If track names do not show in the Track List box, click the Freedb button (the Penguin icon) in the Audiograbber main window. Through your computer's active online connection, Audiograbber can access Freedb's giant online database of CD track information. If track names still don't show up, you have to enter them manually. It's worth doing even though it's time consuming; it's better than chasing down obscure Track 1 and Track 2 names in your folder.

NOTE

The free version of Audiograbber only allows half of the tracks on any given CD to be recorded at once. You can restart the program multiple times to have it re-do the random selection of which tracks are available for ripping.

7. With your settings and your tracks selected, click the Grab button. Audiograbber rips the files from the CD. Ripped files are then placed in the folder you specified. Your files have gone from your CD to your computer (see Figure 2.4)!

FIGURE 2.4

Click Grab to begin ripping your selected tracks with Audiograbber.

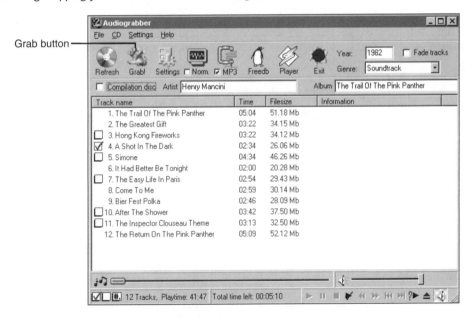

STEP-BY-STEP: Ripping from CD to a Digital File Using iTunes

1. Insert an audio CD into the CD-ROM drive of your Macintosh computer.

2. Run the iTunes program.

3. After a few seconds, iTunes recognizes the CD and attempts to retrieve track names and info by using your active online connection to look up the CD on the CDDB database. If your CD is not recognized by CDDB, you should enter that information manually to avoid being saddled with confusing default names like Track 1, Track 2, and so on.

4. Go to Edit, Preferences (⌘+Y) to set your importing preferences.

5. Choose the Importing tab within the Preferences dialog box and then choose AIFF Encoder. This setting tells iTunes to make the ripped file into an AIFF. For Configuration within the Preferences dialog box, leave the default Automatic setting, unless you want to change channels, sample rate, or sample size, in which case you can select Custom (see Figure 2.5).

6. Click OK to exit Preferences.

NOTE

Within the Preferences dialog box, click the Advanced tab and make a note of your Music Folder Location. You'll want to know where this is. It's where your ripped AIFF files are placed.

FIGURE 2.5

Set the Importing option to "AIFF Encoder" in the iTunes Preferences window.

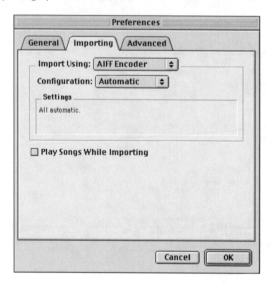

7. In the Source windowpane on the left side of the main iTunes window, press ⌘+1 to display the main iTunes window if it is not already visible. Then select the CD name, which displays the track list of your CD.

8. Next it's time to choose your tracks for ripping. iTunes chooses all the tracks on the CD by default. If you don't want all the tracks, simply uncheck the box next to the appropriate track name.

9. Click the Import button in the top-right corner of the iTunes main display. iTunes is now ripping your chosen tracks to the Music folder. When the ripping process is complete, a chime sounds and a green checkmark appears next to each imported (ripped) track (see Figure 2.6).

FIGURE 2.6

Click the Import button to start iTunes ripping your chosen tracks from CD into AIFF format.

10. Go to your music folder location and take a look to see that it's there. You now have happy uncompressed AIFF audio files ready for manipulating in any number of fun ways!

In the following two examples, you'll convert a song from an audio source to a digital (raw, uncompressed) audio file on the computer desktop.

NOTE

Directly after completing either of the following two Step-by-Step tutorials, take a moment to remove what is called DC offset from your newly created digital file. DC offset occurs as low frequency inaudible noise resulting from equipment grounding problems. If present, DC offset can skew the results of subsequent digital edits. Use the DC offset removal function in Peak or SoundForge (or any other waveform editor) immediately after recording a digital audio file from an analog source.

STEP-BY-STEP: Converting from an Analog Source to a Digital File Using a Waveform Editor (SoundForge for Windows)

1. Plug your audio source stereo RCA outputs into the stereo ⅛" miniplug input on the back of your Windows machine. (Refer to the section titled "Cabling" earlier in this chapter.)

2. Stick the plastic piece of recorded audio into the medium's player.

3. Open SoundForge on your Windows computer.

4. Click the big glowing red Record button (Ctrl+R).

5. In the dialog box that appears, look at Recording Attributes and make sure the settings read as follows: 44,1000 Hz (sample rate), 16-bit (sample size), and Stereo. If you want other settings, simply click New and set them accordingly.

6. Check the Monitor box to have the meters display the input level (see Figure 2.7).

FIGURE 2.7

Select Monitor in SoundForge's recording window.

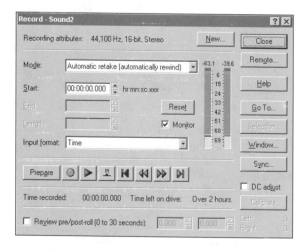

7. With your tape cued to the loudest section of the piece of music you are converting, start your source audio. Watch the vertical lights reflecting the input levels coming in to the waveform editor. Make sure the lights stay green. Red lights mean the input signal might be too loud and could distort the file. If necessary, change the input level to ensure a smooth recording. Numbers above the input levels tell you the peak level reached. These numbers need to remain negative to ensure that distortion doesn't occur. Use the standard Windows Volume Control application to adjust the volume accordingly. To open Volume Control, go to Start, Programs, Accessories, Entertainment, Volume Control. After you have Volume Control open,

go to Options, Properties and select Recording in the Adjust Volume For section of the dialog box. Select the appropriate input device (in this case, use Line Input). Adjust the volume slider until the input level lights are green again (see Figure 2.8).

FIGURE 2.8

The default Windows Volume Control Panel in Recording mode.

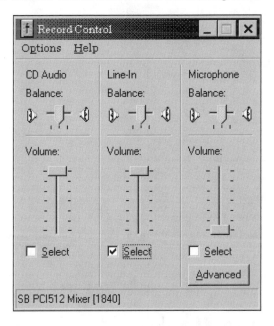

8. You can also use the Volume Control utility that came with the software included in your soundcard. This piece of software might have more features, and you might find it easier to use than the Windows Volume Control application. Either way, changing the settings on the former also changes the settings on the latter.

9. Position your source audio to the start of the song.

10. Back in SoundForge, in the Record dialog box, click Prepare. A blinking green box will say [Prepared] and show recording time available on your hard drive.

11. Start your source audio and then press the big glowing red Record button. Input level meters, elapsed time recording, and time left on drive are shown in the dialog box. The [Prepared] blinking green light changes to a blinking red [Recording] (see figure 2.9).

FIGURE 2.9

Click SoundForge's glowing red Record button to start recording.

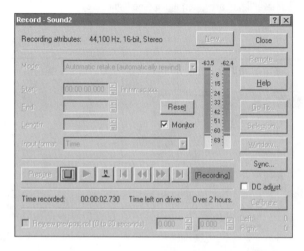

12. At the end of the song, stop the source audio and press the Stop button in the Recording dialog box. Save your completed WAV file to your music folder (naming it ending in .wav). The uncompressed WAV file is now ready to be manipulated in any number of clever digital ways.

STEP-BY-STEP: Converting from an Analog Source to a Digital File Using a Waveform Editor (Peak for Macintosh)

1. Plug your audio source stereo RCA outputs into the stereo ⅛" miniplug input on the back of your Macintosh. (Refer to the section titled "Cabling" earlier in this chapter.)

2. Position the start point of your source audio.

3. Open Peak on your Macintosh computer (see Figure 2.10).

4. In Peak, select Audio, Record Settings. Within the Record Settings dialog box, set the file format to AIFF. Click Device and Sample Format, and within that dialog box, choose 44.1KHz sample rate, 16-bit sample size, and Stereo. Set Compression to None. Set Source to the computer audio input connected to your analog source. (In this case, choose Sound In.)

FIGURE 2.10

Set the correct settings in Peak's Record Settings window.

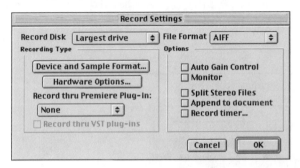

5. Still in the Source pop-up, and with your source audio cued to the loudest section of the piece of music you are converting, start your source audio. Watch the horizontal lights reflecting the input levels coming into the volume setting panel. Make sure the lights stay green. Red lights mean the audio input is too loud and will distort the file. If necessary, move the Gain slider to adjust the input level and ensure a smooth recording (see Figure 2.11).

FIGURE 2.11

Set the volume gain accordingly.

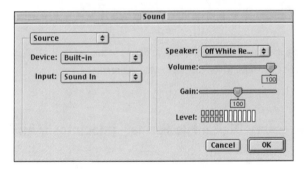

6. Click OK to exit Record Settings.

7. Position the start point of your source audio.

8. In Peak, go to Audio, Record (⌘+R or click the Record button on the main toolbar). A Record dialog box appears.

9. Click the Record button on this dialog box. Start your source audio. You'll see the waveform displayed in the Record box while the song is playing. It tells you how much available record time is left on your hard drive. When the song is finished, click Stop on your computer, and then stop the source audio (see Figure 2.12).

FIGURE 2.12

Click Peak's record button to begin recording your song.

10. Enter the filename and save it into your music folder as prompted by Peak. Peak requires saving to the same drive onto which the audio was recorded.

11. An AIFF digital file is now yours to command.

Converting to the Necessary Digital File Format (Macintosh/AIFF and Windows/WAV)

You can use your waveform editor to convert digital sound files to different file formats (AIFF to WAV and vice versa). Both SoundForge and Peak will read and play both AIFF and WAV files, among others. Use your waveform editor to Save As in your chosen digital file format.

Brief General Overview of Online Music Legal Issues

Up until the early 1990s, the U.S Government took a hands-off approach to the Internet and its uses. The Digital Millennium Copyright Act (DMCA), passed in 1998, has attempted to address copyright issues relating to use of music on the Web. As of this writing, recent changes show some hint of relaxing the stranglehold that the music business is attempting to enforce over online use of copyrighted music. This is important because it means people who want to create online radio stations using others' music now have a simple way to get permission to do so.

If you aren't interested in educating yourself about this hot big money topic, that's fine. But do remember that when it comes to creating streaming audio files online, the simple and safe approach works best. If you own the rights, you can do whatever you want with your audio. If you use audio from another source—a source to which you don't own the rights—you are bound by local copyright law. Like all laws, you are responsible for toeing the line. Ignorance is no excuse! Turn to the Appendix for resources that provide more in-depth information about how those laws work.

Summary

Now you've got a handle on some of the key issues around authoring your own streaming audio and, heck, you've now got a digitized, uncompressed raw audio file on your desktop just begging to be encoded and streamed. Let's get to it!

PART II

How To Do It (Processes)

Part II: How To Do It (Processes)

Aggressive competition for market share between the companies behind the big streaming formats has been both good and bad. On the one hand, it means a broad user base for authors, rapid technological development, and lower (or free) prices for software tools. On the other hand, it means a dizzying array of new products with very similar features released many times each year. The good news is that the importance of backward compatibility is being recognized in new encoding software releases. This means that content authored using today's encoding and production tools will still play using next year's version.

A note of definition: Content we author for on-demand streaming we call "files" and when authoring live streams we use "streams."

If you don't already have a free format-specific player on your computer, now would be a good time to download and install it. You'll need it soon enough to listen to your encoded files and check out what (and how) others author their streaming audio.

The Step-by-Step tutorials in this Part make the following assumptions:

- **On-demand Files**   You'll take raw source AIFF (Mac users) or WAV (Windows users) files and encode them into compressed streaming files. For help capturing to AIFF or WAV files, see the Step-by-Step, "Getting Your Source into Digital Format," in Chapter 2, "Preparing Yourself."

- **Live Streams**   You'll be feeding a live input into your authoring computer's soundcard.

- **Target Audiences**   Both on-demand files and live streams will be authored for two listening audiences: 56k dial-up modems and 384k DSL users.

- **Audio Content**   You'll be encoding music with vocals in stereo as your source audio.

For more information on any format, see the Appendix, "Tools and Resources."

CHAPTER 3

Using RealMedia

RealNetwork's RealAudio is a popular and easy-to-use format for streaming audio. The name *RealAudio* defines the audio component of the RealMedia streaming system. RealMedia is, in turn, one portion of the company's RealSystem iQ platform, which allows users to create, stream, and archive all manner of media-related file types including video, slideshow, text, and pictures (all with their standard *Real* prefix). The platform also includes e-commerce and digital rights management components.

One of RealNetworks' advantages is its SureStream technology. SureStream provides a simple way to encode a file only once to be delivered at optimal quality for users with different connection speeds. The SureStream technology is incorporated during the encoding process by embedding multiple audio streams in the encoded live stream or on-demand file. SureStream also enables the RealMedia player to switch bit rates in real time, offering some insurance for a smooth delivery of the stream across networks of fluctuating bandwidth.

NOTE

SureStream should not be delivered via HTTP/Progressive streaming. Refer to Chapter 1, "Introduction to Streaming Audio," for more information.

Software Encoders: Free Versus Pay

RealNetworks provides the RealProducer software product to author RealMedia content and also licenses their encoding libraries to third-party software companies. You can use these third-party companies' waveform editors to author on-demand RealMedia files. For live stream authoring, you can use RealProducer or other third-party tools such as Discreet's Cleaner Live. The third-party tools cost money and are not specific to the RealMedia format. In addition to RealProducer 8.5, these Step-by-Step tutorials will use Sonic Foundry's Sound Forge (Version 5.0) and Bias Inc.'s Peak (version 2.62 TDM) waveform editor programs to author RealMedia on-demand files.

RealProducer is the preferred software for authoring and encoding RealMedia streaming content. It's available in two flavors: Basic (free) and Plus ($199.95, with a 30-day money-back guarantee). Is it worth it for you to spend the money? It depends on your needs. The Plus version has advanced features that benefit the committed streaming audio author. The Basic version is perfectly acceptable for beginning authors.

Both versions can create RealMedia audio and video files for uploading to a RealServer. Both support encoding on-demand files and can also capture live audio and video for delivering live streams. Both versions support batch encoding (helpful if you're working with multiple files), although the Plus version allows for more flexibility and is better at doing its job in the background while you use the same computer for other activities. The Plus version also enables authors to generate backward-compatible RealMedia streams. Backward-compatibility is helpful as not everyone downloads every new version of the RealPlayer. RealProducer Plus also includes two other potentially useful tools: an on-demand file editor for files that are already RealMedia-encoded, and a simulator to show how various bandwidth conditions affect a live stream.

Target audience is also a factor in choosing which version of RealProducer is most appropriate for your needs. *Target audience* refers to how RealProducer describes the connection speed of your projected listeners (such as 56K modem, DSL, and so on). Using the SureStream technology, RealProducer includes multiple bit rates in your encoded stream for each selected target audience. RealProducer Basic can author up to two target audiences. The Plus version can author up to eight. The actual bit rate and codecs that are used during the encoding process are determined from default settings within RealProducer. Advanced RealProducer Plus users can override these defaults, choosing specific bit rate and codec combinations to fine-tune their on-demand files and live streams.

A full comparison of features for both RealProducer Plus and RealProducer Basic is available at www.realnetworks.com/products/producer/comparison.html. RealProducer Basic is available for download at www.realnetworks.com/products/producer/related_products.html. The Plus version can be purchased and downloaded at www.realnetworks.com/products/producer.

If you're just starting out as a RealMedia content author, download the Basic version. If you're planning on doing a lot of streaming or if you're one of those who have to have the latest, greatest, most full-featured version of any product and don't mind spending the money, RealProducer Plus will make you happy.

The examples in this book use RealProducer Plus. If there's any task that's accomplished using Plus that cannot be accomplished using Basic we promise to point it out.

Choosing Your Encoding Settings

Authoring streaming media requires choosing certain encoding settings. The settings decisions you make are based on limitations of, among other things, the current state of software engineering, computer processing and the subjective nature of human hearing. Thankfully, how you make these encoding settings decisions is generally similar across all formats.

Any audio file that can be opened in a waveform editor can be converted to a RealMedia file.

NOTE

Do not encode already-encoded files. Encoded files sound better if you begin with uncompressed source audio.

Whether your source audio is spoken word, sound effects, or music, you must choose the bit rate, codec, and channel (mono or stereo) settings that are appropriate to your own and to your projected audience's needs prior to encoding. It's all about file size versus audio quality. Obviously you want your streaming audio file to sound as good as the available technology and bandwidth will allow. But you must also take steps to ensure that the stream reaches the user intact. Not everyone has broadband connectivity, so it's recommended that you choose the lowest bit rate setting you can get away with that still sounds acceptable. For instance: If you're authoring content that contains only a human voice (mono) speaking under normal conversational conditions, it isn't necessary to encode the streaming file at anything over 56Kbps (28Kbps is also recognizable). The voice will be heard and understood at 28- or 56Kbps, and you won't consume unnecessary bandwidth. If you're authoring encoded music files in stereo, however, listeners will have a more enjoyable sonic experience if you offer the streaming file at a higher bit rate (56Kbps minimum and above).

In these tutorials you'll use a 32Kbps (mono) encode setting for 56Kbps users and a 128Kbps (stereo) encode setting for DSL (or any other broadband format) users. It's possible to encode at higher bit rates but the sound quality isn't all that much better and, by keeping the high quality setting at 128Kbps, broadband users have headroom to use their connection for other tasks.

The encoder invisibly selects a codec based on your encoding settings. Advanced users can and may want to choose a specific codec.

RealMedia Stream Attributes

Every RealMedia on-demand file or live stream contains many attributes that not only describe the content, but also include instructions for the server and player. These attributes, also called metadata, are separate from the encoded audio and the specific codec. Filling out this information might seem a little time consuming, but it's good to do. It's frustrating to hear good music and have no idea who is performing it. Most RealMedia file attributes are referred by the same names across different encoding tools, but a few exceptions exist. RealMedia's available attributes are outlined here, noting when some software tools call them by other names:

- **Author**—A blank text field for entering the author of the content of your stream.
- **Title**—A blank text field for entering the title of your stream.
- **Copyright**—A blank text field for entering copyright information for your stream.

- **Description**—A blank text field for entering a short description of your stream. (Consider putting a relevant URL here!)

- **Keywords**—A blank text field for entering a few keywords that describe your stream. Three or four words are enough.

- **Audience Rating**—A blank text field or a list, such as General—All Ages, Parental Guidance Recommended, Adult Supervision Required, and Adults Only, that provides moral judgment about your stream.

- **File Should Not Be Indexed By Search Engines**—An option that is only relevant for your on-demand RealMedia files. Checking this option adds a header tag that most search engines accept to ignore the file when updating its search database. If you're creating content for a private audience, this is useful. Of course, if you want to be indexed by search engines, leave this box unchecked.

- **Perfect Play**—An on/off check box that allows RealPlayers that are connected at low modem speeds to play higher bit rate files in real-time by using heavy buffering. It's nice to provide this feature to listeners who have slow connections, so select this option when possible.

- **Allow Recording**—An on/off check box that allows some RealPlayer Plus users to save local copies of your stream on their computer. Typically, authors don't want to allow this. Peak calls this feature *Copy-protect* and reverses the on/off meaning accordingly.

- **Allow Download**—An on/off check box that allows people with an audible-ready handheld device to download a RealMedia clip. More info on this is available at www.audible.com. Older versions of Sound Forge call this option *Mobile Play*.

- **File Type**—Typically a radio-button selection that enable authors to choose between RealNetworks' proprietary SureStream or Single Rate. SureStream requires playback through a RealServer, and Single Rate works with both RealServers and Web servers. SureStream will be selected wherever possible.

- **Target Audience**—Typically a multiple choice checkbox to determine the correct bit rate and codecs for a given file. Available with recent RealProducer encoders that support G2 (and later) versions.

Authoring an On-Demand RealMedia File

To author in the RealMedia format, you'll need to use the RealProducer tool or a third-party application that supports the RealMedia plug-in. You'll learn how to use RealProducer (on Windows and Macintosh), Sonic Foundry's Sound Forge (Windows), and Bias's Peak (Macintosh). Sound Forge and Peak are both shipped with the RealMedia plug-in.

RealProducer—RealNetworks' Authoring Tool

RealNetworks has its own innate encoding tool, RealProducer, to author RealMedia streams. RealProducer enables you to author both live and on-demand RealMedia streams through a consistent interface on both Windows and Macintosh platforms. One advantage to using RealProducer is that you're assured of having the latest underlying codecs. Third-party applications typically take a little while to catch up.

You're going to use RealProducer to encode a song with vocals for delivery to a target audience of listeners who have connections ranging from dial-up (56Kbps) to broadband (DSL 384Kbps). (Refer to Chapter 2, "Preparing Yourself," to learn how to create an AIFF or WAV file.) Because this is an on-demand file, you get to upload and stream it from a RealServer. (See the section called "Creating a Server," later in this chapter, and Chapter 7, "Serving Your Audio.")

STEP-BY-STEP: Using RealProducer to Author an On-Demand RealMedia File

1. Launch RealProducer on your Windows or Macintosh computer. RealProducer offers two options:

   - *The default is to use the Recording Assistant, which walks you through a series of simple steps to choose the source file and set up your encoding preferences. A series of dialog boxes prompts each step for encoding options.*

- *More advanced users can manually set all of their options. To prevent the Recording Assistant from starting every time RealProducer is launched, check the "Don't show this when RealProducer starts" check box in the Recording Assistant's first screen.*

This book uses the Recording Assistant. The Recording Assistant includes short descriptions for each step of the encoding process and a Help button for more detailed information. A Back button is also available to return to previous windows. The Recording Assistant automatically starts when RealProducer is launched (see Figure 3.1). Advanced users will notice an option not to show the Recording Assistant when they start the program.

FIGURE 3.1

RealProducer's Recording Assistant offers you three choices to create a RealMedia file.

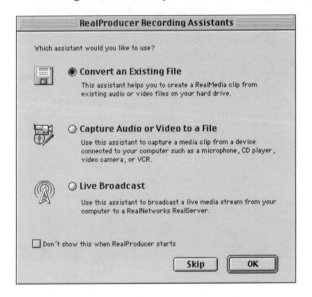

The first page of the Recording Assistant asks which of three Recording Assistants you would like to use: Convert an Existing File, Capture Audio or Video to a File, or Live Broadcast.

2. Because you're creating a RealMedia encoded file from an uncompressed digital music (WAV or AIFF) file in your computer, choose Convert an Existing File and click OK. Recording Assistant now prompts you for the location of that source audio file.

3. Click the Browse button in the Record from File screen of Recording Assistant to locate the file you want to encode. After you have found the file, click Next. This takes you to the RealMedia Clip Information screen (see Figure 3.2). Fill out the title, author, copyright, description, and keyword attributes for this soon-to-be-encoded file. (For more information on RealMedia Clip Information, see RealMedia Stream Attributes above.)

FIGURE 3.2

Enter your stream's media attributes into RealProducer's Clip Information window.

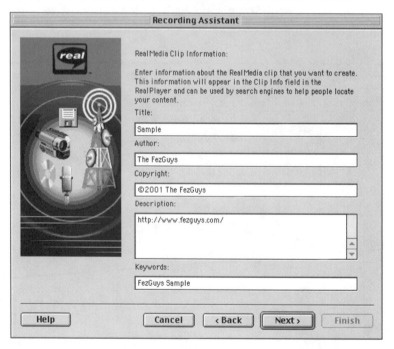

4. After filling in the file information, click Next. Recording Assistant moves along to File Type (see Figure 3.3), where you can choose either SureStream or Single Rate. Because you're streaming your on-demand files from a RealServer, select SureStream. If you prefer to create a single bit rate-encoded file (or use HTTP/progressive streaming—see Chapter 1), you can choose Single Rate. After choosing, click Next.

FIGURE 3.3

Choose SureStream or Single Rate for your file type.

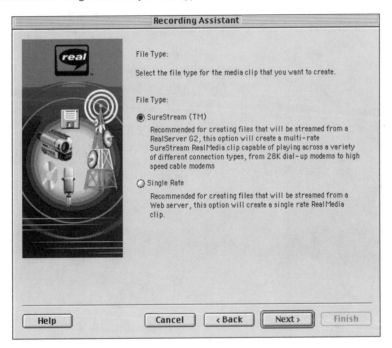

5. The Target Audience window appears (see Figure 3.4). For more information on RealMedia target audience, see RealMedia Stream Attributes above. Eight connectivity speed choices (RealProducer Basic users will only be able to select two) are arrayed in ascending order, from 28K dial-up modem to 512K DSL/cable modem. Because you expect your listening audience to have connectivity in the broad range (a purely arbitrary choice, but still a safe bet) from 56K modem to 384K DSL, check all boxes except 28K modem and 512K DSL/cable modem. After choosing your target audience, click Next.

NOTE

RealProducer Basic users will only be able to select two settings from this window. Given the same expected audience as the preceding scenario, Basic users should select the low end (56K) and the high end (384K) of your expected user connectivity.

FIGURE 3.4

Choose as many audiences as desired from the Target Audience window.

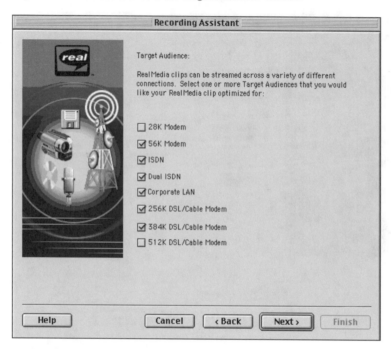

6. The Audio Format window (see Figure 3.5) appears. RealProducer chooses an appropriate codec to encode your audio based on one of four choices: Voice Only, Voice with Background Music, Music, and Stereo Music.

   Because you're encoding a stereo file of music and will be encoding it up to high enough bit rate levels to take advantage of 384K broadband connectivity, choose Stereo Music. If you're only encoding at 56K or below, you could save space (and do your part to ease network traffic) by encoding your file in mono. After making your choice, click Next.

NOTE

Stereo Music cannot be chosen if your source file is mono. RealProducer automatically selects the codec and bit rate settings, based on your Audio Format setting combined with your target audience selection.

FIGURE 3.5

Choose your number of channels in RealProducer's Audio Format window.

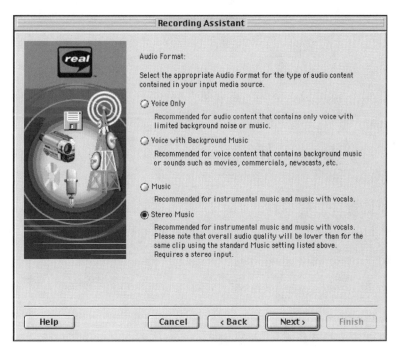

7. The Output File window in the RealProducer Recording Assistant will try to guess a suitable filename and location for saving your encoded file. If you want to use a different name, simply click Save As... and enter your info. Click Next.

8. Finally, you arrive at the Prepare to Record window, a summary of your chosen settings so far. If all is in order, click Finish. At this point, you are returned to the main screen of RealProducer with all of your chosen settings selected. You are ready to encode.

NOTE

Now might be a good time to take a quick look at other less common (but useful) preferences in RealProducer. Within RealProducer, go to Options, Preferences and choose the General tab for RealMedia File Properties options (see Figure 3.6). Make your selection for the Allow Download, Allow Recording, File Should Not Be Indexed by Search Engines, and Audience Rating boxes based on your needs (see RealMedia Stream Attributes above for full descriptions). After you have finished, click OK out of the Preferences box.

FIGURE 3.6

Configure RealProducer's General Preferences based on your needs.

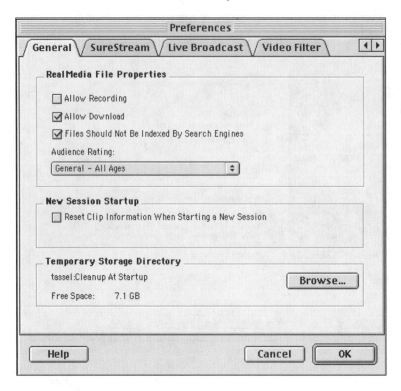

9. If you're satisfied that you're ready to author a RealMedia on-demand file, click the Start button (Figure 3.7) to begin encoding. A progress bar shows the status of the encoding process, and two vertical light bars (which can be turned off from View, Show Audio Meter) show your audio levels. As seen in Figure 3.8, if you want to know more about the encoding process, select View, Statistics (Mac shortcut: ⌘+E) to show extended information including computer performance, time remaining until the completion of the encoding process, and the different bit rates that are being encoded. This is particularly helpful for SureStream encoded files as you can observe the bit rates that users on different bandwidths will be receiving.

FIGURE 3.7

Press the RealProducer's Start button to begin encoding your file.

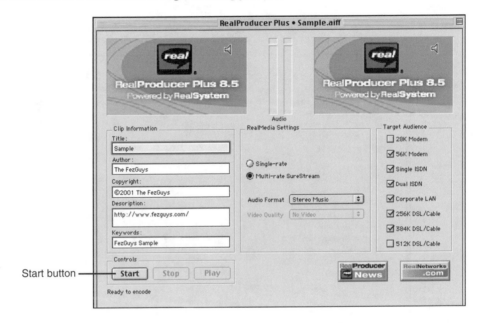

FIGURE 3.8

RealProducer's Statistics window updates information about the encoding process and output file in real-time.

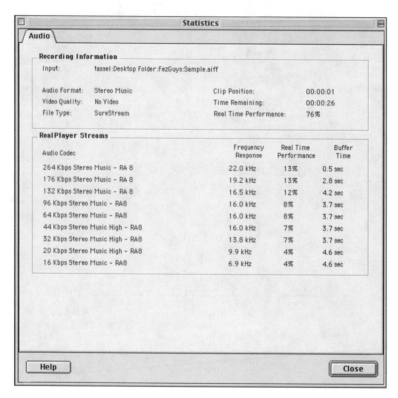

10. When the file is complete, a Processing Complete window appears showing the input and output file location and the duration of the file. More extensive statistics can be viewed here as well. When you're finished perusing this data, click Close.

To preview your newly encoded RealMedia on-demand streaming file, click the Play button, which launches your RealPlayer (see Figure 3.9). Because you're playing back the file from a "local" setting (your computer), RealPlayer plays back at the highest bit rate at which the file was encoded regardless of the value set in RealPlayer's Connection Speed preference. If you're playing back your files from a local setting, you aren't necessarily hearing the encoded file under real-world conditions. Nonetheless, you now have a RealMedia encoded file on your computer ready to upload to a RealServer (see "Creating a Server" later in this chapter).

NOTE

If you don't have a copy of the RealPlayer yet, go online to download your free copy from
`www.realnetworks.com`.

FIGURE 3.9

Test playback of your encoded file using RealPlayer.

Using Sound Forge for Windows

Sonic Foundry's Sound Forge is a popular Windows-only waveform editor. It
can open and save to many different file formats, including RealMedia.
Available at `www.sonicfoundry.com`, Sound Forge comes in two flavors: full or
"streamlined." This book uses the full version, Sound Forge 5.0.

NOTE

A typical Sound Forge installation includes the codecs that are required to do a Save As to the
RealMedia format. If you see RealMedia listed as an option in your Sound Forge Save As file
types, then all is well. If, however, you don't see RealMedia listed as an option in your Save As file
types, first check your installation documentation. Previous versions of Sound Forge might have
different RealNetworks format options available in the Save As dialog box. If you're running a version of Sound Forge prior to v5.0, you might need to select RealNetworks G2 instead. If you're
given a choice between multiple RealNetworks options (RealMedia and RealNetworks G2), select
RealNetworks G2, as it's the most recent release of the two.

STEP-BY-STEP: Using Sound Forge to Author an On-Demand RealMedia File

1. Launch Sound Forge on your Windows computer.

2. Select File, Open (Ctrl+O) to locate your source WAV file and select Open. See Chapter 2, "Preparing Yourself," to find out how to create a WAV file. You'll see the waveform of your chosen file displayed in the main Sound Forge window.

FezGuys' Tip

It's a good idea to play the file to make sure it's the one you intend to encode. Sometimes multiple versions of a file have similar names.

3. Go to File, Save As and select the correct RealNetworks type as your Save As file type (see Figure 3.10). In Sound Forge v5.0, select RealMedia.

NOTE

Sound Forge does a good job of guessing where you would like to save your encoded on-demand file and defaults to saving that file in the same directory as your source audio WAV file, changing the .wav file extension to the RealMedia default of .rm. Change as you see fit.

FIGURE 3.10

Select RealMedia from Sound Forge's Save As file type options.

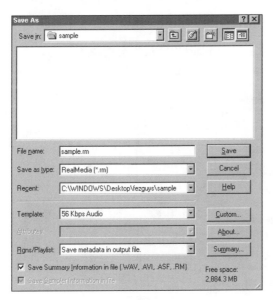

4. After you select the Save As type, a new option appears in your Save As pop-up for choosing the template with which to encode your clip. This is roughly equivalent to RealProducer's Target Audience setting. (For more information on target audiences and other RealMedia settings, see RealMedia Stream Attributes, above). Because you'll encode for 56K modem users first, select 56Kbps Audio.

5. Click the Custom button to set various encoding options (see RealMedia Stream Attributes earlier in this chapter), including author, title, and description for the encoded file.

   1. *From the Custom pop-up window, select Encoding Settings from the subpanel of different tabs at the bottom of the window (Figure 3.11).*

   2. *Target Audience Player Compatibility allows authoring of RealMedia encoded files compatible to previous versions of the RealPlayer. For this example, choose G2 RealPlayer to take advantage of SureStream technology.*

   3. *Next, choose from the list of target audiences. You've already selected 56K modem, and that's reflected in this window. Select 384K DSL/Cable Modem and everything in between that and 56K as additional target audiences.*

   4. *Choose SureStream for your file type.*

FIGURE 3.11

Select your preferred Sound Forge RealMedia encoding settings.

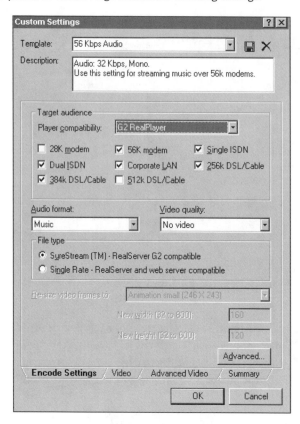

5. *Click the Summary tab and set your Media Clip (title, author, and so on) information (see Figure 3.12).*

FezGuys' Tip

Older versions of Sound Forge might also have a few additional options that aren't mentioned here. You can safely leave these in their default settings. Also you don't need to check Automatically Generate RAM File. This book covers metafiles (including RAM files) in Chapter 7, "Serving Your Audio."

6. *Click OK to accept your settings and close the Custom Settings window.*

FIGURE 3.12

Set your media attributes and other RealMedia custom settings within Sound Forge.

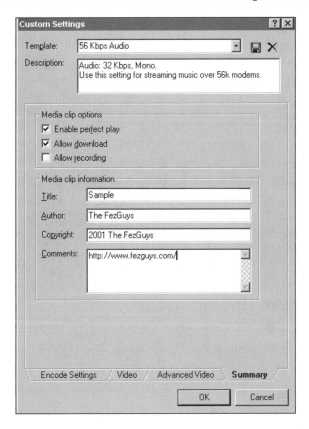

6. Click Save. Sound Forge begins encoding your WAV file into a RealMedia on-demand stream-ing file. During the process, a status bar zips across the bottom-left part of the screen listing the percentage of the file that is encoded and providing a Stop button in case you want to cancel the process.

7. When the encoding is finished, a dialog box pops up telling you the name of your encoded file and prompting you to play it using the Associated Player—in this case, RealPlayer. Click Yes and make sure everything sounds all right.

NOTE

Because files are played back from a local setting (your computer), RealPlayer plays back at the highest bit rate at which the file was encoded regardless of the setting preference for the connec-tion speed set on the local copy of RealPlayer. That means you won't necessarily hear the encoded file under real-world conditions.

You now have a RealMedia encoded file on your computer ready to be uploaded to any RealServer into which you can hack (just kidding about the hacking part). This chapter covers the RealServer setup a little later.

Using Peak for Macintosh

Bias Inc.'s Peak is a popular Macintosh-only waveform editor. It can open and save to many different file formats, including RealMedia. It is available at www.bias-inc.com and comes in four flavors, including the affordably priced LE version. This book uses the full TDM version, Peak 2.62.

NOTE

A typical Peak installation includes the codecs required to do a Save As to the RealMedia format. If you see RealAudio 5.0 listed as an option in your Peak Save As file types, then all is well. If you don't see RealAudio 5.0 listed as an option in your Save As file types, check your installation media and documentation.

STEP-BY-STEP: Using Peak to Author an On-Demand RealMedia File

1. Launch Peak on your Macintosh computer and go to File, Open (⌘+O) to open your AIFF source file. You'll see the waveform of your chosen file displayed.

FezGuys' Tip

It's a good idea to play the file to make sure it's the one you intend to encode. Sometimes multiple versions of a file have similar names.

2. Go to File, Save As (Shift+⌘+S) and, as seen in Figure 3.13, select RealAudio 5.0 for your file type. The RealAudio Encoder dialog box pops up (see Figure 3.14). (Click the Options button on the Peak Save As dialog box to reopen the RealAudio dialog box at any time.)

FIGURE 3.13

Select RealAudio 5.0 in Peak's Save As file type option list.

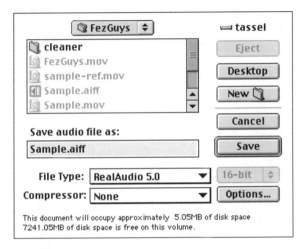

3. From the three Source options (Voice, Music, and Voice and Music) choose Music; you're encoding an on-demand file for 56Kbps dial-up modem users.

4. In the Encoder pull-down menu, select RealAudio 5.0—32Kbps Mono. (Choosing Mono improves the audio quality and 32Kbps ensures the file will be compatible with 56Kbps modem users.)

5. Fill out the Title, Author, and Copyright media attributes.

6. Leave the Bandwidth Negotiation check box option unchecked.

7. Unless you want to set the encoded file's title to be the same as the source audio filename, leave Use Source Document Name unchecked and fill in your own name. Otherwise, check this option. (This item is generally a time-saver for batch encoding.)

8. For information about Copy Protect and Perfect Play, see RealMedia Stream Attributes earlier in this chapter.

9. For Embed Markers as URLs, leave unchecked. (This is an advanced authoring option that this book doesn't use.)

10. For Use Peak Sample Rate Converter, leave this box checked. (Peak's sample rate converter is higher quality than the standard RealAudio encoder tool.)

11. Check the Filename .rm Suffix box if you're not good about remembering to place the .rm suffix at the end of RealAudio-encoded on-demand files. Checking this box automatically adds the .rm suffix to your encoded file's name, whether you've already added it or not.

FezGuys' Tip

It's a good idea to use the correct file suffix on all your files. Not only is it informative, but when transferring files between different operating systems, it's typically required.

12. Check the box Strip / From Filename. Unlike Windows or Unix, the Macintosh OS allows / in a filename. Having a / in your encoded filenames makes your files incompatible with Unix- or Windows-based server computers (and those are the only operating systems on which the RealServer runs).

FIGURE 3.14

Set your RealAudio encoder settings from within Peak.

13. After the information is filled out correctly, click OK in the encoding box to close the RealAudio Encoder window (see Figure 3.14).

14. Choose a destination folder for your encoded files and an appropriate filename.

15. Click Save in the Peak Save As dialog box.

The encoding begins. The progress is marked by the scrolling horizontal bar and a counter detailing the seconds until completion. Check your encoded file using your local RealPlayer. (The free RealPlayer download is available at `www.real.com`*.)*

NOTE

Because files are played back from a local setting (your computer), RealPlayer plays back at the highest bit rate at which the file was encoded regardless of the setting preference for the connection speed set on your local copy of RealPlayer. That means you won't necessarily hear the encoded file under real-world conditions.

You now have a RealMedia encoded file on your computer ready to be uploaded to any RealServer you can steal space on (just kidding). We'll get to the RealServer setup a little later in this chapter.

Authoring a Live RealMedia Stream

In this section, you'll create a live RealMedia stream on your authoring computer. That is, source audio enters your computer uncompressed and exits as an encoded live stream. The RealServer forwards the live stream, in turn, to your listeners on the Internet. Make sure your audio source is plugged into your computer's audio input. Use the same audio input level guidelines that you used to create a digital file (see Chapter 2).

Your source audio quality is crucial here. This is because no further opportunities (such as waveform editors) are typically available to optimize the signal between encoding and outputting that audio as a live stream. Make sure your signal is as clean as possible and that your level is set accurately—not so low that it can't be heard and not so loud that it will distort; both scenarios prevent the encoder from doing a good job. You might want to place some audio hardware (such as a compressor) in your signal path to smooth the signal and increase the encoder's efficiency. (See Chapter 11, "Advanced Audio Optimization.")

This might seem a little like putting the cart before the horse, but now is a good time to mention that, when sending a live stream to the Internet, your authoring computer's software needs to connect to a separate computer that is running RealMedia streaming server software. Therefore, an important early step is to either lease or borrow someone else's server, or have already config-ured your own (see "Creating a Server" at the end of this chapter). You'll also need a reliable Internet connection between the encoding authoring computer and the server computer. In addition, you'll need a valid username and pass-word ready to plug in as you configure your RealMedia encoder to create a live stream. If you're running your own server, you already have that informa-tion handy; otherwise, make sure you've received it from your server provider.

Prior to beginning the live stream, it's strongly recommended that you have, if possible, another test computer available to do a listening test. Short of calling your friends on the phone (which also works), this is the best way to make sure your live stream sounds okay and is actually making it out to the Internet intact. The most realistic test is having your listening test computer on a com-pletely different Internet connection from your live encoder computer. In addition, if you're encoding and streaming for modem users, make sure you test your live stream with a modem connection (not broadband or DSL) to get a realistic experience.

NOTE

Although it's possible to use the same computer to simultaneously author from and run your streaming server, doing so is not recommended for handling more than a dozen listeners.

STEP-BY-STEP: Using RealProducer to Author a Live RealMedia Stream

As in encoding your on-demand files, RealProducer functions basically the same for both Windows and Macintosh computers. We'll note where they differ. The Windows version of RealProducer is a bit more stable (fewer random crashes in heavy use). If you have the option, choose the Windows OS for your live encoder platform.

1. Launch RealProducer on your Windows or Macintosh computer. From the Recording Assistant, select Live Broadcast and click OK (see Figure 3.15).
   A Live Broadcast Recording Assistant window opens.

FIGURE 3.15

Choose RealProducer's Live Broadcast Recording Assistant.

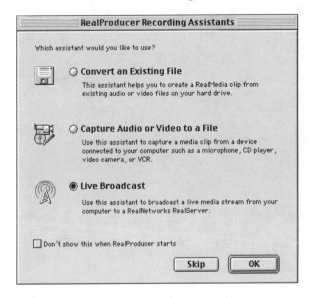

2. Check Capture Audio (leave Capture Video unchecked as you're encoding audio only) to select your audio input device (see Figure 3.16).

FIGURE 3.16

Make sure Capture Audio is selected for RealProducer's input source.

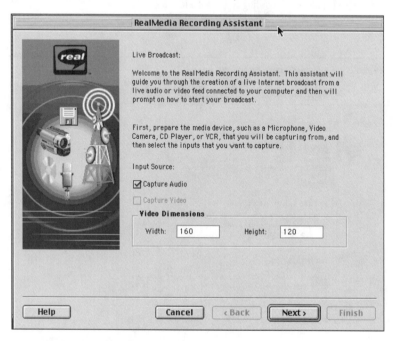

 Windows users might have multiple audio input devices listed below the Capture Audio check box. Leave the default setting. The OS set this when your sound card was installed. The default audio input setting should work and will likely be named something that includes *Wave* or *Wave Recording* in the title (see Figure 3.17). If you're not receiving audio from the default audio input setting, try selecting any audio input that uses the word *Wave* somewhere in the title. Click Next.

FIGURE 3.17

Make sure the correct input device is chosen from your input source.

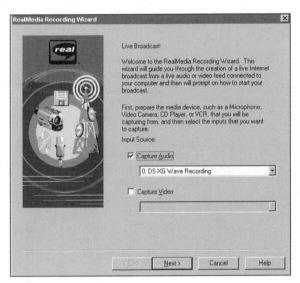

Mac users won't have input devices from which to select. This configuration is handled later on in the process. Click Next.

3. On the RealMedia Clip Information screen (see Figure 3.18), faithfully fill out title, author, copyright, description, and keywords for your file (see RealMedia Stream Attributes earlier in this chapter). After filling in the file information, click Next.

FIGURE 3.18

Fill out your media attributes in RealProducer's Clip Information window.

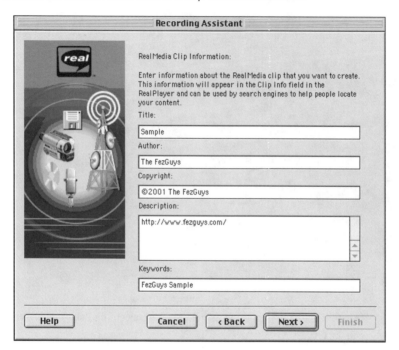

4. Options on the File Type window (Figure 3.19) are SureStream or Single Rate. Because you'll be broadcasting to more than one target audience using SureStream, select SureStream and click Next.

NOTE

If you want to create a backward-compatible single bit rate encoded stream (compatible with much older versions of RealPlayer), choose Single Rate.

FIGURE 3.19

Select your preferred setting from within RealProducer's File Type window.

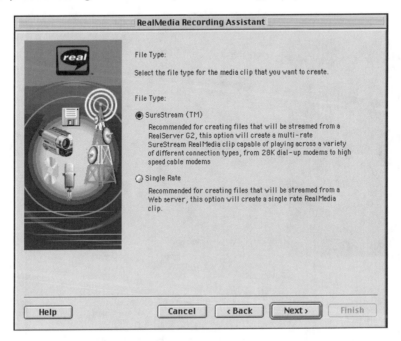

5. The Target Audience window (Figure 3.20) has eight connectivity speed choices (RealProducer Basic users will have two choices) arrayed in ascending order, from 28K dial-up modem up to 512K DSL/cable modem. Because you expect your listening audience to have connectivity in a broad range (a purely arbitrary choice, but still a safe bet) from 56K modem to 384K DSL, check all boxes except the 28K modem and 512K DSL/Cable Modem choices. Click Next.

FIGURE 3.20

Select the appropriate target audience settings in RealProducer.

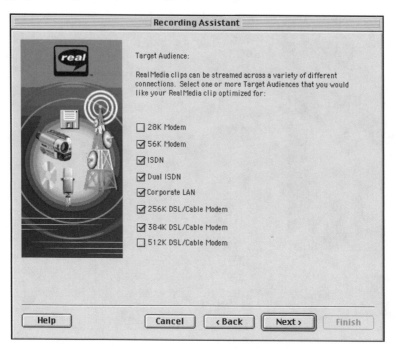

NOTE

RealProducer Basic users can only select two settings from this window. Given the same expected audience as the preceding scenario, Basic users should select the low end (56K) and the high end (384K) of expected user connectivity.

6. From your selection in the Audio Format window (Figure 3.21), RealProducer chooses the appropriate codec to encode your audio. Select from one of these choices: Voice Only, Voice with Background Music, Music, or Stereo Music. Because you're encoding a stereo file of music for up to 384K broadband users, choose Stereo Music. If you were encoding only at 56K or below, you could increase the audio fidelity by encoding your file in mono. Stereo Music cannot be chosen if your source file is mono. After you've made your choice, click Next.

FIGURE 3.21

Choose your audio format in RealProducer based on your audio source and target audience settings.

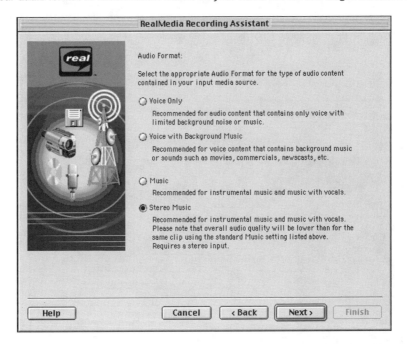

7. In the Media Server window (see Figure 3.22), enter the configuration information about the RealServer to which you're sending your encoded stream for redistribution. (See "Creating a Server," later in this chapter, to learn where this information comes from).

- *RealServer—Enter the host name (or IP address) of your RealServer.*

- *Server Port—Enter the port number of your RealServer. (The default is 4040.)*

- *Filename—Enter the pathname to your live stream.*

- *Username—Enter the username authorizing you to send your stream to the RealServer.*

- *Password—Enter the password for your username.*

- *Archive Broadcast to File—This allows you to save a local copy of your live stream. This saved local copy has many potential uses. It can be edited and uploaded later for on-demand use as well as serving as a backup. If you want to save a local copy, check this box and select the location for this file.*

NOTE

Remember to have enough available disk space on your hard drive for the archived stream. Although an encoded live audio stream takes up much less space than uncompressed audio, it will still pile up, especially if the stream goes on for hours or days.

FIGURE 3.22

Confirm RealProducer's Media Server settings for your live stream.

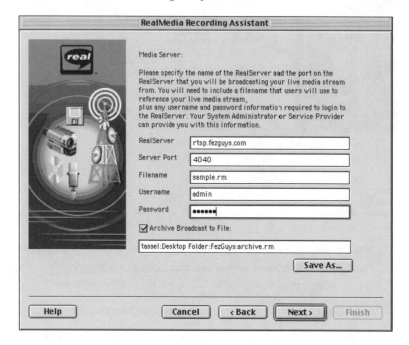

8. Click Finish.

9. In the pop-up Summary window, confirm that your displayed settings are correct.

10. Start your input device (or just press Play on your cued up audio source) or, if they are around, tell the band to begin their sound check. While the audio is playing, check your input levels.

To see input levels for Macintosh:

Go to Options, Audio Capture settings. This brings up the Sound input window (Figure 3.23). Select the appropriate setting in Device and Input (mic, line, CD, and so on). You should now see level display (a blinking horizontal light meter). Set the input level to avoid clipping.

FIGURE 3.23

Check the audio input levels through the Sound input panel.

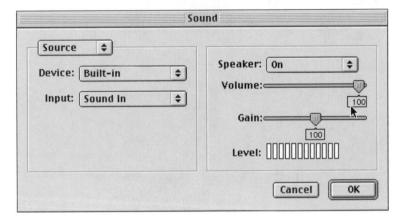

To see input levels for Windows:

Depending on whether you use mic input, line input, or a CD as your source audio, check that the correct input is selected. As seen in Figure 3.24, use the standard Volume Control panel (as described in Chapter 2). A shortcut is available for launching the Volume Control panel through RealProducer. Go to Options, Audio Capture Settings, Volume Control. Set the input level to avoid clipping.

FIGURE 3.24

Check the audio input levels through the standard Windows Volume Control utility.

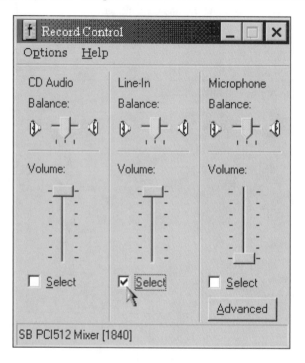

Source audio is now coming into your computer, the input levels are clean, your RealServer (remote or local) is correctly configured, and RealProducer is ready to begin the live, encoded stream. You might want to select View Statistics (Figure 3.25) during this input level test, before beginning the actual stream. This gives you a reminder of what bit rates you're encoding, among other helpful statistics. If you're satisfied that everything looks good, click Stop on your source audio (remember to reset the start point of the source audio) or tell the band to take a break.

FIGURE 3.25

View RealProducer's Encoding Statistics to see what bit rates you will be encoding and other useful
information.

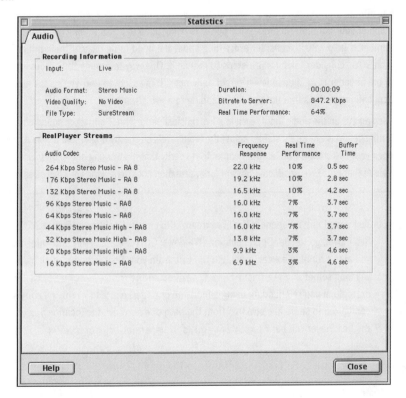

NOTE

Macintosh users will not be able to do anything else with their computer while encoding; however,
if you first open the View Statistics window, you can place it on the screen such that you can see
important information that is not obscured by the main RealProducer window.

NOTE

Windows users can view statistics as well as perform other functions during the live stream, but
don't do it just because you can. It's recommended that you leave your live encoding/authoring
computer alone while streaming.

11. When you're ready to begin the live stream, click Start on the RealProducer main window to
begin sending your stream to your RealServer. Press Play on your source audio or tell the band
to begin playing.

FezGuys' Tip

Pay attention to the real time performance value (in your Statistics window) that tells you how much of your computer's processing power is being used to encode the live stream. If that number is below 90%, consider everything under the hood to be okay. If the number is higher than 90%, consider taking a few steps to reduce it. One way to reduce the processing demands of the encoder is to choose fewer target audiences. It is assumed that you're not running other applications at the same time you're encoding to a live stream.

Keep an eye on the audio input level. In a live musical performance situation, sound check and performance levels are rarely stable. Adjust the input levels on-the-fly if necessary. Take a moment to open your live stream from another computer to verify that it's working and sounds acceptable (see Authoring a Live RealMedia Stream for information about checking your live stream.

12. Test everything by opening the live stream URL in your RealPlayer (Figure 3.26). In your RealPlayer, go to File, Open Location (Windows: Ctrl+L, Mac: ⌘+L) and enter the URL. If you aren't running a RealServer, get the URL from your RealServer administrator. The URL will look something like this: `rtsp://server.host.name/encoder/filename.rm`. For example, if you're encoding using a filename of `sample.rm` to `rtsp.fezguys.com` configured to serve live streams from the path of `encoder`, the location you will enter into the RealPlayer will be: `rtsp://fezguys.com/encoder/sample.rm`.

FIGURE 3.26

Enter your live stream's URL in your RealPlayer to test that it's working properly.

Congratulations! You are now streaming live through the Internet. Of course, it's possible that certain issues are preventing the stream from working. Be patient. Some elements to the equation are out of your control (bandwidth or even the band) but with a little perseverance, tenacity, and troubleshooting, you will stream!

Creating a Server

What's a RealServer and where do you get one? Although the system might not yet be as ubiquitous as setting up residential phone service, it's out there. We're going to tell you how to get (and use) it.

For serving on-demand files, you can use either the RealServer for real-time streaming of on-demand files or any Web server for HTTP/Progressive streaming. For live stream authoring, you must use the RealServer, which is available for Unix (Linux, FreeBSD, and so on) and Windows NT/2000. For the purposes of the Step-by-Step tutorials in this chapter, you'll be using the RealServer for both live and on-demand.

NOTE

> HTTP/Progressive on-demand RealMedia files can be streamed through HTTP/Progressive streaming from a Web server. See Chapter 2 for an explanation of the differences between progressive (for on-demand only) and real-time (both on-demand and live) streaming. See Chapter 7 for examples on how to do both.

For more general information on issues relating to serving your streams, see Chapter 7.

RealServer 8.0 (Free Versus Pay)

RealNetworks offers four RealServer products, and they're all available from the RealNetworks Web site. Each of these products is different, so if you want to know more, go to www.realnetworks.com/products/servers/comparison.html for links to information and purchase (download) of all four products.

- **RealSystem Server 8.0 Professional**—This supports multicasting and includes a 100-user concurrent stream license (expandable to 1,000). The price starts at an eye-opening $5,995. Higher number licenses are available. You will want a real budget and compelling content to justify the purchase of this product.

- **RealSystem Server 8.0 Plus**—This supports multicasting and includes a 60-user concurrent stream license. (More concurrent users are available by upgrading to the Professional edition.) You can get this product for around $1,995, which is still pricey, but is good for people with smaller budgets who want to get their feet wet. This product does have a few limitations: no advertising and authentication extensions, a limited RealSystem administrator, absence of control over client IP connections, and lack of stream capacity segmentation.

- **RealSystem Server 8.0 Intranet**—This is specifically configured to support corporate intranets. This product supports scalable multicasting (efficient for this environment) and includes a 200 user concurrent stream license (expandable to 500). The price starts at $3,995.

- **RealSystem Server 8.0 Basic**—This supports multicasting and includes a 25-user concurrent stream license (not expandable). The best news is that it's free. Limitations include lack of advertising and authentication extensions, a limited RealSystem administrator, no control over client IP connections, and absence of stream capacity segmentation.

For the purposes of this book, you'll learn how to install RealServer Server 8.0 Basic on a Unix (FreeBSD) computer and also a Windows NT v4.0 computer.

STEP-BY-STEP: How to Set Up Your RealServer

The RealServer application functions basically the same for both Windows and Unix computers.

1. Download RealServer Basic from www.realnetworks.com/products/servers/ basic.html. Download instructions are included on this Web page. Be sure to select the RealSystem Basic download and not the Plus. Fill out the information and choose your operating system (either FreeBSD 3.0 or Windows NT/2000) from the Download dialog box choices. Your license key will be e-mailed to the e-mail address you entered in the Download Information area. The Basic license is free for one year.

NOTE

If you downloaded the installer to your desktop computer, you need to transfer the installer to the server computer that will be running RealServer Basic. If you're transferring via FTP, use binary mode.

FreeBSD users must have the 3.0 compatibility libraries installed on the computer where the RealServer will reside.

2. Open your e-mail and save your license attachment to a file. If necessary, also transfer the license to your server computer (again as a binary transfer). Now you are ready to install.

3. Run the installer program. The RealServer installation greeting appears. Select Next. You will do this repeatedly throughout the installation process even though it's not mentioned again.

4. Enter the full filename to your license file.

5. Read and then continue, assuming you agree to the licensing terms.

6. Specify the directory where you want to install RealServer Basic 8.0.

NOTE

Make sure that the directory you select has plenty of free space. The installed program requires 25MB of disk space and the server's log files that also reside in this directory can quickly grow to gigabytes (see Chapter 2 for server computer hardware requirements).

7. Create a username and password that will be used for accessing the RealSystem administrator, monitor, and live encoder. You'll need to enter this information into your RealProducer so that it can broadcast live streams to the RealServer.

8. Accept the default port setting of 7070 for the RealServer to listen for PNA connections.

9. Accept the default port setting of 554 for the RealServer to listen for RTSP connections.

10. Accept the default port setting of 8080 for the RealServer to listen for HTTP connections.

NOTE

If you're not running a Web server on the same computer as RealServer Basic, you might want to choose the default Web server port 80. Port 80 is more likely to be allowed through most firewalls than Port 8080.

11. Accept the random port that the installer selects for the admin port. This value determines on what port RealServer's administration system will listen for Web browser requests. Make note of this number for later post-installation configuration purposes.

NOTE

If you're installing RealServer on a Windows NT/2000 server, you'll have the option to install RealServer Basic as an NT Service. The default of checked (accepted) is fine.

12. The installer will show a summary of your installation settings. Finish the installation. (For Unix, press F. For Windows, click Finish.)

13. After the installation process is complete, you'll be prompted to start the RealServer and the RealSystem Administrator. Choose Yes.

RealSystem Server 8.0 Basic for Unix (FreeBSD) and Windows NT/2000 is now ready to use. Live streams sent to the server are available to the RealPlayer in the default /encoder pathname (rtsp://myserver.mydomain. name/encoder/streamname.rm).

You can upload on-demand files into the Content directory of your RealServer installation directory and then access them with a URL such as rtsp://myserver.mydomain/ondemandfile.rm.

Sample sound clips are included with the installation, so you can easily test your server. A link is available to play these sample sound clips through the RealSystem Administrator (Figure 3.27). Extended documentation and help is also available from within the administrator, which you can access with your Web browser (where adminport is the port number chosen during installation) at http://myserver.mydomain:adminport/admin/index.html.

FIGURE 3.27

Open the RealSystem Administrator in your Web browser to perform additional configuration.

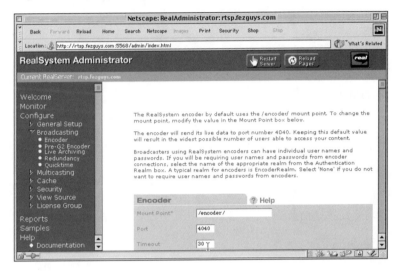

Summary

After you have uploaded your on-demand content and started your live streams, link them into your web site (see Chapter 7), announce them on your mailing lists, put the announcement in your e-mail signature, and so on. Make a point to periodically check for upgrades to the RealMedia player, server, and encoder applications. Streaming audio technology continues to innovate at a rapid pace. Although your RealServer should work with future versions for years to come, you might want to take advantage of new features often released annually.

CHAPTER 4

Using Windows Media

Windows Media is Microsoft's streaming media system, native to the Windows operating system and with limited authoring support for other platforms. As in most things, Microsoft wants its streaming media system to be your one and only, offering software free of charge and not worrying about the Windows Media platform turning a profit. Consequently, Microsoft hasn't made much effort to provide its tools (except for the Windows Media player, which is available for almost everything) for other operating systems to author and serve Windows Media content.

NOTE

 Macintosh users can get a product called Cleaner (www.discreet.com/streamingmedia) to encode on-demand Windows Media—as well as RealMedia and QuickTime—files on the Macintosh OS. Similarly, Cleaner Live, another product by Discreet, can author Windows Media and RealMedia live streams on a Macintosh. Cleaner is covered in Chapter 13, Media Process, as part of a discussion on batch processing tools.

Serving Windows Media-encoded content via real-time (as opposed to HTTP/Progressive) streaming requires a Windows NT/2000 server platform. Windows Media servers will be covered later in this chapter, "Creating a Server."

Software Encoders (Free Versus Pay)

Microsoft provides the Windows Media encoding software free. You can also use many waveform editors to create on-demand Windows Media files. For live stream authoring, you can use the free Windows Media encoder or other third-party tools such as Discreet's Cleaner Live. The third-party tools cost money and are not specific to the Windows Media format. Most of these third-party tools run only on Windows.

For the purposes of this book, you'll use both the Microsoft Windows Media Encoder and Sonic Foundry's Sound Forge waveform editor to create on-demand Windows Media streaming files. For authoring live Windows Media-encoded streams, you'll use the Windows Media encoder.

Choosing Your Encoding Settings

Authoring streaming media requires choosing certain encoding settings. The settings decisions you make are based on limitations of, among other things, the current state of software engineering, computer processing and the subjective nature of human hearing. Thankfully, how you make these encoding settings decisions is generally similar across all formats.

NOTE

Don't encode files that are already encoded. An encoded file sounds better if you begin with uncompressed source audio.

Any audio file that can be opened in a waveform editor can be saved (converted) as a Windows Media file.

Whether your source audio is spoken word, sound effects, or music, you must choose the bit rate, codec, and channel (mono or stereo) settings that are appropriate to your own and to your projected audience's needs prior to encoding. It's all about file size versus audio quality. Obviously you want your streaming audio file to sound as good as the available technology and bandwidth will allow. But you must also take steps to ensure that the stream reaches the user intact. Not everyone has broadband connectivity, so it's recommended that you choose the lowest bit rate setting you can get away with that still sounds acceptable. For instance: If you're authoring content that contains only a human voice (mono) speaking under normal conversational conditions, it isn't necessary to encode the streaming file at anything over 56Kbps (28Kbps is also recognizable). The voice will be heard and understood at 28- or 56Kbps, and you won't consume unnecessary bandwidth. If you're authoring encoded music files in stereo, however, listeners will have a more enjoyable sonic experience if you offer the streaming file at a higher bit rate (56Kbps minimum and above).

In these tutorials you'll use a 32Kbps (mono) encode setting for 56Kbps users and a 128Kbps (stereo) encode setting for DSL (or any other broadband format) users. It's possible to encode at higher bit rates but the sound quality isn't all that much better and, by keeping the high quality setting at 128Kbps, broadband users have headroom to use their connection for other tasks.

The encoder invisibly selects a codec based on your encoding settings. Advanced users can and may want to choose a specific codec.

Windows Media Stream Attributes

Every Windows Media on-demand file or live stream contains many attributes that not only describe the content, but also include instructions for the server and player. These attributes, also called metadata, are separate from the encoded audio and the specific codec. Filling out this information might seem a little time consuming, but it's good to do. It's frustrating to hear good music and have no idea who is performing it. Most Windows Media file attributes are referred by the same names across different encoding tools, but a few exceptions exist. Standard Windows Media available attributes are outlined here, noting when some software tools call them by other names:

- **Author**— A blank text field for entering the author of the content of your stream.

- **Title**— A blank text field for entering the title of your stream.

- **Copyright**— A blank text field for entering copyright information for your stream.

FezGuys' Tip

To quickly get a copyright symbol on Windows, press Alt+Ctrl+C.

- **Rating**—A blank text field to enter a moral judgement about your stream.

- **Description**— A blank text field for entering a short description of your stream. (Consider putting a relevant URL here!)

Authoring an On-Demand Windows Media File

If you have decided to author in the Windows Media format, you need to use the Windows Media Encoder tool or a third-party application that supports the Windows Media plug-in. This chapter walks you through using the Windows Media encoder and Sonic Foundry's Sound Forge. Sound Forge is shipped with the necessary Windows Media plug-in.

Windows Media Encoder—Microsoft's Authoring Tool

Microsoft has its own innate encoding tool, the Windows Media Encoder, to author both live and on-demand Windows Media streams. One advantage to using the Windows Media Encoder is that you are assured of having the latest underlying codecs. Third-party applications typically take a little while to catch up.

This chapter uses the Windows Media Encoder to encode a song with vocals for delivery to a target audience of listeners with connections ranging from dial-up (56Kbps) to broadband (DSL 384Kbps). (See Chapter 2, "Preparing Yourself," to learn how to create a WAV file.) Because this is an on-demand file, you are required to upload and stream it from a Windows Media Server. (See the section called "Creating a Server" later in this chapter and Chapter 7, "Serving Your Audio.")

To download the free Windows Media encoder (v7.01 or later) on your Windows computer, go to www.microsoft.com/windowsmedia and click on the Windows Media Encoder link.

After installation, follow this Step-by-Step tutorial.

STEP-BY-STEP: Using Windows Media Encoder to Author an On-Demand Windows Media File

1. Launch the Windows Media Encoder on your authoring computer. The encoder opens a New Session Wizard, which speeds basic tasks. Options include the following: Broadcast a Live Event from Attached Device or Computer Screen, Capture Audio or Video from Attached Device or Computer Screen, and Convert an Audio or Video File into a Windows Media File.

2. Choose Convert an Audio or Video File into a Windows Media File (see Figure 4.1). You will also see a check box for Begin Converting When This Wizard Finishes. Don't check this for now. Later, after you are more comfortable with the process, you might want to incorporate this time-saving feature. Click Next.

NOTE

Back buttons are available at every step if you need to change information. The Windows Media Encoder's New Session Wizard also includes a Help area for most questions.

FIGURE 4.1

Select Convert an Audio or Video File into a Windows Media File in the Windows Media Encoder Session Wizard.

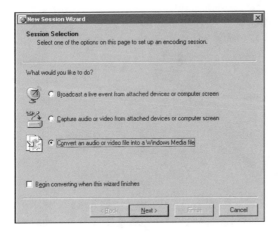

3. From the File Selection page (see Figure 4.2), choose a file to convert by clicking Browse and locating your WAV file (see Chapter 2, "Preparing Yourself," to learn how to create a WAV file).

4. The Windows Media Encoder Wizard inserts its best guess for the filename and location for that soon-to-be-encoded file. If the Wizard's best guess is not what you want, click Browse, specify your desired destination file, and click Next.

FezGuys' Tip

It's helpful to create a naming standard for yourself when encoding a single piece of source audio to multiple bit rates. You might want to try something along the lines of `myfile-56k.wma` or `myfile-low.wma`. Make sure that the filename ends in `.wma`.

FIGURE 4.2

Choose your source and destination filenames from the Windows Media Encoder's File Selection window.

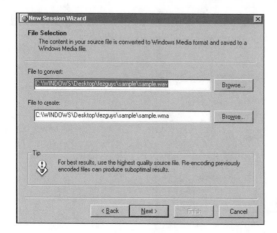

5. In the Profile Selection window (see Figure 4.3), specify the bit rate to encode your source audio. Choose from a menu of eight audio-only encoding choices. (You can ignore the video-relevant choices for now.) From the eight audio-only bit rate encoding options, choose Audio for Dial-Up Modems (56Kbps Stereo) from the Profile Selection window. Click Next.

NOTE

Advanced users can create custom profiles to control individual codecs, bit rates, sample rates, and number of channels (mono or stereo).

FIGURE 4.3

Choose Audio for Dial-Up Modems (56Kbps Stereo) in the Windows Media Encoder Profile Selection window.

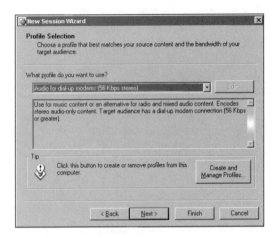

6. In the Display Information window, enter your file's attributes (see Windows Media Attributes earlier in this chapter), including title, author, copyright, rating, and song description (see Figure 4.4). Click Next.

7. The Settings window displays a summary of your encoding settings. If the information is correct, click Finish.

FIGURE 4.4

Enter your Windows Media file attributes in the Windows Media Encoder's Display Information window.

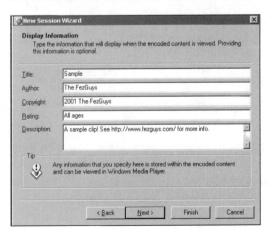

8. Click the Start button (which has blinked a few times to get your attention) to begin encoding your on-demand Windows Media file (see Figure 4.5). The progress bar and window show, among other things, the estimated time to the end of the encoding process, the percent of encoding complete, the bit rate chosen, the encoded file's destination (after it is complete), the amount of disk space remaining, and the audio level meters.

NOTE

The Progress window is split up intelligently. It's easy to ignore if that's what you want, but interested users can find useful details during the quick encoding process. If you don't want to see this panel go to the View menu option and uncheck either Audio Panel, Monitor Panel, or Control Panel and uncheck areas you don't want. Keep in mind, however, that you need the Control Panel to click Start.

FIGURE 4.5

Click the Start button to begin encoding your on-demand file.

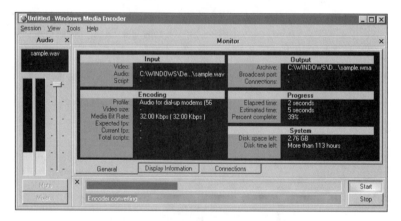

9. After encoding has finished, an Encoding Results dialog box (see Figure 4.6) appears. If you don't want to see this dialog box again, you can uncheck the Show This Dialog Box When Encoding Finishes option.

10. You now have a low bit rate Windows Media encoded file in a folder, ready for uploading to an on-demand Windows Media streaming server. Other options in the Encoding Results window (see Figure 4.6) are View Output File (to play your encoded file using your Windows Media player) and Select New Session (to repeat the process at another bit rate).

FIGURE 4.6

Windows Media Encoder: encoding results.

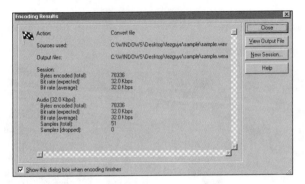

11. Click Select New Session in the Encoding Results window to make a second file, this time a high bit rate on-demand Windows Media encoded file, optimized for broadband 384k DSL users. You can also start the New Session Wizard again by selecting Session, New Session Wizard (Ctrl+W).

12. The New Session Wizard asks if you want to save the current session. Unless you want to repeat the exact encoding configurations for your next file, click No.

FezGuys' Tip

When encoding additional files, make sure to choose a different filename to avoid overwriting previous files.

13. Go through the previous steps 2–10. When you reach the Profile Selection bit rate menu (step 5), choose Audio for CD-Quality Transparency (128Kbps stereo), which is suitable for broadband 384K DSL users. Click Next and continue steps 6–10.

You now have two Windows Audio Media on-demand streaming files in your chosen folder, ready for uploading to a streaming server or Web site. Open them with your Windows Media player and verify that they sound okay (see Figure 4.7).

FIGURE 4.7

Play back your on-demand files in the Windows Media Player to ensure they are okay.

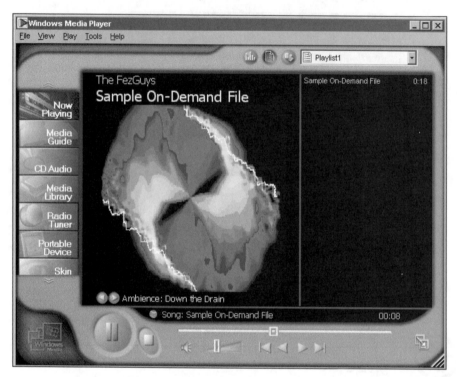

NOTE

Upon launching your Windows Media encoder a second (and subsequent) time, there will be a different introduction screen with these options: Broadcast, Capture, or Convert a File Using the New Session Wizard; Create a Custom Encoding Session; Open an Existing Encoding Session; and Open a Recent Encoding Session. Choose the option Broadcast, Capture, or Convert a File Using the New Session Wizard until you're more comfortable with the software. If you don't want to see this pop-up window upon every launch, uncheck the box Show This Dialog Box at Startup. If you still want to use the Wizard, go to Session, New Session Wizard (Ctrl+W).

Using Sound Forge

Sonic Foundry's Sound Forge is a popular Windows-only waveform editor. It can open and save to many file formats, including Windows Media. It's available at www.sonicfoundry.com and comes in two flavors: the full or the "streamlined" version. The following Step-by-Step uses the full version, Sound Forge 5.0.

STEP-BY-STEP: Using Sound Forge to Author an On-Demand Windows Media File

1. Open Sound Forge on your Windows computer.

2. Within Sound Forge, open your source audio file.

3. Choose Save As and then choose the file type to which you want to save (see Figure 4.8). In this case, select Windows Media Audio V8 or .wma.

FIGURE 4.8

Select Windows Media Audio V8 in Sound Forge's Save As Type option list.

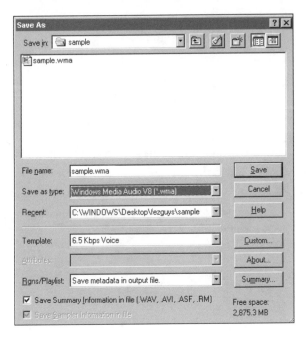

4. From the Template pull-down menu, choose 56 Kpbs Stereo for a target audience of 56 Kbps dial-up modem users (see Figure 4.9).

FIGURE 4.9

Select the 56 Kbps Stereo setting in the Sound Forge Save As window.

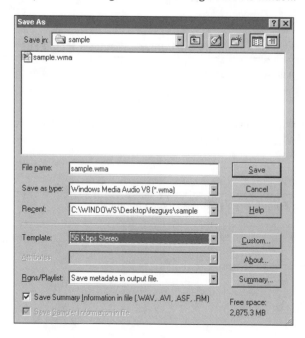

5. Click the Custom button to enter the Custom Settings window. The Audio tab within the Custom window is selected by default.

6. Click the Summary tab and enter your file's media attributes, including title, author, copyright, description, and rating (see Figure 4.10). After filling in the information, click OK to close the Custom Settings window.

FIGURE 4.10

Enter your Windows Media file attributes in the Summary tab of Sound Forge's Custom Settings window.

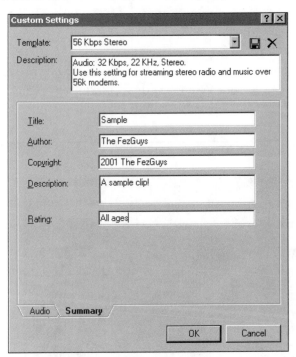

7. After verifying that the destination filename is correct, click Save to begin the encoding process. A horizontal progress bar marches across the bottom of the screen, detailing percent complete. A Cancel button is also available.

8. After saving as a Windows Media encoded file, Sound Forge asks if you want to reopen the file from your newly encoded version. The application is asking if you want to close your raw audio and instead open the compressed Windows Media file. Because you will use the same source WAV file to author on-demand files at other bit rates, make sure to click No. Clicking Yes opens the completed and compressed Windows Media file. You don't want to recompress an already compressed file.

9. Repeat steps 3–7 above to create an on-demand file for 384Kbps DSL users. In step 4, select the 128 Kbps CD Transparency Audio template and, in step 7, make sure to name the new encoded file something different from your 56K version so you don't overwrite it.

NOTE

The highest setting of the default encoding templates is 160Kbps, although Sound Forge can encode to 192Kbps through the Custom settings.

Verify that your Windows Media encoded files sound okay by playing back the newly encoded files in your Windows Media player (see Figure 4.11).

FIGURE 4.11

Test your on-demand file with Windows Media Player.

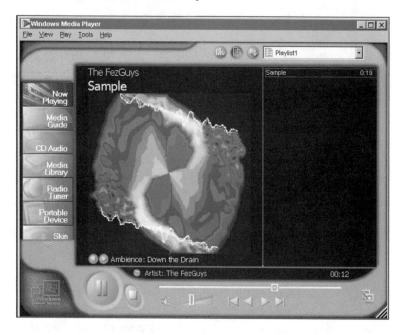

You now have two Windows Audio Media on-demand streaming files in a chosen file, ready for uploading to your streaming server or Web site.

Authoring a Live Windows Media Stream

In this section, you will create a live Windows Media stream on your authoring computer. That is, source audio enters your computer uncompressed and exits as an encoded live stream. The Windows Media streaming server forwards the live stream, in turn, to your listeners on the Internet. Make sure your audio source is plugged into your computer's audio input. Use the same audio input level guidelines that you used to create a digital file (see Chapter 2).

Your source audio quality is crucial here. This is because no further opportunities (such as waveform editors) are typically available to optimize the signal between encoding and outputting that audio as a live stream. Make sure your signal is as clean as possible and that your level is set accurately—not so low that it can't be heard and not so loud that it will distort; both scenarios prevent the encoder from doing a good job. You might want to place some audio hardware (such as a compressor) in your signal path to smooth the signal and increase the encoder's efficiency. (See Chapter 11, "Advanced Audio Optimization.")

When sending a live stream to the Internet, your authoring computer's software (in this case, the Windows Media Encoder) needs to connect to a computer running Windows Media streaming server software. Therefore, an important early step is to either lease or borrow someone else's server, or have your own already configured. (See "Creating a Server" at the end of this chapter.) You'll also need a reliable Internet connection between the encoding authoring computer and the server computer. In addition, you'll need a valid username and password ready to plug in as you configure your Windows Media encoder to create a live stream. If you're running your own server, you should already have that information handy; otherwise, make sure you have received it from your server provider.

Prior to beginning the live stream, it's strongly recommended that you have, if possible, another test computer available to do a listening test. Short of calling your friends on the phone (which also works), this is the best way to make sure your live stream sounds okay and is actually making it out to the Internet intact. The most realistic test is having your listening test computer on a completely different Internet connection from your live encoder computer. In addition, if you're encoding and streaming for modem users, make sure you test your live stream with a modem connection and not broadband or DSL to get a realistic experience.

NOTE

Although it's possible to use the same computer to simultaneously author from and run your streaming server, doing so is not recommended for handling more than a dozen listeners.

The Step-by-Step below walks you through the process of using the Windows Media Encoder to create a live stream suitable for streaming to 56Kbps dialup modem users. If streaming to 384Kbps DSL users, encode to a 128Kbps stream in step 6.

STEP-BY-STEP: Using Windows Media Encoder to Author a Live Windows Media Stream

1. Launch the Windows Media Encoder and open the New Session Wizard. Options are Broadcast a Live Event from Attached Device or Computer Screen, Capture Audio or Video from Attached Device or Computer Screen, or Convert an Audio or Video File into a Windows Media File. You will also see a check box for Begin Converting When This Wizard Finishes. Leave this box unchecked.

2. Choose Broadcast a Live Event from Attached Device or Computer Screen (see Figure 4.12) and click Next.

NOTE

Back buttons are available at every step to change information. The Windows Media Encoder's New Session Wizard also includes a Help area for most questions.

FIGURE 4.12

Select Broadcast a Live Event from Attached Device or Computer Screen from the Windows Media Encoder Recording Assistant.

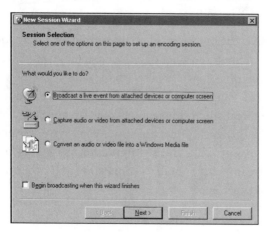

3. In the Device Options window (see Figure 4.13), uncheck Video. Audio is selected by default and cannot be unchecked. The default audio device (soundcard or software) should already be selected in the pull-down menu. Ignore the Configure button (the default settings should be just fine), and click Next.

FIGURE 4.13

Uncheck Video and make sure Audio is checked within the Windows Media Encoder Device Options window.

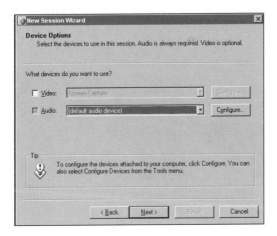

4. In the Broadcast Connection window, leave the default of 8080 for the HTTP Port option.

NOTE

If you're running another network service (another Web server) on your encoding computer that is already using port 8080, check the Find Free Port box and the encoder will choose a new port for you. If you're behind a firewall, make sure to choose a port that is allowed. Ports that are commonly used by Web servers (8080 or 80) are good ports to try. If necessary, consult your network administrator.

5. Lower down in the Broadcast Connection window (see Figure 4.14) is the URL for your Internet or LAN connection. Make note of this URL—you'll need it when you configure your Windows Media server to receive your live stream. If you're satisfied with these choices, click Next.

NOTE

Your authoring computer name might not be displayed in the Broadcast Connection window as a full Internet host name. For example, it might display SERVERNAME instead of the full name SERVERNAME.MYDOMAIN.COM. Although it's sometimes possible to use the short name of your authoring computer on your Windows Media server, it's recommended that you always use its full host name or IP address. You can't change this value from the Windows Media Encoder—it's pulled from the operating system's settings. If your authoring computer's name is only listed in its short form, don't worry. This host name (or IP address) can be entered into the Windows Media server configuration manually. If you aren't certain what your authoring computer's full host name or IP address is, ask your network administrator.

FIGURE 4.14

Set your Windows Media Encoder Broadcast Connection settings according to the instructions in step 5.

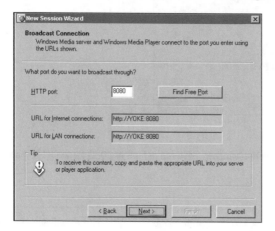

6. In the Profile Selection window, specify the bit rate to encode your source audio. Choose from a menu of eight audio-only encoding choices. (You can ignore the video-relevant choices for now.) From the eight audio-only bit rate encoding options, choose Audio for Dial-Up Modems (56 Kbps Stereo) from the Profile Selection window (see Figure 4.15). Click Next.

NOTE

Advanced users can create custom profiles to control individual codecs, bit rates, sample rates, and number of channels (mono or stereo).

FIGURE 4.15

Choose Audio for Dial-Up Modems (56 Kbps Stereo) in the Windows Media Encoder Profile Selection window.

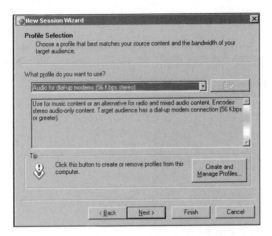

7. From the Archive Option window (see Figure 4.16), you can choose to make a local copy (archive) of your broadcast as it streams. The broadcast archive can serve as a backup and can also be used later for on-demand listening. Choose your location folder for this archive file and remember to make sure you have enough disk space. Click Next.

FIGURE 4.16

Select the location and filename to archive your live Windows Media stream.

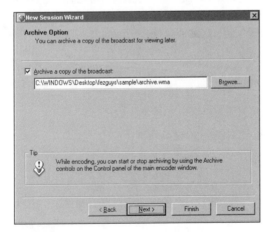

8. In the Display Information window, enter your file's attributes (see Windows Media Stream Attributes earlier in this chapter) including title, author, copyright, rating, and song description. Click Next.

FIGURE 4.17

Enter your Windows Media file attributes in the Windows Media Encoder's Display Information window.

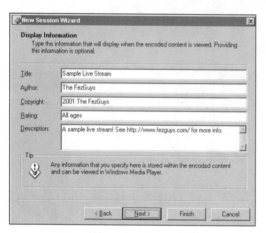

9. In the Settings window, you will find a summary of your configuration information. If everything looks as it should, click Finish.

10. Check your audio input levels. Click the Mixer button under the Audio panel of the main Windows Media encoder window (see Figure 4.18) to launch the standard Windows audio mixer. The Windows Media Encoder saves you a step by automatically setting the mixer for input instead of output levels. (It will be titled Record Control.)

FIGURE 4.18

Click the Mixer button to launch the standard Windows audio mixer and check your input levels.

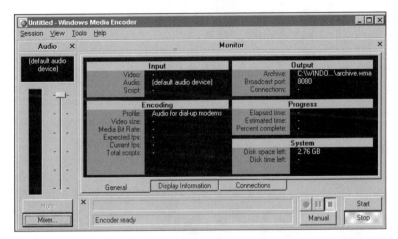

11. Select the correct input from the mixer window and move the Windows Media Encoder window and the mixer window so that they are side by side. Start your input source audio with the loudest musical section and click Start on the encoder. Observe the input levels and adjust them accordingly.

NOTE

Adjust the input level from the Record section of the standard Windows audio mixer (see Figure 4.19), not from within the Windows Media Encoder's Audio display. Windows Media Encoder's volume control and mute button don't appear to work reliably.

FIGURE 4.19

Select your audio input and adjust your input recording levels.

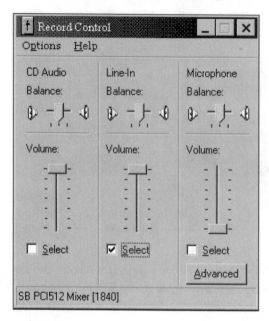

12. If everything looks healthy, press Stop and reset your source audio to the start point. When you're ready, click Start on the encoder and start your audio source (see Figure 4.20). The encoder begins streaming. (See "Creating a Server" for how to set up and configure a Windows Media Server.)

FIGURE 4.20

Click Start in the Windows Media Encoder to begin streaming.

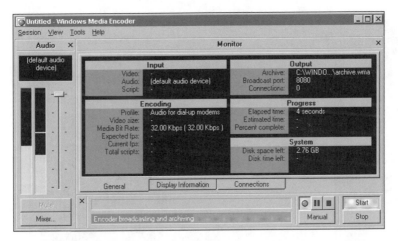

Test your live stream by plugging the URL that your Windows Media server administrator provides into your Windows Media player, ideally on a different computer with a different network connection (see Figure 4.21). If you're running your own server, see the following Step-by-Step tutorial on necessary server configuration.

FIGURE 4.21

Use your Windows Media Player to test your live stream.

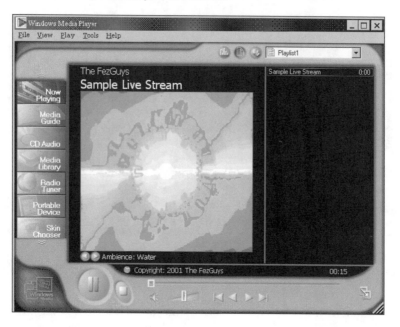

Creating a Server

Now that you have on-demand Windows Media encoded files or a live Windows Media stream on your authoring computer, it's time to serve it to your Internet audience. This means configuring and using (or leasing space on) a server computer to stream those files. This server (and the streaming software on it) is really a go-between that acts as the doorway between your stream's authoring point and the Internet.

A limitation to using the Windows Media format is that only computers running Windows NT/2000 can run the Windows Media streaming server. If you wish to serve your live or on-demand streams via real-time streaming the Windows Media server is required. HTTP/Progressive streaming of on-demand Windows Media streams can be done through the Windows Media server or any Web server. You'll be using the Windows Media Server for all the Step-by-Step tutorials in this chapter.

For more information on issues relating to streaming servers, see Chapter 7.

STEP-BY-STEP: Creating a Windows Media Server (Windows NT/2000)

NOTE

Steps in the install process that are not mentioned here indicate that you should accept the default that the Windows Media Server installer offers.

1. Download the Windows Media Server software for your computer running Windows NT/2000 from www.microsoft.com/windowsmedia/download. (Reminder: The Windows Media Server is not available for Windows 98/ME.)

    1. *From the download Web page, select Windows Media Services.*

    2. *From the download list, select the free Windows Media services for NT. If you need more advanced features, you can also download the Windows Media services add-in.*

2. Install the Windows Media server on your computer running Windows NT/2000.

NOTE

To install the Windows Media server, you need to be running NT v4.0 with Service Pack 4 or later, and be logged in from your authoring computer to your NT server as a user with administrator privileges. If you aren't familiar with this NT-specific process, refer to your NT manual.

3. When prompted for the directory to store your content (Windows Media calls this your Home Publishing Point), enter the appropriate folder or keep the default. This is the directory where all of your Windows Media encoded on-demand files will be placed.

4. You are asked if you want to enable HTTP streaming and distribution. If you aren't running a Web server on the same computer, you might want to enable this service, which allows the Windows Media server to act as a Web server and serve on-demand files using HTTP/Progressive streaming. If you already have a Web server running, you can use it for HTTP/Progressive streaming.

5. An account for the Windows Media service must now be configured. Thankfully, the installer can take care of the finer points of account creation for you. Accept the default option and allow the installer to create a NetShowServices account. This prevents you from having to deal with some of the more arcane user account administration functions of the Windows Media Server within the NT/2000 operating system. If you absolutely must have all the power, select the account you want to use.

6. Upon successful installation, you will be prompted to restart your server computer.

After your server computer has rebooted, you need to configure your Windows Media server software via the Windows Media Server Administrator to do the following:

- Pull live streams from your authoring computer.

- Handle uploading of your on-demand files to the Home Publishing Point specified during this installation. More details on creating metafiles to access this content can be found in Chapter 7.

The following Step-by-Step walks you through the process of using the Windows Media Administrator to configure your Windows Media Server to serve a live stream. In our Step-by-Step, the same server computer will be used to run both the Windows Media Server and the Windows Media Administrator.

NOTE

Although it is recommended that you run the Windows Media Administrator and the Windows Media Server on the same computer, this won't always work. For instance, if your Windows Media Server is physically elsewhere, you can install the Windows Media Administrator on a Windows 98/ME computer and use it to remotely configure your Windows Media Server.

STEP-BY-STEP: Configuring a Live Windows Media Stream Using the Windows Media Administrator

1. Launch the Windows Media Administrator by clicking Start, Windows Media, and Windows Media Administrator.

2. On the main page, under Configure Server, click Unicast Publishing Points.

3. Under Broadcast Unicast Publishing Points, make sure that the "Use wizard" checkbox is selected, and then click the Broadcast button and select New. This launches a QuickStart Wizard.

FIGURE 4.22

Start the QuickStart Wizard by selecting New from the Broadcast Unicast Publishing Points
pull-down menu.

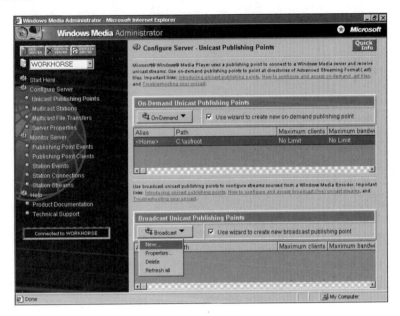

4. Verify that the Windows Media live stream from your encoding/authoring computer is running
   and click Next.

5. Select Create a Broadcast Publishing Point from the QuickStart Wizard Select a Publishing
   Point window (see Figure 4.23) and click Next.

NOTE

The first time you add a live stream to your server configuration, you will need to create a *broadcast publishing point (BPP)*. A BPP is defined as a virtual directory for storing content that is available to clients or for accessing a live stream. The BPP is the folder where the encoded streams reside. That might mean your authoring computer (for live streams), a server computer (for on-demand files), or another computer. Listeners, or clients, reach a BPP through the BPP's URL.

FIGURE 4.23

Select Create a Broadcast Publishing Point from the QuickStart Wizard's Select a Publishing Point window.

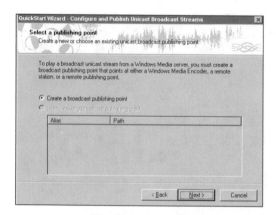

6. On the Specify Source window, select Windows Media Encoder (see Figure 4.24). This tells the server to redistribute a stream authored with the Windows Media encoder. Other choices are Remote Station and Remote Publishing Point for server-to-server broadcasting and more advanced server architecture. Click Next.

FIGURE 4.24

Specify Windows Media Encoder as your encoding source from within the Windows Media Administrator.

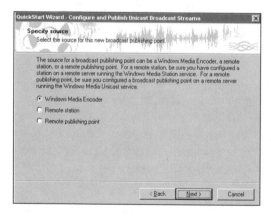

7. In the New Broadcast Publishing Point to a Windows Media Encoder window (see Figure 4.25), enter an alias (the name you give your Publishing Point). You can use the New Session Wizard's suggestion of *LiveEvents*.

FIGURE 4.25

Name your publishing point and enter the URL and port to your encoding source in the Windows Media Administrator.

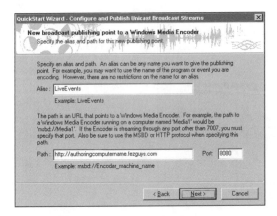

8. Now you must provide a path. This is the URL that points to your Windows Media Encoder (see steps 4 and 5 of the earlier Step-by-Step "Using Windows Media Encoder to Author a Live Windows Media Stream.") For this example, the URL is `http://authoringcomputername.mydomain.com`.

9. Next, enter the port you selected on your authoring computer. If you used 8080, enter that here. Of course, if you used 80, enter that instead. Click Next.

10. Within the Select Publishing Method page (see Figure 4.26), choose the default protocol of MMS and uncheck all publishing options. The publishing options are shortcuts to creating HTML and metafiles or copying related links to your Clipboard for linking Web pages to your live stream. (You will learn more about this in Chapter 7.) Note the MMS URL listed here. This URL will be used in a Windows Media player to test the live stream. Click Next.

NOTE

Your Windows NT/2000 server name might not show up as a full Internet host name on the Select Publishing Method page. This has to do with NT/2000 configuration, and you don't need to worry about it. If your server name is formatted as SERVERNAME instead of SERVERNAME. DOMAIN.COM, simply replace SERVERNAME with the server's complete host name or IP address. If you aren't certain what the full host name or IP address of the server is, ask your network administrator. If you need to change this to the full host name, you can click the Change Server button and enter it there. Doing so updates the URL displayed within the Select Publishing Method page. To be clear, you need two URLs: one to identify the authoring computer and the other to identify the server.

FIGURE 4.26

Select the MMS protocol, uncheck all publishing options, and edit your server name if necessary in the Publishing Method page of the Windows Media Administrator.

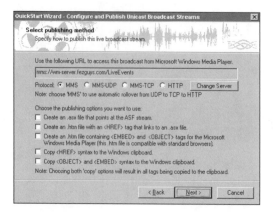

11. If all of the information looks correct on the Ready to Publish page, click Finish.

12. A Publishing Complete window appears, and the live stream becomes operational (see Figure 4.27). Buttons are available to test the stream from the Windows Media Administrator computer.

FIGURE 4.27

The Publishing Complete window of the Windows Media Administrator displays a summary of your new publishing point and provides a link to test your live stream.

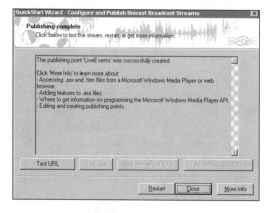

NOTE

Unless you're running the Windows Media Administrator on a separate machine, it's recommended that you open a Windows Media player using a different computer and even a different connection from the server or the encoder. In the player, enter the MMS URL and test this way. If the stream comes through the player, all is well (see Figure 4.28).

FIGURE 4.28

Test playback of your live stream using the Windows Media Player.

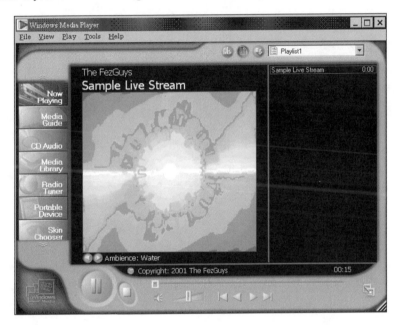

Under the Monitor Server link on the main Windows Media Administrator window are options that allow you to see what streams are running and who is listening to them. Select the Publishing Point Clients link to view current listeners.

Congratulations! You are serving a live audio stream, encoded in the Windows Media format, over the Internet. This is no small accomplishment, especially when using the Windows NT/2000 environment. Give yourself a pat on the back.

Summary

After you have uploaded your on-demand content and started your live streams, link them into your Web site (see Chapter 7), announce them on your mailing lists, put the announcement in your e-mail signature, and so on. Make a point to periodically check for upgrades to the Windows Media player, server, and encoder applications. Streaming audio technology continues to innovate at a rapid pace. Although your Windows Media should work with future versions for years to come, you might want to take advantage of new features often released annually.

CHAPTER 5

Using QuickTime

QuickTime grew out of an early Macintosh OS 6.0 software toolset for transferring large media files. Because of its initial heavy use for visual content, the
standard nomenclature for QuickTime files became (and remains) *movie*. The
regular suffix for QuickTime files is .mov. This can be a little confusing, so
this book will stick to calling QuickTime encoded on-demand files *files*,
although some software will refer to the files as *movies*.

One of the unique elements of the QuickTime streaming format is a process
called *hinting*, which is required when authoring on-demand files to be
streamed through a QuickTime streaming server. This process adds extra
information to an encoded on-demand file and creates *hints* for the streaming
server to deliver the file more reliably to your listener's player.

NOTE

Windows Media and RealMedia formats also include this type of additional information in their
streams, but it's handled transparently during the authoring process. Unlike Windows Media and
RealMedia, QuickTime allows you to author streams without the hinting information, which is
almost always done when serving via HTTP/Progressive streaming. Hinting your QuickTime on-
demand files typically doubles the size of the resulting file.

Audio can be included in QuickTime files in two ways. The first method
uses what is known as a self-contained file, which actually contains the audio
information. The other method uses a file type that is referred to as having
dependencies and is actually a reference, or pointer, to the file that contains the
audio information. Dependencies are helpful if you're making a presentation
with the QuickTime format and using various individual media files on

repeated occasions. Referencing the self-contained files with dependencies frees you from having to include the same audio (a disk space eater) every time that audio is used. Working with files that have and use dependencies can quickly become confusing; therefore, this book only works with self-contained files.

QuickTime 5 is used for all examples.

Software Encoders (Free Versus Pay)

Many third-party audio applications can save audio files as QuickTime on-demand files. Most of these applications only support on-demand encoding of QuickTime files for download-only Web server scenarios, although some third-party products support hinting technology. Because QuickTime Pro is native to the QuickTime environment, it offers the most consistent and reliable user experience across multiple platforms.

When you purchase the Pro license from Apple ($29.99, with a 10-day money back guarantee), you receive a license key. Simply plug the license into your player. The player then becomes a QuickTime encoder, allowing you to save and export to multiple formats for both audio and video.

Choosing Your Encoding Settings

Authoring streaming media requires choosing certain encoding settings. The settings decisions you make are based on limitations of, among other things, the current state of software engineering, computer processing and the subjective nature of human hearing. Thankfully, how you make these encoding settings decisions is generally similar across all formats.

NOTE

Don't encode files that are already encoded. An encoded file sounds better if you begin with uncompressed source audio.

Any audio file that can be opened in a waveform editor can be saved (converted) as a QuickTime file.

Whether your source audio is spoken word, sound effects, or music, you must choose the bit rate, codec, and channel (mono or stereo) settings that are appropriate to your own and to your projected audience's needs prior to encoding. It's all about file size versus audio quality. Obviously you want your streaming audio file to sound as good as the available technology and bandwidth will allow. But you must also take steps to ensure that the stream reaches the user intact. Not everyone has broadband connectivity, so it's recommended that you choose the lowest bit rate setting you can get away with that still sounds acceptable. For instance: If you're authoring content that contains only a human voice (mono) speaking under normal conversational conditions, it isn't necessary to encode the streaming file at anything over 56Kbps (28Kbps is also recognizable). The voice will be heard and understood at 28- or 56Kbps, and you won't consume unnecessary bandwidth. If you're authoring encoded music files in stereo, however, listeners will have a more enjoyable sonic experience if you offer the streaming file at a higher bit rate (56Kbps minimum and above).

In these tutorials you'll use a 32Kbps (mono) encode setting for 56Kbps users and a 128Kbps (stereo) encode setting for DSL (or any other broadband format) users. It's possible to encode at higher bit rates but the sound quality isn't all that much better and, by keeping the high quality setting at 128Kbps, broadband users have headroom to use their connection for other tasks.

You'll be selecting the QDesign music codec for authoring your encoded files for these examples.

NOTE

If you find yourself authoring voice-only content for dial-up modem users, choose the Qualcomm PureVoice codec in the QuickTime encoding software menu. Advanced users might want to sample other codecs.

Because QuickTime Pro is relatively inexpensive, it only includes a basic version of QDesign's codec, limiting you to a maximum bit rate of 48Kbps for encoding files. That's not very high, and will not provide the much-touted near-CD audio quality that all formats promise. To use higher bit rate levels within QuickTime, download QDesign's QDMC Music Codec 2.1 Professional Edition ($399.00) from its Web site at www.qdesign.com. A less expensive option might be to acquire the 2.1 QDesign Pro software as part of a bundle of other encoding products, such as Cleaner Pro or Sorenson Broadcaster.

The bit rate limitation applies only to QuickTime Pro when authoring on-demand files. Software for live streaming (Sorenson or Cleaner) already includes the QDesign Music Codec 2.1 Professional Edition. This book uses the QDesign QDMC Music Codec 2.1.

QuickTime Stream Attributes (and Annotations)

Every QuickTime on-demand file or live stream contains a number of *attributes*, or pieces of information that the software uses to describe the content of the file. Filling out this information might seem time consuming, but it's good to do. It's frustrating to hear good music and have no idea who the performer is. Most of these attributes are referred to by the same names across different encoding tools, but a few exceptions exist. QuickTime's available attributes are outlined in the bulleted list below.

Live streaming QuickTime encoders include a configuration section for entering attribute information in only a limited number of fields. Authoring on-demand files, however, includes many additional descriptions. These additional descriptions are called *annotations* and are accessed by selecting Movie, Get Movie Properties (Macintosh: ⌘+J, Windows: Ctrl+J) from within QuickTime Pro. This opens the Annotations window. You can view and edit existing values or add new ones through a simple interface. These changes can be preserved when you save the file or export it to another compression/ hinting combination. Unless noted otherwise, all fields are simple text fields.

- **Full Name**—A blank text field for entering the title of your stream. The QuickTime player displays this as the title of the player window. The Sorenson Broadcaster (see "Authoring a Live QuickTime Stream" later in this chapter) calls this attribute Title.

- **Author**—A blank text field for entering the author of the content of your stream.

- **Copyright**—A blank text field for entering copyright information for your stream.

FezGuys' Tip

To quickly get a copyright symbol on the Macintosh, press Option+G; on Windows, press Alt+Ctrl+C.

- **Information**—A blank text field to enter a short description of your stream. The Sorenson Broadcaster calls this attribute Info. Tip: Consider putting a relevant URL here.
- **Comment**—A blank text field for other information about your stream. The Sorenson Broadcaster automatically inserts the name and version of itself into this attribute's field.

The Sorenson Broadcaster also has a program URL for including the URL to the Web site so that viewers can access your broadcast.

You can view a summary of attribute and annotation information during playback by selecting Window, Show Movie Info (Macintosh: ⌘+I, Windows: Ctrl+I).

Authoring an On-Demand QuickTime File

If you have decided to author on-demand files in the QuickTime format, you will need to have the Pro version of QuickTime. You can also use third-party applications such as Cleaner.

QuickTime Player Pro—Apple's Authoring Tool

Apple has its own innate encoding tool, which is included as part of QuickTime Player Pro, to author on-demand QuickTime files. One advantage to using QuickTime Player Pro as opposed to third-party applications is that you are assured of having the latest underlying codecs.

This chapter uses QuickTime Player Pro to encode a song with vocals for delivery to a target audience of listeners with connections that range from dial-up (56Kbps) to broadband (DSL 384Kbps). (See Chapter 2, "Preparing Yourself," to learn how to create an AIFF or WAV file.) Because this is an on-demand streaming file, you will upload and stream it from a QuickTime server. (See the section titled "Creating a Server" later in this chapter and Chapter 7, "Serving Your Audio.")

Download the free QuickTime player from www.apple.com/quicktime/download. During installation, select the Full (for Macintosh) or Recommended (for Windows) installation type for QuickTime Pro users and media creators. Then purchase a QuickTime Pro (v5) license from www.apple.com/quicktime/buy. Launch your QuickTime player. The installation places a shortcut on your desktop. After installation, go to Edit, Preferences, Registration. (Windows users might need to select Registration from the QuickTime Settings page.) Enter the license information you received when you upgraded to the Pro version. Close the QuickTime Settings window.

After installation and registration, follow this Step-by-Step tutorial.

STEP-BY-STEP: Using QuickTime Player Pro to Author an On-Demand QuickTime File

1. Launch QuickTime Player Pro on your Macintosh or Windows computer.

2. Select File, Open (Macintosh: ⌘+O, Windows Ctrl+O). Open your AIFF (Macintosh) or WAV (Windows) file. Your file will appear in a newly opened QuickTime player window. Play it to make sure it's the one you want.

3. Set your media attributes (as described in "QuickTime Stream Attributes (and Annotations)") by selecting Movie, Get Movie Properties (Macintosh: ⌘+J, Windows: Ctrl+J). Add and edit your attribute values (see Figure 5.1).

FIGURE 5.1

Set your on-demand file's attributes in the Movie Properties window of QuickTime Player Pro.

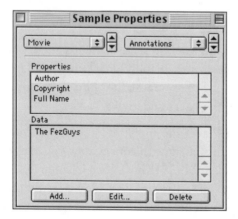

4. Select File, Export (Macintosh: ⌘+E, Windows: Ctrl+E) to open the Save Exported File As dialog box (see Figure 5.2).

FIGURE 5.2

Select File, Export to open QuickTime Pro's Save Exported File As dialog box.

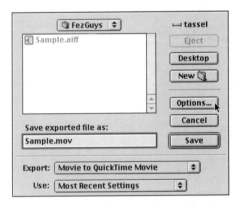

5. Choose Movie to QT Movie in the Export pull-down menu.

NOTE

If you already have a compressed QuickTime movie and only want to hint it for streaming through a QuickTime streaming server, you can export Movie to Hinted Movie, which adds hinting but leaves the other settings such as bit rate, channels, and codec untouched.

6. Click the Options button to open the Movie Settings dialog box. The video portion should be grayed out (unavailable) unless you're including video. Make sure the Sound option is checked (see Figure 5.3).

FIGURE 5.3

Make sure that the Sound option is checked in QuickTime Pro's Movie Settings window.

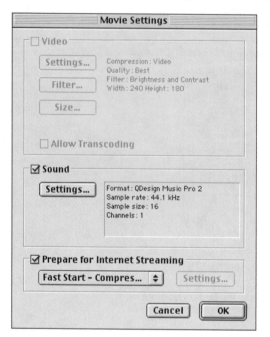

7. Next to the description of your source audio, click the Settings button. A Sound Settings window pops up.

8. In the Sound Settings window, choose QDesign Music Pro 2 for Compressor.

9. Click Options in the bottom left of the Sound Settings window to bring up the QDesign Music Encoder settings window.

   1. In the QDesign Music Encoder settings window, choose the 32 kbits/s bit rate setting (see Figure 5.4). This setting is for 56K dial-up modem users. To author on-demand files for broadband DSL users, choose the high bit rate setting of 128 kbits/s.

NOTE

The QDesign Pro codec only supports bit rate settings up to 128Kbps, which, for our purposes, is sufficient. As noted earlier in "Choosing Your Encoding Settings," if you're using the standard QuickTime Pro encoder (without the full version of the QDesign Music Codec), you will only be able to select bit rates up to 48 kbits/s.

2. *After you select a bit rate, the Recommended Settings text will update the available ranges of sample rates and number of channels (mono or stereo). For your 56K on-demand file, you will be using mono and a 44.1 kHz sample rate. If you choose stereo for your channel selection, consider using a 32 kHz sample rate. This will provide a little extra space for the encoder to use for the second channel. To author on-demand files for broadband DSL users, choose the 44 kHz sample rate and set the number of channels to Stereo.*

NOTE

The sample rate you choose isn't actually entered in the QDesign Music Encoder settings window. You make your decision based on the information in this window and select it when you return to the QuickTime Sound Settings window.

3. *For file optimization, you have two options: Quality or Speed. When authoring on-demand streaming files, always go for audio quality, so select Quality (see Figure 5.4). The speed setting tends to be more useful for the sometimes volatile live streaming environment (see "Authoring a Live QuickTime Stream").*

4. *The Advanced Settings option enables power users to make specific changes to how the codec encodes your audio. Leave this unchecked for now (see Chapter 11, "Advanced Audio Optimization"). Click OK.*

FIGURE 5.4

Select 32 kbits/s bit rate and Quality optimization in QuickTime Pro's QDesign Music 2 Codec options window.

10. In the QuickTime Sound Settings window (see Figure 5.5), set your bit size to 16 (unless your source is 8 bit). Set the sample rate and number of channels based on the recommendations of the QDesign Music window. Click OK.

FIGURE 5.5

Select your desired sample rate, bit rate, and number of channels in QuickTime Pro's Sound Settings window.

11. Your newly selected settings are now displayed in the QuickTime Movie Settings dialog box. Check Prepare for Internet Streaming.

12. Below the Prepare for Internet Streaming check box is a pull-down menu with a choice of three options for your file: Fast Start, Fast Start—Compressed Header, and Hinted Streaming. Depending on whether you are serving your on-demand files via HTTP/Progressive (a Web server) or real-time (QuickTime server), make your selection as follows:

   - *HTTP/Progressive Streaming (Web Server)—Choose either Fast Start or Fast Start—Compressed Header (see Figure 5.6). Both settings enable your file to play while it downloads instead of playing only after it has finished downloading. Like all other HTTP/Progressive streaming, the user receives a local copy and avoids most firewall problems.*

FIGURE 5.6

For HTTP/Progressive streaming, select Fast Start—Compressed Header from QuickTime Pro's Movie Settings window.

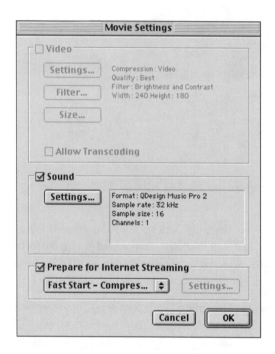

- **Real-Time Streaming (QuickTime Server)**—*Choose Hinted Streaming and click Settings to bring up the Hint Exporter Settings window. Click Optimize Hints for Server (see Figure 5.7). This enables your server to support more concurrent users but results in a file that is nearly twice as large as an unhinted file. Disk space is cheaper than performance, and you want the file to get there efficiently; therefore, click OK to exit the Hint Exporter Settings window.*

FIGURE 5.7

In the Hint Exporter window, check Optimize Hints for Server.

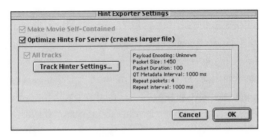

NOTE

QuickTime's real-time streaming server requires on-demand files to be hinted. However, these hints are unnecessary (and increase file size) when delivering your on-demand files via HTTP/Progressive streaming through normal Web servers, so they should not be included.

13. Click OK to exit the Movie Settings window. This returns you to the Save Exported File As window.

14. Select the location and filename for your exported on-demand file. Make sure the filename ends in .mov and click Save. An Exporting Movie dialog box appears with a Stop button. When the process is finished, the Exporting Movie dialog box disappears and the file shows up where you put it.

NOTE

Macintosh users can't do anything else on their computer during the encoding process. Windows users can, but it is recommended that you don't run other applications or perform other tasks on your computer while QuickTime is encoding your file.

15. Go through the previous steps 2–14. When you reach the QDesign Music Codec bit rate option (step 9), this time choose 128 kbits/s that is suitable for broadband 384K DSL users. Continue through the rest of the steps.

You now have two QuickTime on-demand streaming files in your chosen folder, ready to be slapped onto a Web server or tossed into the Movie Directory of a QuickTime server. Open them with your QuickTime player and verify that they sound okay.

Authoring a Live QuickTime Stream

NOTE

The new Macintosh version of Sorenson Broadcaster (v2.0) with QT 5 and Macintosh OS X 10.0 support was not available at the time of this writing. The people who manufacture Sorenson Broadcaster say that the v2.0 user interface will look a little different, and there will be some new features. The Windows tutorial in the next Step-by-Step should help with the authoring process of the new Macintosh version (aside from the inherent differences of the disparate operating systems).

Macintosh OS 9 users can author a live QuickTime stream with Sorenson Broadcaster v1.1 ($199.00), however it requires the out of date QuickTime 4. Other third-party software offering mixed results are CoolStream at www.evological.com and Channel Storm Live Channel at www.channelstorm.com.

In this section, you'll create a live QuickTime stream on your authoring computer. That is, source audio enters your computer uncompressed and exits as an encoded live stream. The QuickTime streaming server then forwards the live stream, in turn, to your listeners on the Internet. Make sure your audio source is plugged into your computer's audio input. Use the same audio input level guidelines you used to create a digital file (see Chapter 2).

Your source audio quality is crucial here. This is because no opportunities (such as waveform editors) are typically available to optimize the signal between encoding and outputting that audio as a live stream. Make sure your signal is as clean as possible and that your level is set accurately—not so low that it can't be heard and not so loud that it will distort; both scenarios prevent the encoder from doing a good job. You might want to place some audio hardware (such as a compressor) in your signal path to smooth the signal and increase the encoder's efficiency (see Chapter 11).

Prior to beginning the live stream, it's strongly recommended that you have, if possible, another test computer available to do a listening test. Short of calling your friends on the phone (which also works), this is the best way to make sure your live stream sounds okay and is actually making it out to the Internet intact. The most realistic test is having your listening test computer on a completely different Internet connection from your live encoder computer. In addition, if you're encoding and streaming for modem users, test your live stream with a modem connection (not broadband or DSL) to get a realistic experience.

NOTE

> Although it's possible to use the same computer to simultaneously author from and run your streaming server, doing so is not recommended for handling more than a dozen listeners.

To create a live QuickTime stream on the Windows operating system for Windows 98, ME, and 2000, Sorenson Broadcaster v1.5 will be used. Sorenson Broadcaster includes a version of the QDesign codec specifically for live streaming that offers a maximum data rate of only 16Kbps. To get higher data rate compression, you have to buy the QDesign commercial codec (www.qdesign.com) or get it with a multimedia software bundle, of which Sorenson Broadcaster is a portion. The Sorenson Broadcaster is also included with a Power Bundle for QuickTime 5 and a Professional Suite for QuickTime 5. These two higher-priced bundles that are available from www.sorenson.com include extra support for video and enhanced production tools.

STEP-BY-STEP: Using Sorenson Broadcaster to Author a Live QuickTime Stream

1. Launch Sorenson Broadcaster v1.5.1 on your Windows computer. An untitled Sorenson Broadcaster window appears (see Figure 5.8). Make sure that your source audio is connected to your authoring computer.

FIGURE 5.8

The Sorenson Broadcaster main window.

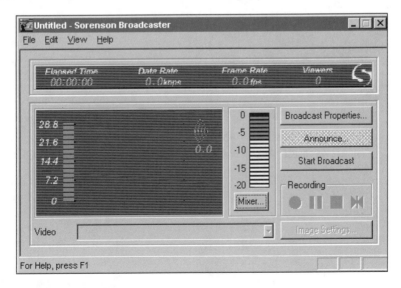

2. Click on the Broadcast Properties button. This takes you to a Sources pane. You have the option of choosing from preset preferences or creating your own. Because a suitable present isn't available for an audio-only 56K live stream, you will configure your settings manually. You can save these settings using File, Save As.

3. Leave Video unchecked. (Note: The Sources pane defaults to this setting if no video is plugged in). The first option in the Audio section is the pull-down menu for your Input Audio Device. The default selection should be allowed. (The OS sets this during the install process.) If you're not certain, choose an option that uses the term *Wave Recording* or *Wave Input*. To the right of the Input Audio Device menu, allow the default Device Config setting. See Figure 5.9 for a summary of the Sources pane settings.

FIGURE 5.9

Leave the Video option unchecked, make sure the Audio option is checked, and verify the Input Audio Device setting in Sorenson Broadcaster's Sources pane of the Broadcast Properties window.

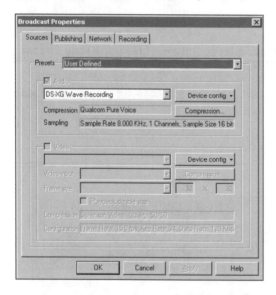

4. Click on the Compression tab, which pops up an Audio Configuration window. For Compressor, choose QDesign Music 2 (see Figure 5.10).

FIGURE 5.10

Select QDesign Music 2 in Sorenson Broadcaster's Audio Configuration window.

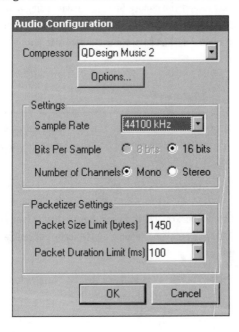

5. Click the Options button, which brings up the QDesign Music Encoder settings window.

6. In the QDesign Music Encoder settings window, choose the 32 kbits/s bit rate setting (see Figure 5.11). This setting is for 56K dial-up modem users. If you are authoring a live stream for broadband DSL users, select 128 kbits/s.

NOTE

The QDesign Pro codec only supports bit rate settings up to 128Kbps, which is sufficient. As noted earlier in "Choosing Your Encoding Settings," if you're using the standard QuickTime Pro encoder (without the full version of the QDesign Music Codec), you will only be able to select bit rates up to 48 kbits/s.

7. After you select a bit rate, the Recommended Settings text updates the available ranges of sample rates and number of channels (mono or stereo). For your 56K live stream, you will be using mono and a 44.1 kHz sample rate. If you choose Stereo, consider using a 32 kHz sample rate, which provides a little extra space for the encoder to use for the second channel. If you are authoring a live stream for broadband DSL users, choose the 44 kHz sample rate and set the number of channels to Stereo.

NOTE

The sample rate you choose isn't actually entered in the QDesign Music Encoder settings window. You make your decision based on the information in this window and select it when you return to the Audio Configuration window.

8. For file optimization, you have two options: Quality or Speed. Select Quality (see Figure 5.11). Only select Speed if your computer has problems keeping up (typically noticeable through dropouts or especially poor sound).

9. The Advanced Settings option enables power users to make specific changes to how the codec encodes your audio. Leave this unchecked for now (see Chapter 12). Click OK.

FIGURE 5.11

Select 32 kbits/s bit rate and Quality optimization in Sorenson Broadcaster's QDesign Music 2 Codec options window.

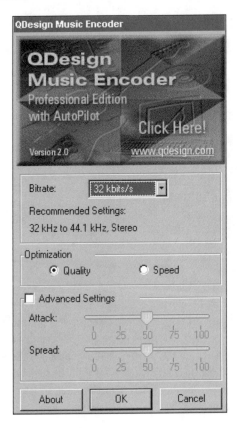

10. In the Audio Configuration window, set your bit size to 16 (unless your source is 8 bit). Set the sample rate and number of channels based on the recommendations of the QDesign Music window. Leave the Packetizer Settings at their default values and click OK.

11. Back in the Broadcast Properties window, click the Publishing tab. Enter your appropriate title, author, copyright, program URL, and other information for your stream (see "QuickTime Stream Attributes (and Annotations)").

12. Within the Publishing tab (see Figure 5.12) is an option to provide a graphics image (called Poster Frame) in your listeners' QuickTime player window. Leave this option unchecked. If you would like to go back later and experiment with offering a groovy little graphic, please do.

FIGURE 5.12

Set your QuickTime live stream attributes in Sorenson Broadcaster's Publishing pane of the Broadcast Properties window.

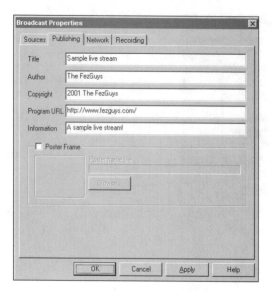

13. Click the Network tab. From the Broadcast Type pull-down menu, select Unicast because you're sending directly to your streaming server (see Figure 5.13). (Users who want to multicast to a local intranet LAN might want to look into the Multicast option.) For Receiver's IP Address, enter the IP address of your QuickTime server. (The IP will be supplied by whomever is in charge of configuring the server. See the section, "Creating a Server" later in this chapter.) Leave the rest of the options on this page as their default settings.

FIGURE 5.13

Select Unicast broadcast type and leave the default values for all other options in Sorenson Broadcaster's Network pane of the Broadcast Properties window.

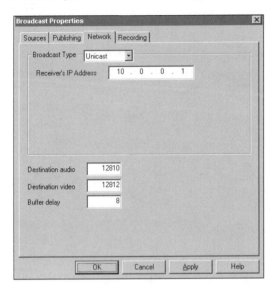

14. If you want to save a local copy of your live broadcast, click the Recording tab and choose the folder to which to save your live streaming file (see Figure 5.14). If desired, check Start Recording When Broadcast Starts to start the Save process as soon as you begin streaming. Regardless of this setting, you can start and stop the archival process while broadcasting using the Record, Pause, and Stop buttons in Sorenson Broadcaster's main window. Click OK to exit the Broadcast Properties window.

FezGuys' Tip

If you choose to archive a local copy of your live broadcast, make sure you have enough disk space available. Long-running programs can quickly consume gigabytes of disk space, and running out of space locally can interrupt your broadcast for all listeners.

FIGURE 5.14

If a local archive of your live stream is desired, enter the archive's filename in Sorenson Broadcaster's Recording pane of the Broadcast Properties window.

15. In the main Sorenson Broadcaster window is a vertical input level meter with a Mixer button. Click that button to open the standard Windows Recording Control utility.

16. Press Play on your input device and make sure the appropriate input (this will most likely be Line Input if you're using an external cassette, CD, and so on) is selected and check your input audio levels (see Figure 5.15). When you're happy with the levels, move the Recording Control window side by side on your authoring computer's screen with the Sorenson Broadcaster Broadcast Properties window to view both simultaneously. Press Stop on your input device and reposition your source audio to the start point.

FIGURE 5.15

Set your input, adjust levels, and place the Recording Control window side by side with Sorenson Broadcaster for easy fine-tuning.

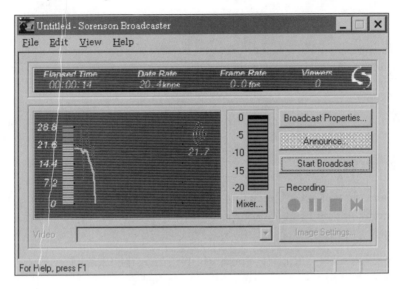

17. You are now ready to stream. Click Start Broadcast button in the main window and start your source audio. You will see elapsed time and data rate information about your broadcast updated in real time.

18. You are now streaming! To announce and test your stream, click on the Announce button on the Sorenson Broadcaster main window. This brings up the Save Broadcast Announcement window.

19. In the filename field, enter the name of your broadcast. It is recommended that you use a simple, short name with no spaces or odd punctuation, such as "live". A file suffix (.mov or .sdp) is automatically added based on what you choose for the Save as Type option.

20. Two options are available for Save as Type: Reference Movie (*.mov) or SDP Text Announcement (*.sdp). Because you're sending your broadcast to a streaming server, choose SDP Text Announcement (*.sdp). If you decide instead to multicast over a LAN or unicast to a single recipient, choose Reference Movie (*.mov). Make your selection and click Save.

21. Using FTP, upload your live.sdp file to the Movie Directory folder of your QuickTime streaming server.

22. Test your stream by opening the streaming file's URL in a QuickTime player (see Figure 5.16) on another computer (and, if possible, another connection). In the QuickTime player, go to File, Open URL (Macintosh: ⌘+U, Windows: Ctrl+U) and enter rtsp://streamingservername.com/live.sdp. Make sure to include subdirectory names if necessary.

FIGURE 5.16

Test your live stream by playing it back using the QuickTime Player.

You are broadcasting a live stream to the Internet! Do your happy dance!

Creating a Server

Where do you get a QuickTime Streaming Server (QTSS)? While the system's not yet as ubiquitous as setting up residential phone service, here's how it's done.

For live stream authoring, you must use either the QuickTime Streaming Server (QTSS) or the Darwin Streaming Server (DSS). The QTSS is available for Max OS X only. The DSS is available for all of the popular operating systems (Macintosh OS X, Windows, and various Unix variants). For serving on-demand files, you can use either the QTSS or DSS for real-time streaming of on-demand files, or any Web server (for HTTP/Progressive streaming). You'll be using both the QTSS and the DSS for all the Step-by-Step tutorials in this chapter.

NOTE

HTTP/Progressive on-demand QuickTime files can be streamed through HTTP/Progressive streaming from a Web server. See Chapter 2 for an explanation of the differences between progressive (for on-demand only) and real-time (both on-demand and live) streaming. See Chapter 7 for examples on how to do both.

FezGuys' Tip

When serving on-demand QuickTime content through a standard Web server, make sure your files have been encoded with the Fast Start feature so that the file streams as it downloads. See the earlier section, "Authoring an On-Demand QuickTime File," for more details.

For more information on issues relating to streaming servers, see Chapter 7.

QuickTime Streaming Server Versus Darwin Streaming Server

The QuickTime Streaming Server (QTSS) is available for Macintosh OS X only. However, the Darwin Streaming Server (DSS), an open-source streaming server, is available for Unix, Windows NT/2000, and other platforms. The DSS is available in precompiled binary or source form, and the use of either requires acceptance of the Apple Public Source License (APSL). You don't have to pay a fee; you simply set up a username and password after accepting the terms.

According to the Apple Web site, OS X is the preferred platform to run the QTSS. In fact, OS X Server software includes it by default (and is the only one covered by Apple Support). Standard OS X (not the Server version) can run the QTSS, albeit without Apple Support at your beck and call. Macintosh OS 9 isn't supported at all. Although the server source code is the same for all platforms, on operating systems other than OS X, the server is referred to by the DSS name. The Web site goes on to mention that, regardless of the OS chosen to run either DSS or QTSS, the features are the same but there are "inherent performance differences as a result of the platform."

Installing the QuickTime Streaming Server on Macintosh OS X

The QuickTime Streaming Server (QTSS) v3.0.2 is included as part of the Macintosh OS X Server software. This section uses a Macintosh G4 computer running OS X Server V.10.1, although QTSS is also available as a separate download for the standard (non-server) OS X platform (although unsupported by Apple Support).

After you have installed the QTSS software on your Macintosh G4 server computer, the QTSS Streaming Server Admin is added to your system dock.

NOTE

The authors downloaded (from www.apple.com/quicktime/products/qtss), installed, and ran QTSS successfully on the standard (non-server) Macintosh OS X platform, but noticed that it doesn't put the Streaming Server Admin icon in the desktop dock. In this environment, simply open your browser and enter the URL http://127.0.0.1:1220 manually.

Clicking on Streaming Server Admin is a shortcut to opening your Web browser to the default URL. You can also manually open a Web browser and enter that URL. The Streaming Server Admin icon uses the default of http://127.0.0.1:1220, but you can also use your server's host name in place of 127.0.0.1 and access the QTSS server admin from another (remote) computer on your network.

NOTE

During initial configuration, if you didn't choose to start the server upon boot, make sure you click Start Server Now in the top right of your Streaming Server Admin screen. Doing so launches a Server Snapshot screen.

At this point, it's a simple matter of plugging your configuration information into the Server Snapshot screen. You're ready to fast forward to the later Step-by-Step in this chapter titled "Configuring a QuickTime or Darwin Streaming Server."

Installing the Darwin Streaming Server on Unix (FreeBSD)

Other Unix installations should be similar to FreeBSD. If you haven't already set up an APSL account, do so at www.publicsource.apple.com/apsl.

Download the latest version of the Darwin Streaming Server (DSS) for FreeBSD v3.5 from www.publicsource.apple.com/projects/streaming. You'll download version 3.0.1 in its binary distribution as opposed to downloading and compiling the source code. If you have version 4 of FreeBSD installed, you'll probably need to install the FreeBSD v3.5 compatibility library distribution (available from the same place you received your FreeBSD install).

The streaming server and administration tool are started as part of the installation.

At this point, it's a simple matter of plugging your configuration information into the Server Snapshot screen. Fast forward to the later Step-by-Step titled "Configuring a QuickTime or Darwin Streaming Server."

Installing the Darwin Streaming Server on Windows NT/2000

The somewhat cumbersome process of installing the Darwin Streaming Server (DSS) on a Windows NT/2000 system requires a little extra patience, but it does work. Installing DSS on an NT/2000 system isn't the typical "click Next" installer-based dialog box process.

Using the Streaming Server Administrator of the DSS for NT requires that the interpreter for Perl v5.004_05 (or above) be installed on your server computer. If necessary, you can get the free download of Perl from http:// people.netscape.com/richm/nsPerl. Read the README file that comes with the Perl download for extra install information. Carefully following the README instructions makes the Perl interpreter accessible to the DSS.

FezGuys' Tip

If you install the Perl interpreter in a different location than the Perl installer places it by default, you might need to update your system path so that the DSS can find Perl.

A simpler solution is to copy the file nsperl.exe into your C:\WINNT directory (which should already be in your system path) and name it perl.exe.

Basic operation of the DSS for Windows NT is similar to FreeBSD and MacOS. You can read about these differences in the last chapter of the AboutDarwinStreamingSvr.pdf file included in your Windows NT DSS installation.

If you haven't already set up a free APSL account, do so at www.publicsource. apple.com/apsl.

Next, download the latest version of the DSS for Windows NT/2000 from www.publicsource.apple.com/projects/streaming. Download version 3.0.1 in its binary distribution as opposed to downloading and compiling the source code.

Running the downloaded file unzips the files into an installation directory. Run the INSTALL.BAT installer. The MS-DOS window, which was opened during the install, will remain open because it is still running the Streaming

Server Administrator. Leave this window open as long as you want the Streaming Server Admin to run. (You can minimize it if you like.)

At this point, it's a simple matter of plugging your configuration information into the Server Snapshot screen. See the following Step-by-Step.

STEP-BY-STEP: Configuring a QuickTime or Darwin Streaming Server

1. Make sure you're logged into the Streaming Server Admin. Point your browser to `http://127.0.0.1:1220`. The default administrator username is *streamingadmin* and the default password is *default*.

2. When you open the Streaming Server Admin, the main Server Snapshot page displays various useful bits of information about your server status. Click Settings to view the General Settings for the server (see Figure 5.17).

3. The Movies Directory setting specifies the folder into which you will upload all your on-demand content. If you're happy with that location, leave it as is and make note of it.

FIGURE 5.17

Set your desired settings in the QTSS/DSS Admin's General Settings page.

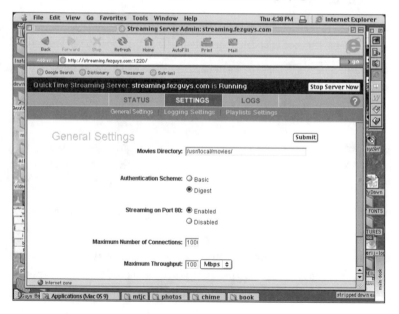

NOTE

Make sure you have enough disk space available. If many people want access to your live stream, a server's log files, which also reside in this directory, can quickly grow to gigabytes. (See Chapter 2 for server computer hardware requirements.)

4. Leave the default Digest for Authentication Scheme. This will require your listeners to have version 5 of the QuickTime player, but it can provide a more secure stream. Of course, if you don't plan to require authentication or want to provide backward compatibility, choose Basic.

5. For Streaming on Port 80, choose Enabled if you are not running a Web server on the same computer as your QTSS or DSS. (This setting is likely to allow your stream through most fire-walls.) Leave the default selection of Disabled if you are running a Web server on the same computer as your QTSS or DSS.

6. The Maximum Number of Connections setting limits how many concurrent users your server will support. The default is 1,000, and you should set this number appropriately for your situation. Keep in mind that if your streams become popular, you will pay fees for every increment of bandwidth you use. Be realistic about what your expectations are and for what you're willing to pay. It's helpful to factor in your server computer's processing power and the available band-width to come up with the appropriate value for this setting.

7. The Maximum Throughput setting is the maximum amount of bandwidth that the server will send out at one time. As mentioned previously, if you don't want to be charged for additional bandwidth by your co-location facility, this is where you limit how much bandwidth the server can use.

NOTE

If the number of concurrent listeners reaches the Maximum Number of Connections setting or the amount of bandwidth in use hits the Maximum Throughput setting, then new users who are trying to connect will get a Server Busy message.

8. In Administrator's New Password, enter (and re-enter in Re-Enter Administrator's New Password) a new password to change the server administrator password. This is highly recommended so that others can't tweak (or do worse things to) your settings.

NOTE

Version 3 of both the QTSS and DSS restrict what characters you can use in your new password. Avoid special characters such as colons (:) and periods (.).

9. Click Submit to finish this first-time QuickTime server configuration.

10. The installation includes a sample movie with which you can test your server. Launch the QuickTime player on another computer (preferably on another connection) and select File, Open URL (Macintosh: ⌘+U, Windows: Ctrl+U). Enter `rtsp://www.myserver.com/sample.mov` and click OK to view the sample movie.

FIGURE 5.18

Test your QuickTime server by playing it back using the QuickTime Player.

Summary

After you have uploaded your on-demand content into your Movie Directory folder or started your live streams, link them into your Web site (see Chapter 7) and announce it on your mailing lists, your e-mail signature, and so on. Make a point to periodically check for upgrades to the QuickTime player, server, and encoder applications. Streaming audio technology continues to innovate at a rapid pace. Although your QuickTime server should work with future versions for years to come, you might want to take advantage of new features that are sometimes released annually.

CHAPTER 6

Using MP3

MP3-encoded audio is far and away the most popular encoding method used to transfer sound across the Internet. Its widespread use might even be the primary reason you hold this book in your hands. MP3 isn't actually a format, however, and only recently has it become popularized as more than an on-demand, download-only codec. The popularity of MP3 for file sharing and music downloads has almost automatically made it a popular streaming format. Manufacturers have quickly jumped on board and added support for the MP3 standard to their encoding and producing tools.

Software Encoders (Free Versus Pay)

For those who are just starting out in streaming audio, it's not necessary to spend money on an MP3 encoder. Freeware and shareware MP3 on-demand file encoders and live streaming tools are available from a wide variety of sources (see the Appendix, "Tools and Resources"). Far more on-demand tools than live streaming tools exist. At some point, however, your streaming audio idea might become part of a business. If you reach that point, consider purchasing a more flexible and robust software or hardware encoding tool.

In this chapter, you'll author on-demand MP3 files using Audiograbber (Windows) and iTunes (Macintosh). You'll use Winamp (Windows) to author live MP3 streams. A generally used Macintosh-based MP3 live stream encoding software tool has yet to be released (at the time of this writing).

Other MP3 software encoders are listed in the Appendix.

Choosing Your Encoding Settings

Authoring streaming media requires choosing certain encoding settings. The settings decisions you make are based on limitations of, among other things, the current state of software engineering, computer processing and the subjective nature of human hearing. Thankfully, how you make these encoding settings decisions is generally similar across all formats.

NOTE

Don't encode files that are already encoded. An encoded file sounds better if you begin with uncompressed source audio.

Any audio file that can be opened in a waveform editor can be saved (converted) as an MP3 file.

Whether your source audio is spoken word, sound effects, or music, you must choose the bit rate, codec, and channel (mono or stereo) settings that are appropriate to your own and to your projected audience's needs prior to encoding. It's all about file size versus audio quality. Obviously you want your streaming audio file to sound as good as the available technology and bandwidth will allow. But you must also take steps to ensure that the stream reaches the user intact. Not everyone has broadband connectivity, so it's recommended that you choose the lowest bit rate setting you can get away with that still sounds acceptable. For instance: If you're authoring content that contains only a human voice (mono) speaking under normal conversational conditions, it isn't necessary to encode the streaming file at anything over 56Kbps (28Kbps is also recognizable). The voice will be heard and understood at 28- or 56Kbps, and you won't consume unnecessary bandwidth. If you're authoring encoded music files in stereo, however, listeners will have a more enjoyable sonic experience if you offer the streaming file at a higher bit rate (56Kbps minimum and above).

In these tutorials you'll use a 32 Kbps (mono) encode setting for 56Kbps users and a 192 Kbps (stereo) encode setting for DSL (or any other broadband format) users. It's possible to encode at higher bitrates but the sound quality isn't all that much better and, by keeping the high quality setting at 192 Kbps, broadband users have headroom to use their connection for other tasks.

The Step-by-Step tutorials in this chapter will take advantage of a piece of technology called variable bit rate (VBR) that is used to optimize MP3 encoding (both on-demand files and live streams). A brief explanation of VBR follows.

Standard MP3 files are encoded at a single (or "constant") bit rate (CBR) through the entire file. That means high-quality, high bit rate streaming files are at the mercy of available bandwidth, potentially dropping out or disconnecting altogether when data rates fall below acceptable levels. This inconsistent connectivity is a typical happenstance for anyone who is subscribed to an ISP that is overselling bandwidth. You know the scenario: Everybody goes online at a certain time, nobody gets anything, and 3 a.m. becomes the optimal time for listening to uninterrupted music on the Internet.

VBR encoding takes advantage of every little bit of bandwidth by looking at an audio file and automatically choosing at what bit rate to encode the file based on how much audio information is present at any given moment. A song that begins quietly or with a single musical instrument will, during that section, be encoded at a lower bit rate than say, the middle of the same song (when all the instruments might be playing together and the volume and frequency range might be greater). Songs with many fluctuations in dynamic range will be encoded at several bit rates.

The key conceptual difference between CBR and VBR might be expressed this way: CBR encoding specifies compression by space, and VBR encoding specifies compression by quality. With CBR, quality might be dropped in the process of maintaining the specified bit rate. With VBR, the bit rate changes to meet the quality level desired. Ten seconds of silence encoded at a CBR of 128Kbps uses the same disk space as ten seconds of full-on stereo opera. VBR encoded files of the same audio would result in a low bit rate for quiet sections and higher bit rates for louder sections. VBR encoding, like CBR, is set at the time the audio is encoded.

The MP3 standard is designed so that information about bit rate encode levels is included throughout the file. This makes it easy for VBR-enabled MP3 players to seamlessly decode and play VBR files just like CBR files. In fact, users are likely to have a more consistent listening experience with the frequent bit rate changes in a VBR-encoded file than with a CBR-encoded file. In a CBR file, when you suddenly reach a more full-range portion of a song, only the same number of bits are available. This can result in unwanted audio artifacts (a "swooshy" sound that is most noticeable when encoding to lower bit rates).

Upgrade your player if you haven't in the past two years. You can choose not to enable VBR if you think your listeners might not benefit, but that's not recommended.

MP3 Stream Attributes

Every MP3 on-demand file or live stream contains a number of "attributes" that not only describe the content but also include instructions for the server and player. These attributes are separate from the actual encoded audio and the specific codec. Filling out this information might seem time consuming, but it's good to do. It's frustrating to hear good music and have no idea who is performing it.

MP3 includes these attributes using a standard format called *ID3 tags* (www.id3.org). Many versions of the ID3 tagging format are available, and older MP3 players might not be able to read the later incarnations. The new version (ID3v2 and later) places this information at the beginning of the stream; the older version (ID3v1 or earlier) placed the information at the end. For this reason, ID3v2 is far more useful for providing information for live streams. As you will see, ID3 tags are geared primarily toward audio files. They originated to add information about downloadable and traded music. ID3v2 will be used in this book wherever possible as all common MP3 players have updated to support it.

Most MP3 file attributes are referred by the same names across different encoding tools, with a few exceptions. MP3 available attributes are outlined in the following bulleted list, noting what other software tools used in this book might call them. (Dozens of attributes are available, with varying practical use.)

- **Artist**—A blank text field where you enter the author of the content of your stream.

- **Album**—A blank text field where you enter the album to which the stream is related, if any.

- **Comments**—A blank text field where you enter a short comment about your stream. Tip: Consider putting a relevant URL here.

- **Genre**—This is either a blank text field or a selection from a list of genres where you enter or select a musical style classification.

- **Year**—A blank text field where you enter the year the stream (or stream content) was created.

- **Track Number**—A blank numerical field used for audio from released material—what track number it is on the release.

Authoring an On-Demand MP3 File

Although you'll be using previously prepared uncompressed audio files in these examples, in creating on-demand files, both Audiograbber and iTunes support one-step ripping and encoding directly from a CD into an MP3-encoded file. If you don't need to do additional processing (EQ, compression, and so on), don't bother making the separate steps of ripping CD audio to WAV or AIFF files and then encoding those files to MP3.

Using Audiograbber and LAME

Audiograbber doesn't automatically come with a codec to encode to MP3. When Audiograbber is launched on a Windows computer, it detects an MP3 encoder (if any) within the Windows OS. Because Audiograbber usually chooses a Windows add-on with limited capabilities, you can download a free plug-in for Audiograbber called LAME (for: "Lame Ain't an MP3 Encoder"). With LAME available to Audiograbber, you can encode MP3 files up to 320Kbps.

If you don't have it already on your Windows computer, go to `www.audiograbber.com-us.net/download.html` and download version 3.89 or later. As of this writing, a fully enabled version of Audiograbber costs $29.95 and is well worth having.

Download the free LAME plug-in for Audiograbber from `www.win32lame.com`. The download is free (see the Appendix, for information about licensing and using LAME). Follow the instructions on the download site to extract the files into your Audiograbber directory (the default location is `c:\audiograbber`). After installation the LAME plug-in is automatically detected when Audiograbber is launched as an available MP3 encoding engine.

You're going to use Audiograbber and LAME to encode a song with vocals for delivery to a target audience of listeners who have connections ranging from dial-up (56Kbps) to broadband (DSL 384Kbps). (Refer to Chapter 2, "Preparing Yourself," to learn how to create an AIFF or WAV file.) Because this is an on-demand file, you get to upload and stream it from a SHOUTcast or Web server. (See the section called "Creating a Server," later in this chapter, and Chapter 7, "Serving Your Audio.")

STEP-BY-STEP TITLE: Using Audiograbber and LAME to Author an On-Demand MP3 File

1. Launch Audiograbber and select Settings, General Settings. This is where you set the music folder for your encoded files. You can also choose any number of simple (or complex) methods for how to name them and sub-directories in which to put them.

    1. Next to Directory to Store Files in the General Settings window, click on the Browse button to select your desired main music folder directory.

    2. Under Create Filenames From, check the boxes next to the items on which you would like your encoded file's names to be based.

    3. Under Sub Directories, (see Figure 6.1) you can select directories in which to place your files (under the main music folder). Some of these values are pulled from the track's ID3 values and are especially useful when ripping large numbers of CDs into a music library. For individual on-demand file creation, Audiograbber's defaults are fine, so don't bother wasting time weighing the different options.

    4. When finished, click OK.

FIGURE 6.1

Select the destination directory and method to name new files in Audiograbber's General Settings window.

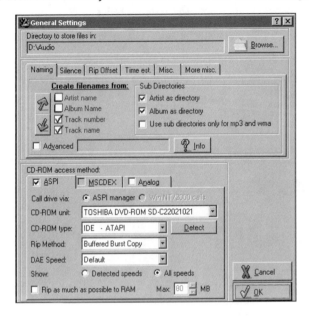

2. Click on the MP3 icon or go to Settings, MP3 to bring up the MP3 Settings window (see Figure 6.2).

3. Select your MP3 Encoding Engine by checking Internal Encoder (in the middle of the MP3 Settings pop-up window). Select the LameEnc DLL from the pull-down option list directly below the Internal Encoder checkmark.

4. Select Constant Bit Rate. Do this because the LAME encoder doesn't support a variable bit rate below 90Kbps, and you're encoding to a 32Kbps on-demand MP3 file.

5. Choose 32 on the horizontal slider to set 32Kbps for your 56Kbps modem users. If you are creating for broadband users, select 192 for 192Kbps.

6. For the number of channels, choose Mono for your 56Kbps modem users. For your broadband users, choose the setting Stereo.

NOTE

Dual Stereo uses half of the total bit rate for each channel. This is what you're used to with uncompressed CD audio. Choosing Stereo varies the bit rate used for each channel as needed. Choosing Joint Stereo (the best choice for bit rates under 128Kbps) encodes certain frequencies in mono to save space.

7. From the choices Voice, Low, Normal or High, choose High. (Only select Voice when you are encoding spoken word.) You won't notice a huge audio quality difference between Low and High, but if you're not in a rush, High will sound slightly better.

8. Leave the Bitstream Flags as they are. Most format players don't pay attention to them.

9. Leave the Encoder Priority slider at Normal. Only adjust the slider if you want to do other tasks on your computer and don't want the encoder to take up all your processing resources while encoding a large number of files.

FIGURE 6.2

Choose the appropriate settings for your on-demand MP3 file in Audiograbber's MP3 Settings window.

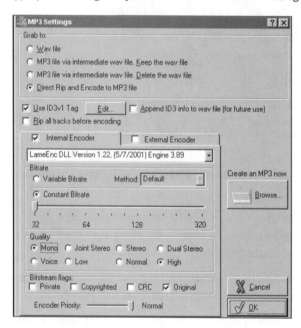

10. Check the Use ID3v1 Tag option to include ID3 tag information in your encoded file and click Edit to bring up the ID3 Tag Editor pop-up window (see Figure 6.3). Fill out the information and click OK.

NOTE

The title you enter in the ID3 Tag Editor window is only used if you are encoding a single file. When batch encoding (see Chapter 13), the filename of each source file is used to determine the title in the encoded MP3 file's ID3 tag.

FIGURE 6.3

Enter your MP3 file attributes in Audiograbber's ID3v1 Tag Editor.

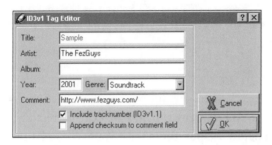

11. Under the Create an MP3 Now text, click the Browse button to locate and select your source WAV file(s). After selecting the desired files, click Open and the encoding process begins immediately. A status window appears including elapsed time and time remaining to completion (see Figure 6.4). When the status window disappears, the encoding process is complete.

FIGURE 6.4

The Audiograbber status window shows the file's encoding progress.

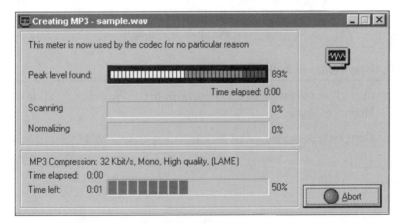

12. Test your file(s) using a local (on the same computer) MP3 player.

13. To encode a file for your prospective 384Kbps DSL broadband listeners, repeat steps 4–12. Choose Variable Bit Rate in step 4 (leave the VBR Method set to Default and select the highest quality on the horizontal slider) and select Stereo in step 6.

NOTE

> When you run the encoder again for this high bit rate file, the encoder will add a suffix to the file-name to avoid overwriting the first one. For example, if your source WAV file is `sample.wav`, your first encoding will be `sample.mp3` and your second encoding will be `sample-1.mp3`. You should rename them as you see fit.

You now have two MP3 on-demand streaming files in your chosen folder, ready to be slapped onto a Web server or tossed into the correct directory of a SHOUTcast server (see below). Open them with your MP3 player and verify that they sound okay.

Using iTunes

Make sure you're running the latest version of iTunes. Macintosh computers purchased after July 2001 might have it already installed. To get the free download of the iTunes system, go to `www.apple.com`. You must be running Macintosh OS 9.0 (minimum) or later to install and use iTunes.

As in the Audiograbber Step-by-Step, you're going to use iTunes to encode a song with vocals for delivery to a target audience of listeners who have con-nections ranging from dial-up (56kbps) to broadband (DSL 384Kbps).

STEP-BY-STEP: Using iTunes to Author an On-Demand MP3 File

1. Launch iTunes on your Macintosh computer. Go to Edit, Preferences (⌘+Y) to bring up the Preferences window.

2. Select the Importing tab and set the Import Using option to MP3 Encoder (see Figure 6.5).

FIGURE 6.5

Set your iTunes importing preferences to use the MP3 encoder.

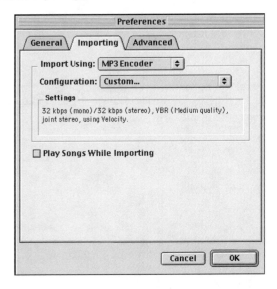

3. For Configuration, select one of the three available built-in default bit rates; alternatively, choose Custom to create your own, which pops up a new MP3 Encoder window (see Figure 6.6).

NOTE

For the purposes of this book, you'll choose Custom because none of the default templates provide VBR or encoding below 128Kbps.

4. Select 32 Kbps for both Mono and Stereo within the Custom pop-up window and check Use Variable Bitrate Encoding (VBR). Unlike some VBR-enabled, MP3 encoding software, iTunes uses the specified bit rate as the guaranteed minimum bit rate. For VBR Quality, start at Medium (you might want to play with this value because it slightly changes both the audio quality and size of the encoded file).

5. Keep the default values checked for Smart Encoding Adjustments. (This allows the iTunes MP3 encoder to choose sample rate or channel number if either of those individual choices is set to Auto.) Also keep the default for Filter Frequencies Below 10Hz and Sample Rate at Auto.

6. Select Mono from the Channels option for your 56K modem users setting. For your broadband users, choose Auto, which encodes to the same number of channels as your source file.

7. In the Stereo Mode setting, choose Normal when authoring for broadband users. This setting is ignored when Channels is set to Mono (as is done when you are authoring for 56K users).

NOTE

Choosing Normal for Stereo Mode varies the bit rate used for each channel as needed. Choosing Joint Stereo (the best choice for bit rates under 128Kbps) encodes certain frequencies in mono to save space.

8. Click OK to exit the MP3 Encoder window.

FIGURE 6.6

Select your desired custom settings in iTunes' MP3 Encoder Preferences window.

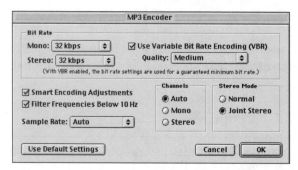

9. In the Preferences window, click the Advanced tab to set your Music Folder Location (see Figure 6.7). Click Change if you want to specify a different folder than displayed. This is where your iTunes MP3-encoded files are placed. Remember this location!

10. Click OK again to exit Preferences.

FIGURE 6.7

Select your desired music folder location in iTunes' Advanced tab of the Preferences window.

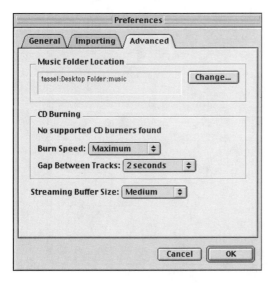

11. Choose Advanced, Convert to MP3. A Choose Object window opens.

12. Select your AIFF source file(s) and click Choose. iTunes immediately begins encoding the source file(s). The files that you have selected to encode appear in the main iTunes window, and a status bar tells you the process of the encoding (see Figure 6.8).

FIGURE 6.8

iTunes's main window shows the encoding status of your on-demand MP3 file.

13. It's possible to listen to music from your iTunes playlist during the encoding process. A chime sounds indicating that your file(s) are finished. Look in your Music Folder Location and test the files with the iTunes player (see Figure 6.9).

FIGURE 6.9

Test your encoded file by playing it back in iTunes.

14. Re-encode your source file for broadband listeners by repeating steps 2–13, setting the bit rates to 192 Kbps in step 4, and Channels to Auto in step 6.

You've just used a shortcut to speedily convert a source audio file into the MP3 format, bypassing the ID3 tag settings (name, artist, album, and so on). Because iTunes uses ID3 values to determine where in the Music Folder hierarchy to place your MP3 files, the files will most likely end up in the Unknown Album folder below the Unknown Artist folder in the Music Folder. If your source AIFF file already has ID3 information, that ID3 information is included in the encoded MP3 file, which is then placed in the appropriate artist and album name subfolders in the Music folder. If your encoded MP3 files don't have the ID3 information, add this information by following the instructions under "Changing Your On-Demand File Attributes" in Chapter 7, "Serving Your Audio."

Authoring a Live MP3 Stream

In this section, you'll create a live MP3 stream on your authoring computer. That is, source audio enters your computer uncompressed and exits as an encoded live stream. The server forwards the live stream, in turn, to your listeners on the Internet. Make sure your audio source is plugged into your computer's audio input. Use the same audio input level guidelines that you used to create a digital file (see Chapter 2).

Your source audio quality is crucial here. This is because no further opportunities (such as waveform editors) are typically available to optimize the signal between encoding and outputting that audio as a live stream. Make sure your signal is as clean as possible and that your level is set accurately—not so low that it can't be heard and not so loud that it will distort; both scenarios prevent the encoder from doing a good job. You might want to place some audio hardware (such as a compressor) in your signal path to smooth the signal and increase the encoder's efficiency. (See Chapter 11, "Advanced Audio Optimization.")

This may seem a little like putting the cart before the horse but now is a good time to mention that, when sending a live stream to the Internet, your authoring computer's software needs to connect to a computer that is running the SHOUTcast server. Therefore, an important early step is to either lease or borrow space on someone else's SHOUTcast server, or have already configured your own (see "Creating a Server" at the end of this chapter). You'll also need a reliable Internet connection between the encoding authoring computer and the server computer. In addition, you'll need a valid username and password ready to plug in as you configure Winamp to create a live stream. If you're running your own SHOUTcast server, you already have that information handy; otherwise, make sure you've received it from your server provider.

Prior to beginning the live stream, it's strongly recommended that you have, if possible, yet another computer available to do a listening test. (That totals three computers: an authoring computer to encode the live stream from the source audio, a server computer to send the encoded live stream out to the Internet, and a test computer on another connection to make sure it all works!) Short of calling your friends on the phone (which also works), this is the best way to make sure your live stream sounds okay and is actually making it out to the Internet intact. The most realistic test is having your listening test computer on a completely different Internet connection from your live encoder computer. In addition, if you're encoding and streaming for modem users, make sure you test your live stream with a modem connection (not broadband or DSL) to get a realistic experience.

NOTE

Although it's possible to use the same computer to simultaneously author from and run your streaming server, doing so is not recommended for handling more than a dozen listeners.

Using Winamp's SHOUTcast Plug-In

You'll use the popular Winamp MP3 player software enabled with the SHOUTcast DSP plug-in to create a live MP3 stream from your Windows computer. This plug-in adds live broadcasting capabilities for Winamp to send to a SHOUTcast server.

If you don't already have Winamp installed, you can get the free download from www.winamp.com (any version above 2.65).

If you don't already have the free SHOUTcast plug-in, you'll need to download and install it from www.shoutcast.com/download. From the main page, click on Be A DJ. This page also includes detailed download and installation instructions.

NOTE

Version 1.8.2 (which these examples use) of the SHOUTcast DSP plug-in for Winamp varies greatly from previous versions. If you have an older version, you should upgrade to this or the most recent version.

Allow all defaults during the installation of both Winamp and the SHOUTcast plug-in.

You'll need the SHOUTcast server configuration settings (server name or IP address, port number, and password) for the server to which you'll be sending your live stream. If you're running your own server, you'll need to have the SHOUTcast server software already installed and configured and know what the settings are (see the next section, "Creating a Server"). If you're sending to someone else's SHOUTcast server, you'll need to get these configuration settings from the server administrator.

Alright, enough talk, let's get on with creating a live MP3 stream!

STEP-BY-STEP: Using Winamp and the SHOUTcast Plug-In to Author a Live MP3 Stream (Windows)

1. Launch Winamp on your Windows computer and press Ctrl+P to bring up the Preferences menu.

2. Select DSP/Effect from the Plug-ins section of the left column and then click on Nullsoft SHOUTcast Source DSP v1.8.2 (or whichever version you have) from the right column (see Figure 6.10).

FIGURE 6.10

Choose DSP/Effect from the Plug-ins section of Winamp's Preferences window and select Nullsoft SHOUTcast Source DSP.

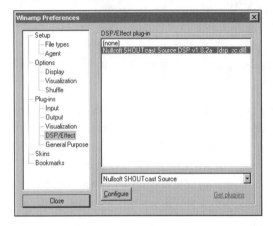

3. A new pop-up window appears labeled SHOUTcast Source. Click Close on the Preferences window (and click the title bar of the SHOUTcast main window to bring it back to the front, if necessary). The SHOUTcast source configuration has four tabs.

   - *Main—Encoding stream summary information*

   - *Output—Server settings*

   - *Encoder—Encoding codec settings*

   - *Input—Source audio input settings*

4. Make sure your audio source input is connected to the computer and that the signal is coming through to test your levels.

5. Select the Input tab of the SHOUTcast source configuration.

   1. *For Input Configuration, set your input device to Soundcard Input (see Figure 6.11).*

NOTE

Don't use Winamp's default recommended setting as this default is for creating a live stream from existing on-demand files. Instead, you are using an external audio input in this Step-by-Step. The Soundcard Input setting also allows you to use advanced features such as voice-overs and cross fading regardless of your audio source. Additional information is included in the DSP SHOUTcast plug-in `dsp_sc_readme.txt` file (part of the installation).

FIGURE 6.11

In the Input tab of Winamp's SHOUTcast plug-in preferences, select Soundcard Input for Input Configuration.

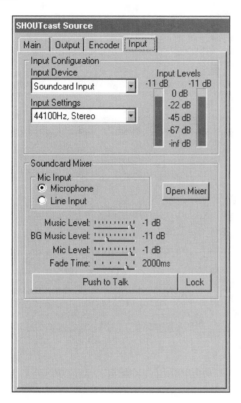

2. Click the Open Mixer button in the sound card section of the Input tab. This opens the standard Windows Volume and Recording panels. Because you'll be using the Record Control window to set your input level (see Figure 6.12), feel free to close the Volume Control panel.

3. Select the appropriate audio input (typically Line, meaning that an external device is plugged into the Line Input of your sound card).

4. Start your source audio and adjust your input levels so that they don't read higher than −4db in the SHOUTcast input meter.

FIGURE 6.12

Select your audio input in the standard Windows Record Control window and adjust your levels.

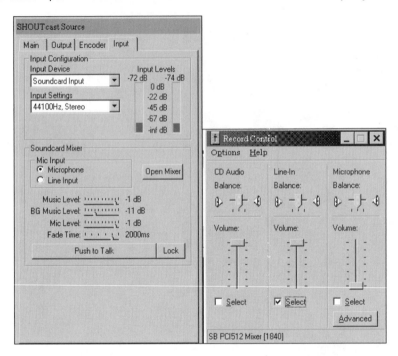

5. Stop your source audio and (if necessary) reposition to the start point.

6. For Input Settings, select your sample rate and number of channels (mono or stereo). Because you can also set the sample rate and number of channels when choosing your bit rate, select 44100Hz, Stereo here.

6. Select the Encoder tab of the SHOUTcast source configuration.

1. Select Encoder 1 from the encoder options list.

2. For Encoder Type, select MP3 Encoder.

3. For Encoder Settings, select 32Kbps, 22.050kHz, Mono (see Figure 6.13)

FIGURE 6.13

Configure the bit rate, sample rate, and number of channels settings for your first Winamp SHOUTcast encoder.

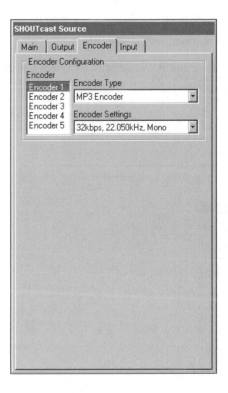

7. Click on the Output tab of the SHOUTcast Source configuration (see Figure 6.14). This is where you link the encoding settings that you just created to an output stream to send to your SHOUTcast server.

   1. *Select Output 1 on the output options list. The status should read Not Connected.*

   2. *Leave the Connect at Startup option unchecked because in this Step-by-Step tutorial, you are only authoring a one-time live stream.*

NOTE

Selecting the Connect At Startup option causes your authoring computer to attempt to connect to this server (Output 1) upon launching Winamp. If you're providing an ongoing live stream, you might want to check this and also configure Winamp to run when your computer boots. This way your stream is always running.

3. *Make sure the Connection button (next to the Yellow Pages button, not to be confused with the Connect button that is higher up) is selected, as it should be by default.*

4. *Enter the settings for the server to which you will be broadcasting (server name, port number, and password).*

5. *Choose Encoder 1 from the pull-down list to select the template you configured earlier.*

6. *Check the Automatic Reconnection on Connection Failure box.*

FIGURE 6.14

Set your SHOUTcast server configuration in Winamp's SHOUTcast output settings window.

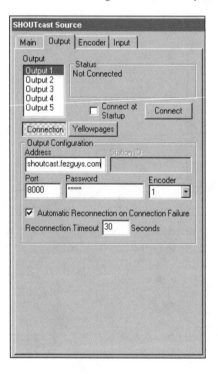

7. *Click the Yellow Pages button to bring up your program's directory listing preferences.*

8. *If you want to have your live stream included in public listings of available programming, select Make This Server Public and fill out the appropriate information (description, URL, genre, and so on).*

NOTE

Checking Make This Server Public makes your program listing appear in the iTunes player and program listings on SHOUTcast.com and Winamp radio. It takes up to 15 minutes after you begin streaming for this information to update in these directories. If your live stream is not intended for the masses, make sure to leave the Yellow Pages button unchecked.

9. *When you feel ready, start your source audio and click the Connect button to connect your stream to the server.*

8. Click Main to see a continuous display of information on server connection status and to see input levels. As your stream progresses, keep an eye on the input levels and, if necessary, adjust accordingly (see Figure 6.15).

FIGURE 6.15

Monitor your broadcast and audio levels from the SHOUTcast plug-in's Main window.

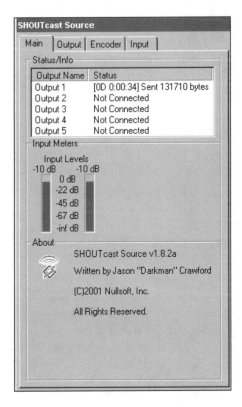

9. Test your stream (see Figure 6.16) through the SHOUTcast administration Web page. Preferably from a separate computer on a separate Internet connection, open your Web browser and go to http://servername:port (where servername is the SHOUTcast server to which you're sending your stream and port is the port on which the server is running). Click on the Listen link.

FIGURE 6.16

Test your live MP3 stream with your MP3 player.

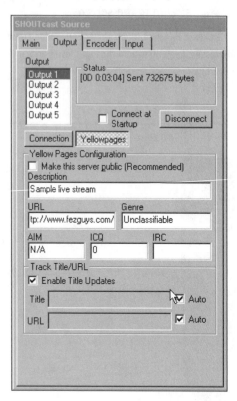

NOTE

MP3 doesn't have a technology (like RealMedia's SureStream) that can author multiple streams for multiple bit rates simultaneously. Authoring another, higher quality stream (for instance, 384K DSL broadband users) requires encoding your source audio as another separate stream to another separate encoder. The good news is that the SHOUTcast plug-in for Winamp makes it possible to do this from the same authoring/encoding computer.

10. To configure a second stream for DSL users, do the following:

1. *Click on the Encoder tab and select Encoder 2.*

2. *Set Encoder Type to MP3 Encoder.*

3. *For Encoder Settings, select 192Kbps, 44.100kHz, Stereo.*

4. *Click back to the Output tab.*

5. *Select Output 2 and point it to your new high bit rate file by choosing 2 for Encoder.*

6. *Enter the server name, port number, and password for your second SHOUTcast server.*

7. *Click Connect. You are now sending a high bit rate live stream.*

NOTE

You can configure up to five different live streams from one encoder, although doing so puts a heavier CPU requirement and additional bandwidth on your authoring computer. Watch the authoring computer's efficiency when encoding and, if necessary, drop the number of streams.

You are now broadcasting your live MP3 stream to the Internet. Create your metafiles and link to them from your Web site (see Chapter 7).

Creating a Server

You have the authoring computer's Winamp encoder ready to crank out your MP3-encoded live stream. Now you need to connect to a server so that listeners on the Internet can hear it. Naturally, you must make some decisions regarding the type of server you will use. How many concurrent (simultaneous) listeners do you need to be able to serve, and at what bit rate? Multiplying the number of concurrent users times the streams' bit rate will provide the total bandwidth requirements for your server scenario.

This test case runs the server computer from home using a 384Kbps sDSL (s for synchronous, meaning 384Kbps upload and download). It is encoding at a bit rate of 32Kbps and supports 10 concurrent listeners. Multiplying the number 10 (listeners) times 32 (the encode bit rate) comes out to around 320Kbps, leaving a little headroom for other tasks, such as testing the streams. Know how much upload bandwidth you have available. Most DSL connections are actually aDSL (a for asynchronous) and usually have much higher download than upload speeds. Check with your ISP customer support to verify your data rates.

If you're using co-located (third-party) server facilities, place limits on the number of users your server will accept. Just because the collocation server facility has the bandwidth to support hundreds of users doesn't mean you should use it. You'll be charged by user access and, if your stream is popular, that can quickly add up to lots of money. Start small.

For live stream authoring, you must use a real-time streaming server such as SHOUTcast or Icecast, which are available for all of the popular operating systems. For serving on-demand files, you can use either of these for real-time streaming of on-demand files or any Web server (via HTTP/Progressive streaming). For the purposes of this book, you'll be using the SHOUTcast server for both.

NOTE

MP3 on-demand files can be streamed through HTTP/Progressive streaming from a Web server. See Chapter 2 for an explanation of the differences between progressive (for on-demand only) and real-time (both on-demand and live) streaming. See Chapter 7 for examples on how to do both.

One feature that the SHOUTcast server has over a Web server when streaming on-demand files is that it becomes more difficult for listeners to save copies of your content. The SHOUTcast server does this by only allowing certain client players to request the stream, disallowing the Web browser from saving it to a local file. This limitation has workarounds, but it's a good first line of defense against people saving your MP3-encoded on-demand files.

For more information on issues relating to streaming servers, see Chapter 7.

Other MP3 Streaming Servers

SHOUTcast is just one of many servers that support on-demand and live streaming MP3-encoded audio. RealMedia, Windows Media and QuickTime have varying capabilities for using the MP3 codec. When MP3 files are served via real-time streaming from RealMedia, Windows Media, or QuickTime servers, the corresponding players to these formats must be used to play the streams. For example, iTunes cannot play back a Windows Media MP3-encoded stream. The great advantage to using SHOUTcast to encode MP3 streams is that 99% of all the common MP3 players can hear it.

SHOUTcast's closest cousin is Icecast, which is fully compatible with SHOUTcast. Icecast is more of an open-source project, making it easy for software developers to contribute new features. Advanced users can create extensive tools to perform various tasks. With Icecast, developers can easily fine-tune the authoring of live streams from static files (unlike SHOUTcast, which must encode through Winamp) and run those files from remote locations. Icecast's liveice tool supports cross fades and live mixing for live MP3 streams. While Icecast is not as user friendly as SHOUTcast (and other formats) that support MP3-streaming, it does offer more flexibility for advanced users. Go to www.icecast.com to learn more about this suite of tools.

Installing a SHOUTcast Server

SHOUTcast is a popular and free server for streaming live and on-demand MP3-encoded files. It's possible to turn your collection of MP3 files into rotating (and repeating) playlists for users to hear online. This is one way to become an Internet radio station.

NOTE

Older versions of the SHOUTcast server cannot stream on-demand MP3-encoded files, so make sure you're using the latest version.

The Server can run on Windows, Mac OS X, Unix (FreeeBSD, Linux, and Solaris) platforms. This chapter uses the SHOUTcast server v1.8.3 for Windows and FreeBSD.

NOTE

Due to size constraints, this book can only cover the basic processes to stream MP3-encoded on-demand files and live audio. Many deeper levels of complexity and flexibility are available for these applications and their processes. Refer to the README file in your SHOUTcast Download folder for detailed installation, configuration, and operation instructions for SHOUTcast tools. Novice Unix users especially will find this helpful.

Go to www.shoutcast.com/download and click on Be a Server.

 Download and run the installer, which puts an entry in your Startup menu. Launch the SHOUTcast server by selecting Start, Programs, SHOUTcast DNAS, SHOUTcast DNAS GUI. Click Edit config. The default text editor (most likely Notepad) opens the configuration file for the SHOUTcast server. Follow the Step-by-Step tutorial that follows.

 Download and unpack. Edit the sc_serv.conf file according to the Step-by-Step tutorial.

STEP-BY-STEP: Configuring a SHOUTcast MP3 Server

1. Open the SHOUTcast server's configuration file, as noted earlier (see Figure 6.17).

2. Set MaxUser to 10. This specifies how many concurrent users can connect to your server.

NOTE

Setting the MaxUser value appropriately ensures that your server's Internet connection isn't overloaded. The scenario mentioned earlier assumes enough bandwidth to support 10 concurrent users with 32Kbps streams. Remember that even though you set MaxUser to 10 doesn't automatically mean that 10×32Kbps (320Kbps) is in use at all times. The server only uses bandwidth for actively connected users.

3. Set the SHOUTcast server's Password to something other than the installer default value. Anyone who is broadcasting a live stream to this server will need this password to connect.

4. The PortBase value can be left at its default setting of 8000. This value will also be needed for anyone who is broadcasting a live stream through your server.

5. The rest of the values can be left as they are for regular operation. (Feeling adventurous? If you want to play with some neat stuff, take a look at the IntroFile setting.)

FIGURE 6.17

The SHOUTcast DNAS server configuration is accomplished by editing a text file.

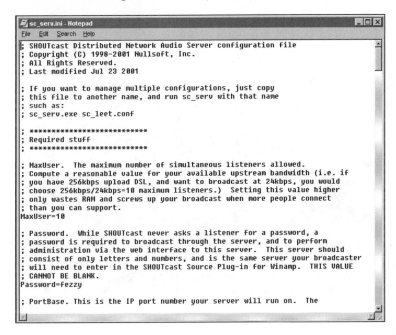

```
sc_serv.ini - Notepad                                            _ □ ×
File   Edit   Search   Help
; SHOUTcast Distributed Network Audio Server configuration file
; Copyright (C) 1998-2001 Nullsoft, Inc.
; All Rights Reserved.
; Last modified Jul 23 2001

; If you want to manage multiple configurations, just copy
; this file to another name, and run sc_serv with that name
; such as:
; sc_serv.exe sc_leet.conf

; ****************************
; Required stuff
; ****************************

; MaxUser.  The maximum number of simultaneous listeners allowed.
; Compute a reasonable value for your available upstream bandwidth (i.e. if
; you have 256kbps upload DSL, and want to broadcast at 24kbps, you would
; choose 256kbps/24kbps=10 maximum listeners.)  Setting this value higher
; only wastes RAM and screws up your broadcast when more people connect
; than you can support.
MaxUser=10

; Password.  While SHOUTcast never asks a listener for a password, a
; password is required to broadcast through the server, and to perform
; administration via the web interface to this server.  This server should
; consist of only letters and numbers, and is the same server your broadcaster
; will need to enter in the SHOUTcast Source Plug-in for Winamp.  THIS VALUE
; CANNOT BE BLANK.
Password=fezzy

; PortBase. This is the IP port number your server will run on.  The
```

6. After you are finished making the necessary changes, save the file and exit your text editor.

7. Close the text editor and start the SHOUTcast server application.

Windows users need to stop the server by choosing Kill Server from the SHOUTcast server console menu. If you accidentally closed the console window, you can bring it back by clicking on the SHOUTcast icon in your system tray (next to the clock). After successfully closing the server, select Start, Programs, SHOUTcast DNAS, SHOUTcast DNAS GUI to start it back up using your new configuration file.

Unix users simply start the server (named sc_serv) for the first time. If you had started it earlier, you would need to stop and restart it so that it will use your new configuration settings.

8. With your server running, open a Web browser to access the SHOUTcast Administrator (see Figure 6.18). Go to http://servername:port, where servername is the name (or IP address) of your server, and port is the install port (typically 8000). This Web page shows a page with stream status and a link to test the stream. (Click Listen.) The SHOUTcast Administrator also allows you to log in (using the password you set for the server) and perform various administration tasks, including editing restrictions on who can listen, view log messages, and so on.

FIGURE 6.18

Access the SHOUTcast Administrator through your Web browser.

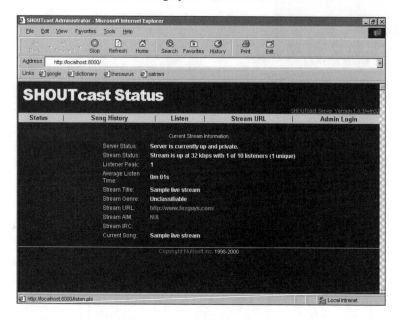

With your SHOUTcast server configured and running, make your on-demand files available for streaming by uploading them into the Content subdirectory where the SHOUTcast server software resides.

NOTE

There is a bug in version 1.8.2 of the SHOUTcast server for Windows that requires you to include a trailing slash on the directory that you specify for ContentDir (used to enable on-demand streaming). For example, ContentDir=C:\Program Files\SHOUTcast\content\.

For live streams, configure the encoder on your authoring computer to match your server name, port, and password settings.

ate SHOUTcast server for each live stream that you want to receive,
be run on different ports on a single server computer. See the
le and documentation for more information on how to do this.

ure the encoder on your authoring computer to match
and password settings.

on-demand and live streams, link to them in your
'), announce them on your mailing lists, put them in
nd so on. Make a point to periodically check for
nd encoder applications because the technology
a rapid pace.

CHAPTER 7

Serving Your Audio

When hosting your streaming audio, you have two options: local or remote. To effectively decide which of these suits your needs, consider the following questions.

Where to Host?

Will you be streaming to a lot (more than 50) concurrent users? If so, don't do this locally. Typical broadband home and office connections are shared by other ISP subscribers and are subject to wild bandwidth fluctuations, especially on Friday night. In addition, purchasing a more reliable network connection, such as a T1, is prohibitively expensive for a simple network. Co-location and content delivery network (CDN) companies offer a reliable solution for securing the necessary bandwidth. *Co-location* means leasing physical space and bandwidth at an ISP and placing your own server computer on their network. A *CDN* is a third-party service that charges to host live and on-demand audio streams as well as other content.

Are you streaming on-demand files only? If so, you have the option of using HTTP/Progressive on-demand streaming with a simple Web server instead of real-time streaming. You might already be paying for a limited amount of disk space and Web bandwidth as part of your existing Internet access. Check with your ISP to find out how much space and bandwidth you have available. As noted in Chapter 1, "Introduction to Streaming Audio", there are a few limitations when streaming with HTTP/Progressive, but it's a less expensive solution.

How much money do you want to spend? Perhaps you're creating a Web site for your band and can't afford additional hosting fees for your streaming audio. In this case it makes more sense to handle your own server needs. Worry not: Hosting and serving your streaming audio is a lot simpler than it was five years ago, and it's becoming more straightforward all the time. In the end, running a local server is more work, but it's potentially a lot cheaper and also provides that fabulous, hands-on educational experience.

If you're still considering serving locally or at a co-location facility, look at whether you might enjoy configuring and maintaining server computers and related networks. Choose a CDN if you don't want to be responsible for those issues.

You must be aware of another basic physical limitation if you've decided to run your own local server. Those who are lucky enough to attract more listeners to their server than the server can handle will find that their popularity actually brings their streams to a screeching halt by democratically cutting off everyone. Those lucky people should reconsider hiring a CDN or co-location facility that can guarantee bandwidth flexibility.

With all these issues in mind, add the time required for installing and maintaining your own server and balance that with the price of leasing outside services. Remember to temper this balanced equation with your expected return for providing streaming audio. Follow this somewhat convoluted equation for happy streaming.

Running Your Own Server

If you've decided to do the hosting yourself, either locally or remotely with a co-location facility, you'll need to install, configure, and maintain your own streaming server computer.

Co-location facilities have a tremendous amount of bandwidth and aisles of grounded metal racks on which to place your server computer, which is then plugged into their network. The facilities handle all the connectivity and secure backup electrical power in case of outages. At co-location facilities (unlike CDNs), you provide your own server hardware and software, remotely administering and maintaining that hardware and software through an online connection. Co-location facilities provide a much more reliable form of connectivity and that improves the quality of your stream.

If, however, you've decided to run your own streaming server on your own local network, make sure you have enough bandwidth. An absolute minimum of 128Kbps ISDN is recommended (128Kbps ISDN guarantees the same data rate for upload and download). 128Kbps allows you to author a live 32Kbps stream to three concurrent users using 56Kbps dial-up modems and still have the bandwidth necessary for a little headroom. If you have a DSL connection, find out exactly what your upload speed is. Typical DSL connections are actually asynchronous digital subscriber line (aDSL) and have greater download (data from others to you) than upload (data from you to others) capability. That means you'd have plenty of bandwidth to download from the Internet, but you would have considerably less available to stream outward.

Remote Hosting

If you've decided to rent a server from another provider, you have several options. Unless you're lucky enough to borrow server space from a friend, expect to pay a modest fee. This fee should relate to actual use based on the number of maximum concurrent users over a specific time period and overall bandwidth used, and it typically includes a flat startup fee and base monthly fee.

Your ISP might offer a real-time streaming server to host your live and on-demand streams. Most ISPs also provide standard Web site hosting accounts that support HTTP/Progressive streaming for on-demand files only. Don't be dismayed if the customer support people at your ISP have no idea what you're talking about. You're now officially on the cutting edge of streaming audio. If your ISP doesn't provide streaming service, ask if they know who might.

If you've decided to host with a CDN and aren't sure where to start, take a look at the short list in the Appendix, "Tools and Resources." Shop around and go with one that has employees you can talk to and who take the time to answer questions to your satisfaction. Find out if they are available 24/7. If your live stream needs attention at 3 a.m., it's important that your CDN's customer support team is available. With the global reach of the Internet, 3 a.m. in your city is the middle of the afternoon on the other side of the earth. You can also search online by adding the word *Hosting* to the streaming format of your choice. For example, search on *Windows Media Hosting*.

Hosting your stream on someone else's server can be a breeze. You don't have to download, install, or set up anything. Your provider will give you all the information necessary to upload your on-demand content and connect your live stream. When working with on-demand files, all you have to do is plug in the provided configuration information into your file transfer program and then upload your files. If you're authoring a live stream, it's a simple matter of plugging in the provided configuration information into your live encoder and starting your broadcast. After that, all you have to do is create your metafiles and link to them from your Web site.

CDNs typically provide additional tools to help deliver an efficient stream. For example, your stream's URL might first connect to a specialized server that decides which streaming server to connect a listener, based on the listener's geographical location. Each CDN has its own unique technological approach to supplying high-quality and reliable streams to your listeners.

Streaming audio is a complex problem—a balancing act in some ways—and a simple solution or industry standard doesn't yet exist. But, like anything else, never settle for poor service. The industry is highly competitive and still small enough that quality of service is important.

Uploading Your On-Demand Files

In this section, you'll use software tools to upload your on-demand files and move them to the correct local folder on your streaming server. If you're using the same computer for both authoring and serving your streams, the process is only a quick copy from one folder to another. If you're authoring and streaming from different computers, you'll need to use a file transfer protocol (FTP) program to move your on-demand files. An FTP program moves files from one location to another across any kind of network. Using FTP programs requires plugging in the host name or IP address of your streaming server as well as your username and password.

NOTE

Skip this section if you're authoring live streams. An FTP program is unnecessary because the entire configuration for sending your stream to the server is handled as part of your authoring software.

Using CuteFTP (Windows)

CuteFTP is a simple and commonly used Windows-based FTP program. If you dig around online, you can also find many freeware FTP programs. Spending a few dollars gets you a better product as well as someone you can yell at if there are problems.

Download and install the 30-day free evaluation copy of CuteFTP v4.2.5 for Windows (compatible with 98, ME, and 2000) from www.cuteftp.com. After the 30-day evaluation period ends, CuteFTP will cost $39.95.

STEP-BY-STEP: Using CuteFTP to Upload On-Demand Files via FTP

1. Launch CuteFTP on your Windows authoring computer. CuteFTP, by default and on first launch, brings up a Site Manager (see Figure 7.1). If the Site Manager window doesn't appear, go to File, Site Manager (F4).

2. Click the New button to create a new site entry for your streaming server. By creating a new site, you won't have to constantly re-enter your streaming server's information each time that you upload new on-demand files.

3. In Label for Site, give your new site entry a name. (In this case, FezGuys Streaming Server was chosen.)

4. For FTP Host Address, enter your host name or IP address. (In this case, streaming.fezguys.com was chosen.)

5. For FTP Site User Name, enter your username. (In this case, fezguys was chosen.)

6. Fill in your username password for FTP Site Password.

7. Leave the default value of 21 for FTP Site Connection Port.

8. From the three choices of Login type (Normal, Anonymous or Double), leave the default of Normal.

FIGURE 7.1

Set the appropriate Site settings when adding a new site within CuteFTP's Site Manager.

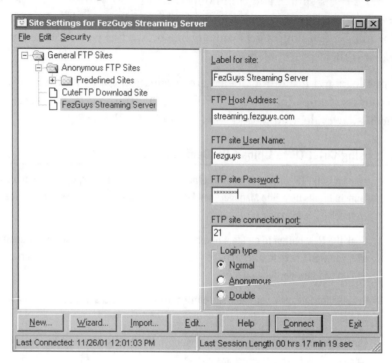

9. Click Connect and CuteFTP will connect your authoring computer to your server computer.

10. After connecting, you'll get a login message pop-up window. Click OK to continue. This places you back in the main window. You're now logged in and ready to transfer your on-demand files to your server.

11. Within the main CuteFTP window are four panes:

   • *Log Window* (at top)—This pane shows the commands you've sent to your server and your server's responses, indicates completed transfers, and can be useful if there are errors. Unless a problem exists, you can usually ignore the contents of this window.

   • *Local Window* (at center left)—This pane is where you select the local copies of your on-demand files for uploading.

   • *Remote Window* (at center right)—This pane shows the files and directories that are contained on your connected server.

- *Queue Window* (at bottom)—This pane shows the files that you're currently transferring to the server or the files you want to transfer later.

Locate the directory containing your local files in the left center Local Window.

12. Verify that the directory into which you're logged (in the right center Remote Window) on your
streaming server is correct. You can change to a different remote directory in CuteFTP by
selecting Commands, Directory, Change Directory (Ctrl+D) or create a new one with
Commands, Directory, Make New Directory (Ctrl+M).

13. Drag your files and directories from the Local Window and drop them into the correct server
directory in the Remote Window (see Figure 7.2).

FIGURE 7.2
_____

Drag your files from CuteFTP's local window to the remote window to begin the upload process.

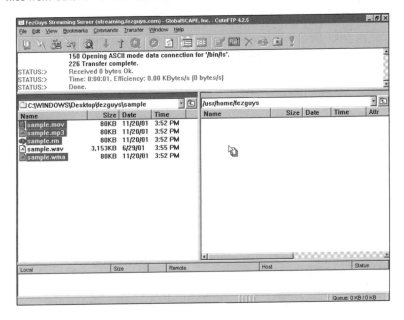

14. Have a cup (or two) of tea while your files upload. The files will appear in the bottom Queue
Window until the transfer is complete (see Figure 7.3).

NOTE
_____

Depending on the size of the file and the speed of your connection, it can take anywhere from a
few seconds to several hours to upload your files. It doesn't matter how long it takes to get to
your server as long as the file streams efficiently to your users after it's there.

FIGURE 7.3

CuteFTP's Queue window shows the status of files that are being uploaded.

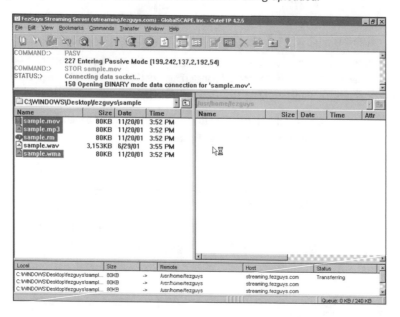

If you're working with more than one format, you'll either upload your files to a different streaming server for each format or to different directories on the same server. The specifics will vary based on how and where you host your on-demand streams.

After the transfer is complete, the uploaded files in your selected directory on your streaming server will be displayed in the Remote window.

Using Fetch (Macintosh)

Download Fetch v4 from www.fetchsoftworks.com and install it on your Macintosh computer. The demo is free for 15 days and then requires a single $25 payment for lifetime use. If you're running Macintosh OS X, you must use version 4 (unless you have OS 9 also installed to run in Classic mode). Pre-OS X Macintosh operating systems can run version 3 or 4. Although Fetch Softworks pushes version 4, it also provides a link to the free and fully functional download of version 3 on the site. This book uses version 4 under OS X.

STEP-BY-STEP: Using Fetch to Upload On-Demand Files Via FTP

1. Launch Fetch on your Macintosh computer. A New Connection window opens. In the window, click Cancel because you'll most likely be uploading on-demand files to your streaming server more than once. You'll instead create a new shortcut that remembers your server settings, making it easy to connect each time you launch Fetch.

2. Select Customize, New Shortcut, which brings up a Shortcut Editor window where you choose your parameters (see Figure 7.4).

   1. *Name—Choose a name for your shortcut or leave as the default value. (In this case, FezGuys Streaming Server was chosen.)*

   2. *Host—Enter your host name or IP address. (In this case, streaming.fezguys.com was chosen.)*

   3. *User ID—Enter the name you want to use to identify yourself. (In this case, fezguys was chosen.)*

   4. *Security—Leave the default setting of Cleartext Password. Advanced users might want to choose a more secure way to connect.*

   5. *Password—Enter your password to the User ID entered in step 3.*

   6. *Directory—If necessary, enter a specific directory to upload your files onto the server.*

FIGURE 7.4

Configure your shortcut in Fetch's Shortcut Editor window.

Shortcut Editor	
Name:	FezGuys Streaming Server
Type:	Folder
Host:	streaming.fezguys.com
User ID:	fezguys
Security:	Cleartext password
	☑ Encrypt session (⌘E)
Password:	••••••••
Directory:	
	Cancel OK

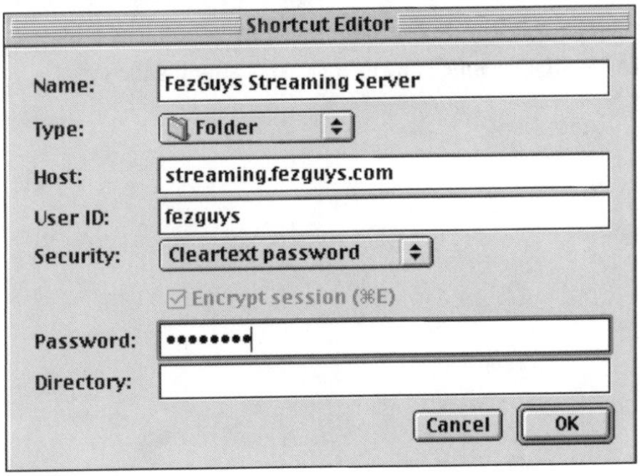

3. Click OK to make your new shortcut available in the Fetch Shortcuts menu.

4. Go to File, Open Shortcut and select your new shortcut to open a new window connected to your streaming server. This window displays your remote files and folders.

FIGURE 7.5

Select your new Fetch shortcut to connect to your streaming server.

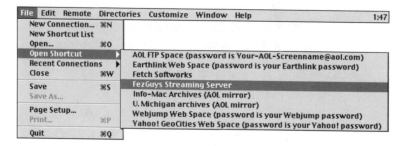

5. Click on the Put files button, select the files you want to put on the server, and click Open.

6. From the Format pull-down menu (default set to Automatic), select Raw Data. This ensures that your on-demand files arrive to the server in the correct format, not mistakenly transferred as text documents.

7. Click OK in the Put File dialog box to begin the transfer (see Figure 7.6).

NOTE

Depending on the size of the file and the speed of your connection, it could take anywhere from a few seconds to several hours to upload your files. It doesn't matter how long it takes to get to your server as long as the file streams efficiently to your users after it's there.

FIGURE 7.6

Fetch displays the status of the files being transferred from a local folder to a streaming server computer.

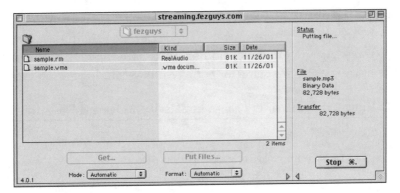

If you're working with more than one format, you'll either upload your files to a different streaming server for each format or to different directories on the same server. The specifics will vary based on how and where you host your on-demand streams.

After the transfer is complete, the uploaded files in your selected directory on your streaming server will be displayed in the main Fetch window.

Streaming Audio Presentation

Now that your streaming audio is ready to go, make sure it has the correct media attributes and is easy for listeners to access from your Web site. This section covers changing on-demand file attributes and creating and using metafiles to link to your stream. It also covers the importance of MIME types.

Changing Your On-Demand File Attributes

It's possible to change the name and any of the other attributes of your on-demand file without completely re-encoding the file. This can be a huge time saver if you realize you've misspelled the author's name or need to add your Web site's URL to a number of previously encoded files.

The tutorials that follow only cover changing your files' media attributes. For more complete information on the tools used in these sections, see the appropriate chapter for the format of your choice in Part II of this book.

Changing RealMedia On-Demand File Attributes

Both the RealProducer Basic and Plus allow you to edit the media attributes (clip information) for on-demand RealMedia files. The RealProducer Plus also allows you to edit other aspects of your on-demand file, such as start and stop times. As a result, Basic and Plus users have slightly different interfaces. The process works the same for both Windows and Macintosh users.

STEP-BY-STEP: Using RealProducer to Change RealMedia On-Demand File Attributes

1. Launch RealProducer.

2. Open the file you want to edit in the RealMedia editor.

   - *RealProducer Basic—Select File, Edit RealMedia File.*

   - *RealProducer Plus—Select File, Edit RealMedia File, which opens the RealMedia Editor. Select File, Open RealMedia File (Windows: Ctrl+O, Macintosh: ⌘+O), and click the Clip Info button to access the window to change the media attributes.*

3. Edit your attributes as desired.

4. Save your edited RealMedia file to a new filename so that you can test your new file before overwriting the original.

   - *RealProducer Basic—Click the Save button.*

   - *RealProducer Plus—Click OK and then select File, Save RealMedia File As.*

After you've verified your new files, you may want to remove the pre-edited version of your files to avoid future confusion.

Changing Windows Media On-Demand File Attributes

The Windows Media Encoder can be used to change your on-demand Windows Media file's media attributes on the Windows platform. Certain third-party tools, such as Discreet's Cleaner 5, offer this feature on the Macintosh.

STEP-BY-STEP: Using Windows Media Encoder to Change Windows Media On-Demand File Attributes

1. Launch Windows Media Encoder and select Convert from an Existing File from the New Session Wizard.

2. In the Wizard, select your previously encoded Windows Media file as your input and enter a new filename for the output.

3. Most importantly, select the identical encoding parameters that were used to author this file. If you don't choose the identical encoding parameters, the encoded file will be re-encoded. Don't re-encode an already encoded file as it results in additional loss of audio fidelity.

4. Click OK, and the Windows Media Encoder creates a new file with your new attribute/name settings.

After you've verified your new files, you may want to remove the pre-edited version of your files to avoid future confusion.

Changing QuickTime On-Demand File Attributes

QuickTime Pro allows you to edit the media attributes (clip information) for QuickTime encoded files. The process works the same for both Windows and Macintosh users.

STEP-BY-STEP: Using QuickTime Pro to Change QuickTime On-Demand File Attributes

1. Launch QuickTime Pro and open your previously encoded file by selecting File, Open Movie (Windows: Ctrl+O, Macintosh: ⌘+O).

2. Select Movie, Get Movie Properties (Macintosh: ⌘+J, Windows: Ctrl+J).

3. Make changes to your attributes (called annotations by QuickTime) and click OK.

4. Select File, Save As to save it to a new file. You can also select File, Save (Windows: Ctrl+S, Macintosh: ⌘+S) to overwrite the file with your changes.

After you've verified your new files, you may want to remove any pre-edited versions of your files to avoid future confusion.

Changing MP3 On-Demand File Attributes

Due to MP3's popularity, there are many tools to update the ID3 tag information in your on-demand MP3 files. This Step-by-Step uses Winamp for Windows and iTunes for Macintosh. Doing an online search for *ID3* provides you with many software options, including shareware tools that can save time when you need to update several files.

STEP-BY-STEP: Using Winamp to Change MP3 On-Demand File Attributes

1. Launch Winamp on your Windows computer and, if necessary, press Alt+E to display the Playlist window.

2. Open (Ctrl+O) your previously encoded MP3 file.

3. Right-click on the song title in the Playlist window and select File info (Alt+3) from the pop-up menu. A new MPEG file info box + ID3 tag editor window pops up.

4. Edit your ID3 tag information and click Update.

STEP-BY-STEP: Using iTunes to Change MP3 On-Demand File Attributes

1. Launch iTunes and (if necessary) select File, Show iTunes Window (⌘+1) to display the main playlist window.

2. Either open a new file with File, Add to Library or select an existing file by locating it in the playlist window.

3. Click on the song's title in the playlist window and choose File, Get Info (⌘+I). A Song Information window pops up.

4. Click the Tags tab in the Song Information dialog box, update your song information, and click OK.

Metafiles: Linking to Your Stream from a Web Page

Metafiles are text files containing pointers to a live or on-demand stream and not the encoded stream itself. Originally designed to be a simple way for Web browsers to hand off multimedia streaming content to an appropriate player application, metafiles now can include other kinds of instructions. Several encoding tools offer options to automatically generate metafiles during the encoding process. Whether you use these tools to automatically generate metafiles (advanced users can write their own scripts for this) or create the metafiles by hand depends on your individual authoring environment.

Without a metafile Web browsers will, by default, download the entire encoded file before passing it to the player. This slow and cumbersome process completely misses the point of streaming.

Any word processor program can be used to create a metafile. Metafiles are only lines of text saved in a regular text file. The minimum information necessary is the full URL to the live or on-demand stream on your streaming server. A metafile typically resides on a Web server, and the stream the metafile points to resides on a streaming server.

In this section, you'll create metafiles in each format, suitable for uploading and linking to from your Web site. See the Appendix for a list of online resources to create and use metafiles.

Linking to Your RealMedia Stream

RealMedia has several types of metafiles from which to choose. `.ram` and `.rpm` files are the oldest and still most commonly used. Although their contents are the same as `.ram`, `.rpm` files cause the browser to use an internal RealMedia plug-in to play the stream inside of the Web page. `.ram` files are used to have the browser launch an external player (on the same computer) for playback. In this section, you'll create `.ram` files. (To create `.rpm` files, see Chapter 13, "Advanced Presentation.")

NOTE

> Synchronized Multimedia Integration Language (SMIL) files represent a World Wide Web Consortium (W3C) standard markup language that provides much more control over how and when streaming files play. RealNetworks pioneered the use of this standard, commonly used when integrating multiple clips of different media types and playing them together as one presentation (see Chapter 13). Advanced users might want to research SMIL technology further. SMIL files are easy to identify by their `.smi` or `.smil` suffixes.

A .ram file, in its simplest form, is merely a text file that contains the URL to your streaming audio. That URL can point to a real-time streaming server (`rtsp://`) or to an HTTP/Progressive streaming Web server (`http://`). For example, to create a metafile for linking to the song `mysong.rm` in the samples directory of the real-time RealServer named `streaming.fezguys.com`, you would create an ordinary text file named `mysong.ram` that contains the following text:

```
rtsp://streaming.fezguys.com/samples/mysong.rm
```

You would then place it on the Web server and link to it like any other Web page. For example, you could place the following:

```
Would you like to <A HREF="mysong.ram">hear a song?</A>
```

on the appropriate page of the Web site. In this example, the phrase *hear a song* (contained within the sentence) becomes the link. When listeners click on this link, their browser retrieves the metafile mysong.ram from your Web server and then launches RealPlayer, passing the metafile file to the player. RealPlayer reads the URL and any other information from within the metafile and connects to the RealServer to play the actual audio stream.

Other text commands such as starting and stopping times and certain (limited) file attributes can be included along with the URL in a .ram (or .rpm) file. These other commands are expressed as:

```
name="value"
```

pairs and must be preceded by a ? (question mark) and separated from each other by an & (ampersand).

Imagine a scenario in which you have a single archived live event of ten bands, all part of the same on-demand streaming file. You want to allow listeners to be able to choose between the individual bands' performances rather than force them to search the entire file for a particular band. To do this, you need to create ten separate metafiles (one for each band). By using metafiles, you avoid having to open the giant four-hour on-demand file in a waveform editor and perform numerous editing operations or, even worse, re-encode from the master file into ten separate encoded files. Instead, you simply create metafiles with the correct start and stop times and names for each band's performance.

In this example, the four-hour 10-band stream's URL is rtsp://streaming. fezguys.com/archive/alltenbands.rm.

The metafile should point to only the first band, so the start and stop times of the first band's 25-minute performance are located and the metafile is created as follows:

```
rtsp://streaming.fezguys.com/archive/alltenbands.rm?start="1:00"&stop="2
6:00"&title="Guster Live"&author="Guster".
```

The RealPlayer also supports including more than one URL in each metafile. You could enter multiple URLs (each on their own line in the metafile), thereby creating a playlist. Using the previous scenario, you could create a single metafile with all ten bands' URLs, including start and stop time, title, and author overrides. Listeners will be able to scroll through each section, or *clip*, from within their RealPlayer.

After creating your .ram metafile, simply upload it to your Web server with your FTP program and link to it from your Web page.

RealServer has a tool called ramgen that generates .ram files automatically. If you don't need to change the attributes contained in your streams, you can use this to save yourself the trouble of individually creating and uploading metafiles.

NOTE

Live events with high attendance typically do not use ramgen because it places an additional load on RealServer.

Ramgen requires the RealServer to be configured to handle HTTP requests. For that reason, you need to know on which port the RealServer is configured to be listening to those HTTP requests. RealServer's installation default port is 8080.

An example of using ramgen to generate a metafile for mysong.rm (residing in the Samples directory of streaming.fezguys.com) is as follows:

```
Want to <A HREF="http://streaming.fezguys.com:8080
/ramgen/samples/mysong.rm">hear a song?</A>
```

This command links directly to ramgen, which outputs the same text content that a metafile would. See your RealServer documentation for more detailed information on using ramgen.

Linking to Your Windows Media Stream

Windows Media has several types of metafiles from which to choose. .asx is an older type, and newer types include .wax (for audio only) and .wvx (for video).

The .asx metafile is still the most commonly used type for linking to Windows Media streams. This is because .wax doesn't always work seamlessly across different (especially older) operating systems and browsers. This book sticks to using the .asx type of Windows Media metafile.

Each .asx file is a text file containing the URL (as well as other elements that define a file as being a Windows Media metafile) to your streaming audio. The URL in that metafile points to a real-time Windows Media streaming server (mms://) or an HTTP/Progressive streaming Web server (http://). For example, to create a metafile for linking to the song mysong.wma in the Samples directory on the Windows Media server named streaming.fezguys.com, you would create a file named mysong.asx that contained the following text:

```
<ASX version = "3.0">
<Entry>
  <Ref href="mms://streaming.fezguys.com/samples/mysong.wma" />
</Entry>
</ASX>
```

After the metafile is created, it is placed on a Web server and incorporated as a link, like any other Web page. For example, you could place this:

```
Would you like to <A HREF="mysong.asx">hear a song?</A>
```

on the appropriate page of the Web site. In this example, the phrase *hear a song* (contained within the sentence) becomes the link. When listeners click on this link, their browser retrieves the metafile mysong.asx from the Web server. The browser then launches the Windows Media player and hands the metafile file to it. The player reads the URL and any other information in the metafile and connects to the streaming server to play the actual audio stream. Other commands can be included in .asx metafiles, such as author, title, copyright, start time, and duration.

Imagine the same scenario (as in the section "Linking to Your RealMedia Stream") in which you have a single archived live event of ten bands, all part of the same on-demand streaming file. You want listeners to be able to choose between the individual band's performances rather than force them to search the entire file for a particular band. To do this, you'll create ten separate metafiles—one for each band. By using metafiles, you avoid opening the giant four-hour on-demand file in a waveform editor and performing numerous edits or, even worse, re-encoding from the master file into ten separate encoded files. Instead, you'll simply create metafiles with the correct start and stop times and names for each band's performance.

If the four-hour 10-band stream's URL is this:

```
mms://streaming.fezguys.com/archive/alltenbands.wma
```

and you want to use a metafile to point to only the first band, you would locate the start time and duration of the first band's 25-minute performance and create your metafile as follows:

```
<ASX version = "3.0">
<Entry>
  <TITLE>Guster Live</TITLE>
  <AUTHOR>Guster Live</AUTHOR>
  <STARTTIME VALUE="1:00" />
  <DURATION VALUE="25:00" />
  <Ref href="mms://streaming.fezguys.com/archive/alltenbands.wma" />
</Entry>
</ASX>
```

The Windows Media Player also supports including more than one URL in this metafile by allowing multiple `<Entry>` (including start time, duration, title and author overrides) sections, thereby creating a playlist. To do this, it's a simple matter of replacing the relevant information within the text of the URL. When including more than one `<Entry>`, you might want to include a `<TITLE>`, `<AUTHOR>`, and `<COPYRIGHT>` for the presentation as a whole so that the information displayed on the Web page makes more sense. Here's how the metafile could look:

```
<ASX version = "3.0">
<TITLE>Ten Live Bands</TITLE>
<AUTHOR>Ten Different Bands</AUTHOR>
<COPYRIGHT>2002 FezGuysLiveCo</COPYRIGHT>
<Entry>
  <TITLE>Guster Live</TITLE>
  <AUTHOR>Guster</AUTHOR>
  <STARTTIME VALUE="1:00" />
  <DURATION VALUE="25:00" />
  <Ref href="mms://streaming.fezguys.com/archive/alltenbands.wma" />
</Entry>
```

```
<Entry>
  <TITLE>Dandeline Live</TITLE>
  <AUTHOR>Dandeline</AUTHOR>
  <STARTTIME VALUE="27:00" />
  <DURATION VALUE="25:00" />
  <Ref href="mms://streaming.fezguys.com/archive/alltenbands.wma" />
</Entry>
</ASX>
```

Keep adding the appropriate information for all ten bands.

After creating an .asx metafile, simply upload it to your Web server with your FTP program and link to it from your Web page.

Linking to Your QuickTime Stream

QuickTime doesn't use metafiles in its streaming system. Instead, you can create a separate QuickTime .mov file that acts like a metafile.

If you link directly to your QuickTime on-demand files from your Web page, a listener's browser will, by default, attempt to open the file using the browser's plug-in. To avoid having this happen, create a small "poster movie" file to link to the actual URL of your QuickTime on-demand streaming file, and then embed this poster movie into your Web page. A poster movie can be an image of any size, which makes it easy to incorporate into the design of your Web site. When clicked, the poster movie launches an external player. Embedding a poster movie simply allows you to access the QuickTime plug-in necessary to launch an external player for a QuickTime stream.

It's not necessary to use the <EMBED> tag (see Chapter 13, "Advanced Presentation," for additional information about this process) when linking to Windows Media, RealMedia, or MP3 metafiles. QuickTime, however, requires some embedding. Although the process might seem confusing or overly complex at times, stick with it. We promise it'll all make sense.

To make a QuickTime poster movie and link it to a QuickTime stream, first choose an image. Anything will do, but you might as well use something that is relevant to the content of the audio. You could also create a simple Play button. The image you use must be saved in a file format that QuickTime Player Pro can recognize and import. All common formats (JPEG, GIF, and so on) are supported.

Launch QuickTime Player Pro on your authoring computer. Select File, Import, locate your image, and click Convert. Next, choose File, Export (Windows: Ctrl+E, Macintosh: ⌘+E) and then Export to QuickTime Movie, making sure your exported file name ends in .mov. Click Options, and in the Movie Settings pop-up window, make sure the video option is checked so that your image will be included. Click Settings under the video check box and choose a compression type for your image. (Photo-JPEG is a safe bet.) Choose a Quality setting. (Medium or above will do, or just match the image quality settings for your Web page.) Ignore the Motion setting because you're working with a still image, close Movie Settings, and, making sure your file ends in .mov, click Save. Upload your saved poster movie to your Web server.

You can use the following HTML sample to link the poster movie to a QuickTime on-demand streaming file for use by any browser that supports Netscape's plug-in architecture. You will embed poster.mov and link it to sample.mov in the samples folder on the streaming server streaming. fezguys.com.

```
<EMBED SRC="poster.mov"
  WIDTH="160" HEIGHT="120"
  HREF="rtsp://streaming.fezguys.com/samples/sample.mov"
  TARGET="quicktimeplayer" CONTROLLER="false"
  PLUGINSPAGE="http://www.apple.com/quicktime/download"></EMBED>
```

Because support for Netscape plug-in architecture has been removed from MSIE5.5 and later (Windows only), you will have to use Microsoft's ActiveX to ensure that the QuickTime poster movie will do its job for listeners who are using MSIE 5 on Windows. You do this by including the ActiveX control <OBJECT> tag around the Netscape plug-in <EMBED> tag in your HTML.

The commands in the previous code sample, when wrapped within the ActiveX <OBJECT> tags, now look like this:

```
<OBJECT CLASSID="clsid:02BF25D5-8C17-4B23-BC80-D3488ABDDC6B"
  WIDTH="160" HEIGHT="120"
  CODEBASE="http://www.apple.com/qtactivex/qtplugin.cab">
  <PARAM NAME="SRC" VALUE="poster.mov">
  <PARAM NAME="CONTROLLER" VALUE="false">
  <PARAM NAME="TARGET" VALUE="quicktimeplayer">
  <PARAM NAME="HREF" VALUE="rtsp://streaming.fezguys.com/samples/sample1.mov">
```

```
<EMBED
    SRC="poster.mov"
    HREF="rtsp://streaming.fezguys.com/samples/sample1.mov"
    WIDTH="160" height="120"
    CONTROLLER="false"
    TARGET="quicktimeplayer">
</EMBED>
</OBJECT>
```

After incorporating these commands into your Web page listeners will be able to click on this poster image to start playing the on-demand file in their external QuickTime player.

Linking to Your MP3 Stream

MP3 streams have a few types of metafiles from which to choose. The most commonly used .pls metafile can be a URL (or a list of URLs), but it can also specify how many streams to play and the location and length of each. An older form of MP3 metafile (.m3u) is simply a URL (or a list of URLs) and doesn't allow additional information. This section uses the .pls MP3 metafile type.

A .pls metafile is a text file that contains the URL, length, and title of your MP3 live or on-demand stream(s). The URL in the .pls metafile points to an MP3 streaming server (such as SHOUTcast) or a standard Web server (both of which are HTTP/Progressive streaming and begin in http://).

To create a metafile for linking to the song mysong.mp3 in the samples directory on the SHOUTcast server named streaming.fezguys.com, you will create a file named mysong.pls that contains this text:

```
[Playlist]
Version=2
numberofentries=1
File1=http://streaming.fezguys.com/samples/mysong.mp3
Title1=My Sample Song
Length1=3:42
```

If you're linking to a live stream, set the Length value to −1.

The Version tag lets the MP3 player know that this is a later version of the .pls metafile that includes the Title and Length tags. The Title and Length tags are only used for streams that are not playing yet. As each stream completes and the MP3 player opens the next URL, the player attempts to extract information from the MP3 stream (if any is present). If you don't care about providing the Title and Length for all streams in your playlist, you can omit them and the Version=2 entry.

After creating the `mysong.pls` metafile, place it on your Web server and link to it like any other Web page. For example, in this text:

```
Would you like to <A HREF="mysong.pls">hear a song?</A>
```

the phrase *hear a song* becomes the link. When listeners click this link, their browser retrieves the metafile `mysong.pls` from your Web server. The browser then launches an external MP3 player and hands the metafile file to it. The player reads the URL in the metafile, connects to your server, and plays the actual audio stream.

As you can guess by this example, you can include more than one song in a .pls file. For example, perhaps you have a language Web site that has five files containing the phrase *Thank You*, with each file in a different language. Instead of creating five different metafiles, you can create one metafile with the appropriate name for each language.

If the URL to the folder that contains the five on-demand files is this:

```
http://streaming.fezguys.com/archive/thankyou/
```

and each version is named by the language it includes, you could include all five as follows:

```
[Playlist]
numberofentries=5
File1=http://streaming.fezguys.com/archive/thankyou/english.mp3
Title1=Thank You (English)
Length1=0:20
File2=http://streaming.fezguys.com/archive/thankyou/spanish.mp3
Title2=Thank You (Spanish)
Length2=0:20
File3=http://streaming.fezguys.com/archive/thankyou/russian.mp3
Title3=Thank You (Russian)
Length3=0:20
File4=http://streaming.fezguys.com/archive/thankyou/latvian.mp3
Title4=Thank You (Latvian)
Length4=0:20
```

```
File5=http://streaming.fezguys.com/archive/thankyou/japanese.mp3
Title5=Thank You (Japanese)
Length5=0:20
Version=2
```

After completing the `.pls` metafile, upload it to your Web server with your FTP program.

Configuring Your Web Server's MIME Types

A Multipurpose Internet Mail Extensions (MIME) type is a way to define the contents of a file. Many programs, including Web servers, use the suffix of a filename to determine the file's MIME type. For example, when you tell your browser to open the page www.fezguys.com/audio/sample.pls, the Web server that handles www.fezguys.com looks up a `.pls` file's MIME type in its configuration. The Web server then returns the contents of sample.pls marked as the applicable MIME type. Each Web server has its own configuration format. If you're unsure of how to change the MIME settings, check the Web server's documentation. An improperly configured Web browser might prevent people from listening to the audio you've spent so much time preparing, so do remember to check this.

NOTE

If you test your metafiles on a Windows computer, you might not notice problems with incorrect MIME type settings. This is because Windows does its own local MIME type check based on the filename after it has been downloaded. As a result, Macintosh users could have problems with your metafiles, and you might not realize it. It's always recommended that you double-check your MIME type settings on your Web server.

Included next is a listing of the correct MIME types and file suffix descriptions for metafiles used in the Step-by-Steps in this chapter. Verify that the Web server that is hosting your metafiles is properly configured for each of these MIME types. Each format also has other, less-common MIME types of which it makes use. Make sure that the MIME types for any other metafiles you decide to use are included in your Web server's configuration.

- **MP3 metafile**—The file suffix is `.pls`, and the MIME type is audio/x-pls.

- **RealMedia metafile**—The file suffix is `.ram` or `.rpm`, and the MIME type is audio/x-pn-realaudio.

- **Windows Media metafile**—The file suffix is `.asx`, and the MIME type is video/x-ms-asf.

- **QuickTime metafile**—The file suffix is `.mov`, and the MIME type is video/quicktime.

Summary

As you can see, streaming audio is a realm with many competing standards. There are many ways to perform many tasks successfully. Some of the processes are labor intensive but result in a smoother system. Other processes get you up and running quickly but are less robust. If you're experienced in streaming audio then this chapter may have increased the efficiency and delivery of your work.

PART III

Case Studies

Part III: Case Studies

Each streaming audio environment requires its own authoring, encoding, design, and serving scenarios. Some streaming audio doesn't require a Web site and some Web sites would benefit from streaming audio. Some must have live streaming audio available 24/7, while others may offer a combination of live, on-demand, and archived streams. Streaming audio may be the entire purpose of a particular Web site while other sites view it as an unimportant add-on.

In this Part we'll document three scenarios for including streaming audio on a Web site.

- The first study will focus on a Web site that primarily uses on-demand files with an occasional live stream for special events.

- The second study is a Web site that offers several live MP3 streams in multiple bitrates.

- The third is the online presence of a standard, terrestrial broadcast radio station streaming its programming.

For each scenario, we'll discuss how the streaming audio is authored and served, and offer some insight into why those choices were made based on what criteria.

CHAPTER 8

Joe Satriani: A Web Site with On-Demand Files in Multiple Formats and Special Event Live Streams

This example details a famous musician's promotional and fan-oriented web site that has many on-demand files of songs authored in multiple formats and occasionally has live streams for special events.

NOTE

Department of Disclaimers

FezGuy #1 is the webmaster/mad genius behind www.satriani.com. But lest anyone think that we're horn-tooting types, let it be known that we chose this site only because it's relevant to the book, and we have an intimate working knowledge of how it all goes together and the reasons those choices were made.

History and Design

The Web site (www.satriani.com) is the online presence for the internationally popular instrumental guitarist Joe Satriani. Over the course of a decade, Satriani has released over 12 albums and toured extensively. His Web site is designed to be informative and useful primarily to his fans, offering standard features such as chat areas, a discography, photographs, and tour information. For the aficionado, the site also offers more detailed technical information about the guitarist's technique and tools.

The design and implementation of the site was handled with the assumption that most visitors to www.satriani.com would already know the guitarist and probably own at least one album. To familiarize visitors with the guitarist's entire catalog (thereby driving increased album sales), a 45-second on-demand streaming clip of every song on every album is provided using an easily navigable design. Only a handful of full-length on-demand songs are available. Recent album releases have offered MP3 downloads and multiple bit rate RealMedia on-demand streams of the first designated single. These downloads are made available to fans before the album is released to radio.

Building and Maintaining Community

Each time Joe Satriani goes on the road with a new album release, a live Webcast is put together to help promote the tour and album to online fans. Satriani is one of the earliest artists to adopt the Internet for direct outreach, doing his first Webcast in March 1996 as an interactive live chat. Previous Webcasts included live video and audio streams in multiple bit rates, and some also featured still photos taken during the show, editorial coverage, and even a promotional giveaway contest for a fan to win gear, a private lesson, complete discography, and other merchandise.

In addition to the Web site's fan-driven bulletin boards, live chats, and member profiles, Satriani has personalized the site by periodically recording short audio and video greetings, which are encoded in several formats. The Web greetings, which set the site apart from the music label or retail Web sites, are typically recorded at a live show. The recording employs a digital video camera, captured onto a Macintosh using Final Cut Pro. After some slight audio compression and video editing, the recording is exported as a raw, uncompressed QuickTime movie. That movie is then encoded into RealMedia using RealProducer Plus (in 34Kbps, 80Kbps, 150Kbps, and 225Kbps bit rates) and compressed into a high bit rate (approximately 128Kbps) QuickTime movie using QuickTime Pro. The files are uploaded via FTP to the Web site, at which time metafiles are created for the RealMedia clips and then linked into the site.

To promote the most recent two album releases, full songs were made available online prior to the designated single's radio release and the album's delivery to retail stores. These songs are available as multiple bit rate MP3 downloadable files and a RealMedia stream.

Streaming Architecture

The audio on the site is authored on a combination of Windows and Macintosh computers using the streaming formats covered in this book (RealMedia, QuickTime, Windows Media, and MP3). The following sections outline many of the tools and processes used for digitizing, encoding, and publishing.

Formats Used

Wherever possible, multiple formats are used for streaming audio on the site. For the 45-second song clips, 56Kbps dial-up modem users are provided with 32Kbps streams in QuickTime, Windows Media, and MP3, as well as a RealMedia SureStream for up to 64Kbps. Full-length tracks are provided as four multiple bit rate MP3 downloads (24Kbps, 96Kbps, 128Kbps, 192Kbps) and a low bit rate RealMedia streaming file. Live Web casts are typically provided in the format that the partner company prefers. In recent years, the site's Webmaster has partnered with QuickTime, although previous Webcasts have included RealMedia.

Encoders

When possible, any Web site that features music should offer low bit rate on-demand clips (segments) of as many songs as possible. Joe Satriani's discography includes approximately 150 songs, and www.satriani.com offers a 45-second clip of each one, authored as on-demand files for Windows Media, QuickTime, RealMedia, and MP3. 150 clips times the four formats equals 600 individual clips. Encoding these files is a potentially time-consuming task. All 600 sound clips were created using a combination of Xing's AudioCatalyst 2.1, Discreet's Cleaner 5.1, and custom Unix script programs.

First, each CD is put into a Windows machine running AudioCatalyst, and then the first 45 seconds of each track is selected to be ripped into an uncompressed WAV file. Certain tracks that begin more slowly (as well as live tracks with applause at the beginning) are set manually for a more appropriate 45-second section.

Before the ripping process begins, AudioCatalyst looks up album and song information through queries to the CD database service CDDB (www.cddb.com) and then configures to save each clip into individual files. Each file is named by song title and track number and placed in a folder named by the album title (handled by AudioCatalyst's useful naming configuration).

After the ripping process, Cleaner 5.1 compresses the extracted excerpts into MP3, QuickTime, RealMedia, and Windows Media on-demand streaming files. Special settings are created for each format desired (see "Formats Used" earlier in this chapter) to set bit rates, fade-ins/outs and author/title metadata and, for formats that had the option, the Comment/URL http://www. satriani.com/.

Because Cleaner 5.1 can only easily output files from each batch into one directory (without manually setting a new destination for each file), files are batch encoded for each album's collection of songs. Each album's folder of uncompressed WAV excerpt files is dragged into a new Cleaner batch window. The files are then selected and the destination directory for the encoded files is set to a new output folder named for the album. With all songs still selected, Cleaner's Advanced Settings option is chosen and all of the desired format settings are selected. After applying the settings, Start is clicked and Cleaner encodes the multiple files, one for each format. When complete, the process is repeated for each album.

When all the tracks have been encoded, a folder with subfolders for each album containing each clip encoded into four different formats is uploaded to the streaming server. A custom Unix script program is used to generate metafiles for the RealMedia, Windows Media, and MP3 files. Metafiles for the RealMedia and Windows Media clips include song title and album title information. This information is retrieved from a simple database of album information by cross-referencing the album name (which is also the name of the folder containing the encoded file) and track number (also in the encoded file's filename). Another custom script is used to insert the song and album information into ID3 tags for the MP3 files. The sound clips are then linked into each album's page within the discography section of the Web site.

Servers and Bandwidth

All on-demand streaming is served as part of the Web site hosting. Because the majority of audio content on the site is short song excerpts, overall bandwidth use is light.

However, when full songs are offered as part of an exclusive promotion for a new release, download popularity temporarily generates a considerable amount of additional bandwidth. Deals are typically set up with the Web site's ISP to trade bandwidth for a logo and link on the site.

Live special event Webcasts also bring in too many listeners to handle using the regular day-to-day streaming servers. Typically, partnerships with other companies are created to stream these Webcasts. Most recently, Apple has assisted in the encoding side, while Apple's streaming partner, Akamai, has handled the serving. Certainly, Satriani's popularity and major music label representation make it possible to form these partnerships. Be that as it may, the streaming audio industry is young enough that some organizations are willing to set aside immediate profit by using these showcases to increase consumer awareness of and demand for the technology.

Summary

Various aspects of the Satriani site are changed on a regular basis, which keeps the site fresh for repeat visitors. In addition, fans post their comments on the site, adding topicality and relevance. This site was created specifically to offer Satriani's online fans a way to stay in touch with him and his music. The site exists because it's useful and because fans use it. Any other band Web site can apply any of the approaches this site uses to strengthen the relationship between the musicians and their fans.

CHAPTER 9

SomaFM: Multiple Live Streams from a Playlist Database

This example details an Internet-only radio station and its Web site offering live streams of (as of this writing) six unique music programs in multiple bit rates.

History and Design

"I couldn't find anything (on the radio) I wanted to listen to."
—R. Hodge

The brainchild of Rusty Hodge, SomaFM (www.somafm.com) first came online in early 2000 with a single 56Kbps live stream. His site's popularity soon convinced him to upgrade his authoring computers, increase the number of programs and bit rate channels, and move the servers to a co-location facility. Less than a year after it began, SomaFM had a SHOUTcast-sponsored repeater service allowing 500 additional concurrent streams. But even that hasn't been enough. Recent peak statistics showed 2,141 simultaneous users and, according to SHOUTcast figures, SomaFM has more than 100,000 listeners per month. Not bad for a streaming Web site with no advertising, no deep pockets, and only word of mouth promotion.

Hodge and a small group of volunteers operate SomaFM, which currently offers six streaming programs in a variety of bit rates. The Web site has a news area for the sporadic posts documenting the trials and victories of running a thoroughly underfunded venture on inspiration and available resources. A typical message found in November 2001: "SomaFM stations accrued 636,974 total listener hours in the last 30 days. On average, we have 884 concurrent listeners. This is significantly higher than many venture-capital funded, commercial Internet broadcasters. You are helping change the way radio works! Thank you so much for listening and being part of SomaFM."

The design of the site is basic, indicating a focus on music. You won't see a Flash intro or blinking objects—just simple links to primary areas: News, Playlists, Listen Now (to the programs), Community, and Donate.

The site asks for donations, providing links to PayPal and the Amazon Honor System. Listeners do contribute (see the next section "Building and Maintaining Community"). Other revenue comes from a link to music retail site Amazon.com. Every time a listener on the SomaFM Web site clicks the link to Amazon.com and buys a CD, a small sum is paid to SomaFM. Listeners also post their comments on the community page. Occasionally, a comment warrants a reply. The Webmaster works full time for a large Fortune 500 company, so he's not able to answer every e-mail.

The physical space is a small room in San Francisco. In the little South of Market squatter's palace are turntables, mics, the authoring computers and a mixer setup for streaming the occasional live performance. Hodge spends between 15 and 20 hours per week maintaining the site, manually tuning the playlists throughout the day based on "what sounds good" and using listener requests to modify the song order. Every week or two, he adds new material.

Building and Maintaining Community

SomaFM depends on its community. An area on the site is available for listeners to post comments. An e-mail link and a telephone number (currently a toll call) are provided for requests and other commentary. Hodge attributes the current load of only five calls per day to the toll charges. A toll-free number is planned. Interestingly, SomaFM's voicemail service makes WAV files of the phone messages, which can be used in the site's programming.

As it is with any commercial-free, listener-supported radio venture, Hodge says: "the trick is to make it pay its own bills." According to information on the site, it costs more than $15,000 a year to run SomaFM, including bandwidth, music publishing fees, hardware maintenance, connectivity, installation charges, and electricity. Site statistics state that almost 5% of the total listening audience contributes to the tune of about $15,000 between 06/01 and 2/02.

Some of the small labels whose music is routinely played on SomaFM have donated CDs, and one has even donated a quantity of its sampler CD to offer as an enticement for listeners who donate $25 or more.

Streaming Architecture

Except for the occasional voiceover or live in-studio programming, all SomaFM music is streamed from pre-encoded on-demand MP3 audio files.

FIGURE 9.1

SomaFM: Diagram of audio pathway from DJ to Internet listener.

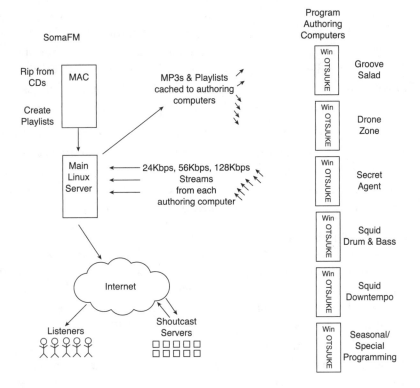

Formats Used

SomaFM broadcasts its programs in the MP3 format, typically providing three bit rates for each program (128Kbps 44.1kHz stereo, 56Kbps 44.1kHz mono, and 24Kbps 22kHz mono). MP3 was chosen as the only format because it's an open standard and server software costs are nil.

Encoders

SomaFM first encoded on-demand MP3 files at 160Kbps, later bumping up to 192Kbps to avoid undesired audio artifacts resulting from re-encoding the on-demand files to lower bit rates as part of the live stream. But while encoding on-demand MP3 files at 192Kbps is suitable for a typical audience listening quietly on computer speakers at the office, it was decided to increase the bit rate to 256Kbps, before settling on a 320Kbps minimum, mostly because disk space is so inexpensive. The higher bit rate encode settings are useful as SomaFM is considering offering its content for satellite radio services.

The majority of these pre-encoded MP3 source files are ripped and encoded from CDs on a Macintosh computer with SoundJam (www.soundjam.com) using the Fraunhofer encoding engine. The SoundJam team was tapped by Apple to help create iTunes and SoundJam is considered the precursor to Apple's music file jukebox software. SoundJam is no longer available, but Hodge remains comfortable with the program's playlist creation features and uses them to maintain master playlist information for each program.

The on-demand MP3 files and program playlists are copied to and stored on a Linux server computer that then shares those files with each of the individual stream's authoring computers. These LAN file transfers are done using the freely available software packages netatalk (the AppleTalk Protocol Suite for Unix) and Samba (Windows file sharing software for Unix).

Each of the program's playlists are updated by hand as new songs are added and old ones removed, or a song's number of plays per program run is changed. To help make things easier, Hodge has a custom-built AppleScript program to automatically copy his playlist onto the Linux server. Each of the programs has a separate playlist folder that includes current songs as well as a list of tracks that have been temporarily removed. To repeat songs within a program Hodge's current approach is to simply list the song multiple times in the appropriate playlist. He acknowledges the solution is inelegant but mentions it's temporary.

Each program has its own dedicated authoring computer that encodes a live stream for each bit rate offered. These authoring computers cost about $350 apiece and are assembled from older hardware found by scouring for good deals at Web sites such as www.pricewatch.com. A typical configuration combines an Intel motherboard with a Celeron processor (400–900MHz), a 20GB hard drive, 128MB RAM, and a Creative Labs Sound Blaster Live "value package" audio card. Prices for memory and disk space have dropped recently, so adding more of both is appealing. Hodge prefers Intel and 3Com networking cards. He feels that other brands have presented problems with SHOUTcast streams, and suggests that the incompatibilities may be a result of the way the network packets are formed.

Each of the individual programs' Windows authoring computers maintains a local copy (pulled from MP3 files on the Linux server) of all the music needed for its specific program. This technique increases the computers' stability and also makes it possible to take the server down for maintenance without interrupting the programs.

To author multiple bit rate streams for each specific program, all authoring computers run a copy of the OtsJuke DJ (www.otsjuke.com) software package for "DJs, radio stations, & music lovers." Free evaluation copies are available from their Web site. This software acts like traditional radio station automation; supporting playlist creation, cross fades, live source mixing, and other features.

SomaFM uses the OtsJuke software's playlist generation feature as a starting point for each stream. Hodge sets up the OtsJuke playlist with a randomly ordered list from his master database and applies a few rules such as "Don't play same artists within 15 tracks" and "Don't play same track name within 100 songs." Some of these rules are of a legal nature (Digital Millennium Copyright Act—see Appendix for more details), and some are simply programming common sense. Because permissions to play about 50% (this number has been steadily rising) of SomaFM's programming comes directly from artists/labels (copyright holders), SomaFM can legally work around many of the DMCA rules. Playlists are fine-tuned while the program streams.

For SomaFM in general and Hodge in particular, the coolest thing about OtsJuke is its direct support for SHOUTcast authoring. OtsJuke has a built-in dynamics processor with automatic gain control (AGC) and a compressor/limiter. The OtsJuke AGC is tunable and, for SomaFM, is currently configured to a fairly long time set. The AGC dynamics processor is only single-band, but it does the job adequately. SomaFM uses dynamic processing slightly differently on each streaming program. For example, the Groove Salad program uses AGC more aggressively than the Drone Zone program. Many listeners are at work, listening on inexpensive computer speakers at low volumes. If they turn their volume up to hear a quiet section, the louder sections of an otherwise unprocessed stream are too loud, and vice versa. AGC dynamics processing is almost mandatory when creating programming with many different kinds of music from many different sources. Streaming programming of this type that doesn't use dynamic processing clearly shows radically unequal volume levels between songs.

SomaFM routes live audio (CD, mic, in-studio performance) through a standalone Behringer 9024 ($400) six-band compressor/limiter prior to including it into a streaming program.

Servers and Bandwidth

All of SomaFM's authoring computers as well as the Web and e-mail server are connected through two 1.5MB sDSL lines. At the time of this writing, one line handles four of a current total of six programs, and the other line hosts the last two programs as well as the Web and e-mail server. All the authoring computers' streams are broadcast to a local SHOUTcast server. Reflector SHOUTcast servers that serve the Internet listeners then pick up one copy of each of the three bit rate streams for every program.

Discounting the Web and e-mail traffic, basic addition seems to show that enough bandwidth exists to stream the current six programs over a single 1.5Mb sDSL connection. Each program streams a 128Kbps, 56Kbps, and 24Kbps feed, totaling 208Kbps per program. Multiply that by six (the number of programs), and the total is 1,248Kbps. That leaves 252Kb of connectivity for administration, e-mail and Web traffic. Unfortunately, it's not that straightforward. Each stream requires a certain amount of headroom for reliability and stability. In fact, Hodge's experience has shown a headroom level of 20% (minimum) over and above each individual stream's bit rate is required. Splitting SomaFM's programming across two connections is necessary to ensure broadcast stability.

SomaFM doesn't have enough cash to afford the bandwidth required for streaming redistribution to listeners from within its own network. Consequently, the streams travel over the Internet to various banks of streaming SHOUTcast server computers. Companies that have spare bandwidth donate servers and bandwidth. These companies have contracted with their ISPs for extra bandwidth to handle their peak usage, and at non-peak times these companies have more bandwidth than they need. Donations of this nature are a strong testament to the positive impact of SomaFM's programming and negotiation abilities. The audience continues to grow, and SomaFM is always on the lookout for more bandwidth. Hodge recently found some in the SHOUTcast developers. SHOUTcast's corporate owner, AOL/Time Warner, had an enormous number of servers and huge amounts of available bandwidth and needed to promote their own streaming services. Through a special offer, certain handpicked stations (of which SomaFM was one lucky recipient) were given access to additional servers and bandwidth. To qualify for the free assistance stations had to fall within certain guidelines, including showing 50–100 peak concurrent listeners consistently. Stations also had to have exceeded their current resources, have no commercials, and show a measure of longevity. As a final decree, SHOUTcast stated it would not offer this promotional service to any streaming station whose programming could be described as "techno."

Although it's possible to serve SomaFM's peak use of more than 2,000 concurrent listeners on fewer (but more powerful) servers, SomaFM's current bandwidth and server arrangements occupy five server computers. In theory, it should be possible to fit eight listeners using 128Kbps streams on 1Mb of bandwidth before saturating a 100Mb (100B-T) connection. SomaFM current guidelines are 600 users per server, although they have peaked to 700 listeners. Most of the SomaFM SHOUTcast servers are running on other people's computers and bandwidth, but Hodge and his crew handle all of the administration duties.

Legal Issues

Currently approximately 50% of the SomaFM's music use permissions come from the actual musicians. SomaFM makes quarterly reports to the BMI and ASCAP collection societies. SomaFM has a Not For Profit license and falls underneath the "revenue cap" for noncommercial use. Their fees (based on the most current listener statistics) hover around $600 annually.

Summary

The SomaFM scenario is a perfect example of "make-do" do-it-yourself creativity. It takes a lot of time and effort and a person has to feel very passionately if it's going to work. But it's clear from the SomaFM example that it can be done, and done well.

CHAPTER 10

KPIG: Traditional Radio Station Streaming Live and On-Demand

This example dissects a Web site for a terrestrial broadcast radio station. The site offers several live streams authored in multiple formats and provides a large selection of archived on-demand programming.

History and Design

"In some ways, the station is a little ahead of its time."
—Wild Bill Goldsmith

On August 2, 1995, KPIG became the first radio station in the world to stream its audio over the Internet. Since that groundbreaking moment it's been streaming continuously. www.kpig.com is the online presence for the Triple A FM radio station KPIG 107.5 in Freedom, California about 90 miles south of San Francisco. Although broadcasting at a meager 2,850 watts (a standard corporate-owned radio station in an urban market is between 50,000 and 100,000 watts), KPIG regularly gets high ratings (based on the Arbitron rating system) in the "Adult 25-54" market. Unlike 90% of the Triple A radio market, KPIG's DJs actually select the music. The station has a decidedly local feel to its programming, with an accent on local events and resources.

KPIG's Web site layout might be described as "rudimentary Americana." It reflects a straightforward design approach that is reminiscent of homespun simplicity with a minimum of glitz. The large site includes archives of live performances, listener feedback areas, Webcam feeds from various locations, and a one-week playlist archive of every song broadcast during that period.

In this extremely comprehensive playlist archive, entries are time-stamped and song titles are linked to a request button, a comment and rating form, or a link to CDNow (an online music retailer).

The site features a large archive containing numerous live streams from past programs of live performances. The individual performances are arranged in chronological order and available for anyone to access, in the same streaming formats as the regular stream programming. Permissions to make these in-studio performances available as archives are provided through the semi-official okay of the performer. Most of the featured musicians are not affiliated with large music business corporations, so including their streams into the archive is welcomed as free promotion. The station is quick to comply should any performer request the deletion of their archived performance from the server computer.

KPIG has a large database of pre-encoded music. Currently above 7,000 songs, new songs are added to the database all the time. DJs have access to the database through a computer in the broadcast booth and create almost all of their on-air programming from the playlist. Custom software enables DJs to create a song order during their shift. They can orchestrate cross fades and preview their edits before publishing them to the separate broadcast and streaming systems.

Online KPIG listeners using dial-up modems can access low bit rate streams in four flavors: a 16Kbps and a 32Kbps Windows Media stream, a 24Kbps MP3 stream that will play through any MP3 player, and the same 24Kbps MP3 stream delivered using a RealMedia metafile, requiring RealPlayer 7+. Broadband users (tuning in to the self-described "Super HiFi CyberPork" streams) can choose between a straight 128Kbps MP3 stream (for use with any MP3 player) and the same 128Kbps MP3 stream delivered using the RealMedia metafile, requiring the RealPlayer 7+. The site also has links to download MP3, RealMedia, and Windows Media players for Windows, Macintosh (old and new), and Linux/Unix (both GUI and Command Line) operating systems.

Listeners are encouraged to register to become part of the KPIG online community. Registrants can save bit rate and player settings, which then automatically launch when the Listen button on the main page is pressed. Registrants can also rate and post comments about songs, save other settings on the Web site, enter online contests, and sign up for the newsletter.

The Web site is the creation of independent consultant Bill Goldsmith (self-described "Chief Cyberswine"). As the primary architect, designer, and programmer for KPIG's online presence, Goldsmith is responsible for the layout, design, graphics, streams, automated systems, Webcams, encoders; pretty much everything. Goldsmith doesn't handle the encode/upload process and day-to-day management of the song database, but he does maintain the site systems and streams. Goldsmith claims to spend about "three to four hours" a month nudging the network and "four to five hours" a week maintaining and updating the Web site.

The KPIG stream typically has a peak concurrence load of 1,100–1,200 listeners. Monthly figures are more difficult to gauge, but it's estimated to be between 60,000–70,000 unique listeners.

Building and Maintaining Community

According to Goldsmith, KPIG's online streaming programs boost and support its standard broadcast reach. Goldsmith mentions that the local feel of the programming feeds what is called an *illusion of inclusion*. Online listeners around the world can still take part in the small town, independent feel of this terrestrial broadcast station by peeking in through their Webcams, adding their own comments, requesting songs and of course, listening to an unapologetically provincial style of programming.

DJs encourage the sense of community through listener ratings. Although not required to use this feedback, DJs can see what listeners think of songs in the form of ratings from 1 ("sucko-barfo") to 10 ("Godlike") and read text comments. This kind of give and take, although not practical for terrestrial broadcast programming, is easy within the online world.

Goldsmith has as much (or more) experience as anyone in this just-emerging realm of streaming radio programming. He observes that competition is much greater in the online world. And with a vastly larger number of competitors, it's a much greater challenge to stand out from the herd. He offers that the quality of the product has "gotta be really good." Goldsmith is not only talking about the programming, either. Quality is also represented by stream stability and Web site ease of use—the entire end user experience. Aiming his comments directly at the online presence of most radio stations, Goldsmith opines: "… mediocrity and lowest common denominator won't work."

Streaming Architecture

KPIG broadcasts both on traditional airwaves and online in multiple bit rates and formats. Consequently, its encoding configuration is a bit more complex than the simple one format, one bit rate Internet-only stream.

FIGURE 10.1

KPIG: Diagram of audio pathway from DJ to Internet listener.

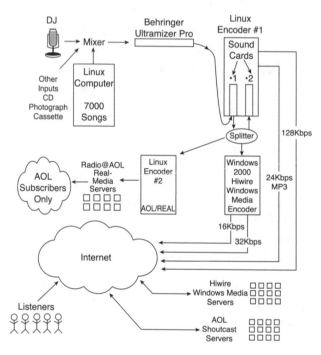

Formats Used

KPIG has always streamed in multiple formats. Starting out with Xing Technologies' MPEG-based Streamworks system, KPIG switched to RealMedia when Xing lost traction in the rapidly expanding streaming media world. (RealNetworks eventually purchased Xing.) A couple of years ago KPIG's streaming partner Magnitude Network (which had contracted with RealNetworks' server network) cut a seven-figure deal with Microsoft to switch all of its 150 stations to Windows Media. KPIG quietly kept a RealMedia feed available to provide a much-needed streaming stability in the early days of Windows Media.

After Magnitude went under, KPIG hooked up with streaming services company Hiwire, also working in the Windows Media format. When MP3 streaming became popular KPIG added it (using server resources from the SHOUTcast developers) and MP3 streams are now the most commonly used (by a margin of two to one). At the time of this writing, KPIG just added a RealMedia feed accessible only by AOL 7 users.

Encoders

Unlike most radio stations, everything at KPIG starts with the DJ's own music selection. Bill Goldsmith created an innovative home-brewed system that KPIG DJs use to select about 95% of their programming. The PIII 933MHz music server system computer has 128MB RAM and runs the Linux operating system. The computer runs Goldsmith's custom software to access a database of more than 7,000 songs encoded as 256Kbps MP3 files. DJs can search for songs by keyword, artist name, and genre, and they can preview and select multiple songs.

Goldsmith uses the Linux-based, command line Ecasound utility (`http://eca.cx`). In addition to many other features, Ecasound handles compression, level control, and fades; it even mixes multiple MP3 files together. An audio output from the Linux computer running Ecasound goes into KPIG's central, mid-Sixties-era, big knob mixing board where the encoded programming can be mixed in with CD, cassette, phonograph, live microphones, or other audio inputs. The final mix is then sent from the control studio to the airwaves and the Internet. The traditional broadcast feed travels via a digital link to the building that houses the terrestrial FM transmitter.

The audio intended for the Internet goes to the next room; first to a Behringer Ultramizer Pro dynamics processor. The Ultramizer performs smoothing and compression on the audio using a multiband processor that handles the bass frequencies separately from the rest of the audio. Out of the Ultramizer, the audio is then fed into a PII 400MHz with 64MB RAM Linux computer that has two sound cards. We'll call this computer "Linux Encoder #1" and its two sound cards "sound card #1" and "sound card #2."

The use of double sound cards in this computer is as follows: KPIG's audio feed is plugged into sound card #1's $1/8$" miniplug input. A cable from sound card #1's output is split and sent to three places: the input of sound card #2 (still within Linux Encoder #1), the input of the Hiwire Windows Media

Encoder computer (PIII 933MHZ with 256MB RAM running Windows 2000), and another Linux encoder computer ("Linux Encoder #2") for the AOL RealMedia stream.

The Linux Encoder #1 computer encodes the audio input received by sound card #2 into two MP3 streams (24Kbps and 128Kbps) using the "liveice" broadcast tool with the LAME (see Chapter 6, "Using MP3") MP3 encoding engine. (Liveice is part of the Icecast system and is compatible with SHOUTcast.) The Linux Encoder #1 then sends the two streams to SHOUTcast's portion of the huge AOL/Time Warner server farm. The Hiwire Windows Media Encoder encodes two streams (high and low bit rate) from the live feed coming into its sound card and sends the Windows Media streams out to the Hiwire streaming servers. The Linux Encoder #2 computer (a PII 400MHZ computer with 64MB RAM) encodes the audio coming into its sound card and uses RealProducer to encode a single 20Kbps RealMedia stream, and sends it off to AOL's server farm for proprietary redistribution to "Radio @ AOL" users. Goldsmith would be happy to send AOL a higher bit rate stream, but that's all AOL wants. Apparently, most AOL users don't want or couldn't use higher bit rate streams anyway.

All outgoing streams from the station to the various streaming servers are sent through the general Internet. The KPIG studio and offices have two 1.2MB sDSL lines, one for the folks working in the offices and the other for the outgoing streams.

The computers and cabling are consumer-grade gear, easily purchased at standard retail outlets. The Linux computers, although a few years old, are dedicated to a single task, so they don't need to have the "latest, greatest whiz-bang" processing power. The sound cards are standard Creative Labs "SoundBlaster Live" products that are available at any local computer store. Some of the cabling is even from Radio Shack.

Servers and Bandwidth

Like everybody else in the broadcasting industry, station management is talking about how to create revenue from streams, but as of this writing, nobody knows how to do that in any substantial way.

By using simple math and multiplying the number of concurrent streams that KPIG serves with the bit rate of each stream, it quickly becomes evident that it would cost upward of $5,000–10,000 a month for bandwidth alone at current market rates. KPIG doesn't receive direct revenue from its Internet streams, and so partners with several organizations to help defray these costs.

All of KPIG's live MP3 streams are served in a partnership with SHOUTcast (included in parent company AOL/Time Warner's server infrastructure). KPIG "helps to promote their software and stress tests (the software) under high usage conditions." This makes KPIG beta testers for SHOUTcast and, in exchange, SHOUTcast "gives" KPIG the necessary bandwidth to support its popular streams. The duration of this relationship in its present form depends on many factors.

Hiwire covers server and bandwidth costs for the Windows Media streams (through iBeam's Content Delivery Network) and sells audio ads in the Internet stream that take the place of ads used in the terrestrial broadcast (see the section later in this chapter: "Ad Replacement"). If Hiwire makes money after covering costs, the revenue is split 50/50 with KPIG. Hiwire's model is perhaps a little ahead of its time. Nonetheless, it appears that this advanced concept is working so far.

The archived MP3 on-demand streams on the KPIG site are handled through Goldsmith's own server computers located in local ISP Got.net's cage at co-location facility AboveNet. In exchange for advertising on KPIG's Web site, Got.net covers the bandwidth needed for those archives.

Song Identification

KPIG's Web site provides an online playlist detailing the programming history of the previous week, a useful feature. Local listeners to the terrestrial broadcast can check KPIG's Web site after hearing a song and find out what it was up to seven days after the fact. The playlist information is posted to the Web site from the DJ's selection computer as each song is played. As each song starts to play, the system creates a new version of the playlist and uploads it to the Web server. When songs are played manually (CD, cassette, phonograph, live in-studio performance), the DJ manually enters the artist and song title information.

The Hiwire encoder is fed a listing of what song is currently playing so that the song can display in the listener's Windows Media player application window. KPIG is working through details to add this same feature to its other format streams.

Legal Issues

Just the same as with its terrestrial broadcasts, KPIG must report its Internet playlists to the appropriate collection societies. BMI and ASCAP receive a report for every song played each fiscal quarter. Other societies, such as SESAC, haven't really figured out how to calculate online usage for their members. (Certain obviously incorrect calculations sorted out to figures higher than terrestrial broadcast use, even as high as six times greater.) Collection societies have different rules for online and traditional broadcast use, and currently it's unclear how to calculate these different usage fees and even whom to pay.

KPIG's staff also uses a policy of self regulation regarding publishing playlists that predates and is actually more restrictive than the DMCA rulings. By abiding to its own stricter code KPIG doesn't have to worry about altering its terrestrial broadcast content prior to streaming.

Advanced Authoring

The glacial pace and inherent misunderstandings of bureaucracy and legislation hold true in the streaming world, like any other. Each live streaming situation has its own special issues to work through, and KPIG is no different.

Ad Replacement

The byzantine fee-payment system for most of the national advertising that runs on a radio station is administered by a trade union that represents the voiceover talent. Someone within the union decided that Internet streaming was very profitable. Based on this decision, the union set rates for Internet use at approximately 300% above the rates for standard broadcast use. As a result, many traditional radio stations have found the costs of running the same advertising on their streams prohibitively expensive and have ceased online streaming entirely. KPIG, showing practicality and common sense, chose to replace the ads in their streams with other content. For their MP3 streams, pre-encoded on-demand MP3 files are inserted in place of the ads. The Hiwire Windows Media system has extra technology built into the listener's player that instead inserts localized ads based on the listener's geographical location.

As mentioned earlier, the Linux Encoder #1 has two audio cards. The mixer output goes through the Behringer processor and into sound card #1. When the DJ's program broadcast is about to play an ad that needs to be removed from the Internet stream, the computer in the DJ booth tells Linux Encoder #1 the start time and length of the ad via direct network (TCP/IP) communication. Goldsmith's custom software on Linux Encoder #1 fades down the live audio input, mixes in some filler audio from a database of on-demand MP3 files, and when the ad is done, fades out the on-demand file and fades back into the live audio. In this way, sound card #1 is acting as an automated mixer between the live audio and on-demand files.

Ad start time and length are also simultaneously sent via a serial signal from the program broadcast computer to the Hiwire encoding computer. Because the Hiwire Windows Media player handles the ad insertion through the player on the listener's computer, no other preparation at KPIG is necessary.

Summary

Although owned by New Wave Broadcasting, a parent corporation that is busy aggregating disparate small- to mid-sized radio stations within specific geographical areas, KPIG's independent approach to programming defies the official industry genre-label of "Triple A." Evolving through what has been called *organic branding*, KPIG has managed to retain its independence in the absurdly sterile and tightly ordered community of institutional corporate radio. A large part of this autonomy is due to the success experienced serving listeners through its online presence.

PART IV

Extra Credit

Part IV: Extra Credit

Once you've got the basics of streaming audio handled, you're ready to expand your knowledge. Whether or not your extra effort makes you financially successful, your listening audience will appreciate it. Actually, your listening audience doesn't really give a damn about how you did it (unless you're featured on a segment of "VH-1: Behind the Codecs"), as long as everything works properly. To ensure everything does work properly, Part IV offers various advanced techniques for streaming stability and presentation uniqueness. There are as many ways to stream audio as there are useless items for sale on eBay, but there's no "right" way.

CHAPTER 11

Advanced Audio Optimization

Most streaming audio tools work well enough, but you can take certain extra steps with your source audio to assist an encoder in doing a better job. These extra steps, sometimes called *audio optimizations*, can be helpful for all streaming audio scenarios, but they're most useful when authoring streams at 64Kbps and below. Using various forms of optimization, you can shape your source audio in numerous ways to improve the chances of delivering the stream to the listener with reasonable sonic legibility.

Naturally, encoding to a low bit rate is going to do some strange things to your audio. With only a small amount of space to represent your source audio, the choice of what to emphasize or throw away is critical. To put it visually, think of making a postage stamp from a painting. What must be lost to make a large image translate to a tiny one? Is the goal to keep the original colors true or to be merely recognizable? You've got to give up something to make it work. The question is: What? While you're thinking about that, consider this: You know your audio source best, so if you're going to remove something, it's better to choose those cuts yourself instead of letting the encoder do it.

Although using somewhat heavy-handed audio optimization for low bit rate encoding has some obvious sonic benefits, there are some risks involved when applying the same optimization for high bit rate encoded audio. Overall, subjective audio quality of high bit rate streams is much closer to the original source audio; therefore the positive or negative effects of your careful optimization will be much more noticeable.

The whole point of optimizing your source audio prior to encoding is to ensure a good quality experience for the listener. Of course, quality is a subjective term. True, you have no control over a listener's environment, but you can make generalizations about whether your listeners are using decent speakers at home or are at work in a cubicle surrounded by ambient noise. To make effective use of the audio optimization process, it helps to clearly outline your goals before you begin. What, exactly, are you trying to gain? When you're encoding for low bit rates, the primary criteria should be basic sonic legibility. At higher bit rates, however, it's useful to have some sense of your projected end user's listening environment.

This book cannot begin to cover all the myriad ways to apply the numerous kinds of audio processing. Many shelves of books have already been written, and many more exist inside the heads of experienced audio engineers. This book can only cover a handful of audio optimization processes, and it's safe to say you could make a lifelong study of compression alone. Expert audio engineers can make something sound better with worse tools than a poor engineer can with great tools. The point is that you shouldn't be afraid to experiment, but also feel free to use the engineered presets as starting points. Let your ears be your guide. Don't expect to master this stuff overnight; many people dedicate their entire career to these subjects.

This chapter focuses on applying audio optimization for the best sonic legibility in low bit rate encoding. You'll learn about equalization, normalization, compression, and a handful of quick and easy modifications to perform on your audio prior to encoding. To use these processes when encoding to high bit rate streams, simply scale way back on the processing values. Less is more.

Here are a few standard approaches (and obvious reminders) for optimizing your source audio prior to low bit rate encoding. It's assumed (since you're in an "advanced" chapter) that you've already taken appropriate steps such as using high-quality cabling whenever possible, having no noisy ground loops, and ensuring that all the toys in your audio chain are plugged into the same power source. (A power conditioner can help here, too.)

- Always get your signal level to be as loud as possible without distorting.

- Remove frequencies that the encoder won't use (see the later section, "Equalization").

- Emphasize those frequencies that the encoding process will diminish (see the later section, "Equalization").

- Reduce the dynamic range (see the later section, "Compression").

- As a comparative tool, encode your audio at low bit rates with no optimization at all. See what it sounds like. Then, try a little optimization and see where that takes you.

- When working in the digital environment, always remember to make sure that the entire file is selected before applying filters.

FezGuys' Tip

When previewing your optimizations, take a moment to listen without observing visual metering guides. Look away from the meters on the computer or simply close your eyes and listen. Visual stimulus can get in the way of the brain's ability to accurately comprehend audio.

If you're optimizing digitized audio files on your computer, it's easiest to use software optimization tools. Most dedicated audio hardware requires sending the audio out in analog form to the unit and back, often going through the digital and analog conversion process two more times. High-end hardware and computer sound cards often use digital interfaces to avoid signal degradation that typically occurs through repeated digital to analog (D/A) and analog to digital (A/D) conversion, but not everyone has access to them.

If you're encoding a live stream from an external source, it's typically easier to route your audio signal through dedicated hardware before it enters the computer. Take the time necessary to properly configure your encoding system, choosing the most appropriate hardware and software audio optimization tools for your environment.

The audio optimization processes detailed in this chapter are starting points. A groovy-looking piece of audio hardware with an anodized faceplate hooked up with oxygen-free gold cabling is not enough. Patience and your good ears will make the difference.

Tools: You Get What You Pay For

All kinds of audio processing tools are available to assist you in your quest for sonic clarity in spite of low bit rate encoding. You can use software on your authoring computer as a discrete package, as a plug-in, or even as part of a larger audio software bundle. You can use a standalone piece of hardware. You can get stuff for free or for almost nothing, or you can pay enormous amounts of money. As the title of this section states, like automobile tires, you get what you pay for. A little research into what kind of gear is best to fold into your particular audio chain will be worth the effort.

Different tools perform in different ways. For example, most waveform editors (such as Peak and SoundForge) operate on existing digital files. However, most standalone hardware (Orban, Telos, and so on) requires a live input source. Other software tools (OtsJuke, Waves, and so on) allow you to optimize live streams from your computer.

Most software and hardware audio tools come with built-in presets that are good starting points. Audio optimization tools marketed for streaming media typically name presets as authoring scenarios (such as "56K dial-up modem," and so on). If you're just getting into audio optimization, start with these presets and experiment.

Various forms of hardware are available to compress and equalize your source audio prior to encoding. This is usually done by placing the hardware in the audio chain before the authoring computer. After your audio is on your computer, it is rarely sent through standalone hardware unless that hardware is extremely high-quality professional gear. Nonetheless, if you have no other option, you can get away with using inexpensive hardware when receiving a live input prior to encoding. This stage finds a hardware equalizer, compressor, or limiter to be useful. When encoding at low bit rates, even an inexpensive compressor is usually better then none at all.

By now, you should be comfortable finding your way around a software waveform editor. All the features described in the following sections behave similarly, regardless of the individual application or operating system. The options are usually named in an obvious way such as, "Equalization," "Normalize," "Fade In/Out," and so on. If you're in doubt about where to find a specific feature, look in the help system or documentation of your waveform editor. Waveform editor software typically comes with basic equalization, DC offset, and normalize features. Some of these products include a compression (or "dynamics filter") feature, whereas other waveform editors need third party plug-ins. For example, SoundForge (Windows) has all of the previously mentioned features, but Peak (Macintosh) requires a third party plug-in to handle compression. The audio software company Waves makes a suite of plug-ins that are commonly used by a wide variety of software tools. These and other plug-in products match seamlessly with waveform editors and multitrack editing software to expand the waveform editor's functionality (see the Appendix).

For more information about common compressors, equalizers, and so forth, see the Appendix.

Normalization

Normalizing, as the name implies, is an audio filtering process that changes the level of digital audio so the peak is at a specified level.

Simple normalization requires a waveform editor such as SoundForge (Windows) or Peak (Macintosh). When using the normalization feature, normalize at a level of 95–99% of the maximum when this level menu option is available. Some encoders have problems with normalized files at 100%; giving up to 5 decibels (dB) of headroom is often necessary.

Compression

As mentioned in Chapter 2, "Preparing Yourself," lossless (as opposed to lossy) audio compression smoothes the audio's dynamic range. Although the concept of compression is similar to normalization, the method and result are rather different. While normalization changes the audio level consistently by the same amount, compression makes softer and louder parts closer to the same level.

When encoding to low bit rates, use compression for audio that has a wide dynamic range to allow the encoder to do a more efficient job. Classical and acoustic music benefit from a healthy dose of compression prior to encoding. Sadly, doing this results in a loss of sonic subtlety, but most streaming audio (especially low bit rate) loses this anyway.

NOTE

The results you get from identical settings will vary between hardware and software compressors due to variations in dB levels and the different ways that analog and digital domains handle clipping. Read your documentation, refer to some of the resources in the Appendix, and experiment to make sure you're getting the most out of your gear.

Adjusting different compression parameters can alter the sound of your audio subtly, dramatically, or anywhere in between. Compressors are available as software, either independently or as part of a bundle or plug-in for Macintosh and Windows, and as standalone hardware. You can acquire serviceable compression tools for less than $100, but you can also easily spend $5,000 on a single channel of classic, mid-sixties, military-spec, all tube compression hardware with a sticky VU meter. Many hardware compressors are available, new and used. A Web search on *compressors* and *compressor plug-ins* quickly reveals a large number of products.

Typically, using lossless audio compression to prepare your audio for encoding doesn't require a heavy hand. A little bit of dynamic range smoothing should be sufficient.

Following are a few key terms and what they mean:

- **Attack**—Indicates how quickly the compressor acts on the input signal. A lower number is a faster attack, measured in milliseconds.

- **Release**—Indicates how quickly the compressor stops acting on the input signal after the signal has gone below your threshold setting. A lower number is a quicker release, measured in milliseconds.

- **Output**—Indicates how much to increase the volume level after the signal has been compressed. This is to make up for any lowering of the overall volume level during compression. This is measured in dB, and a higher number is a louder volume increase.

- **Threshold**—Indicates the audio level where compression starts. This is the point at which the compressor is told to start compressing. Threshold settings are usually marked in dB, measured from a 0dB point (the current setting's point of distortion). The compressor compresses all sound above that threshold.

- **Ratio**—Indicates to the compressor how much to bring down the volume level. A setting of 1:1 has no compression. A higher setting (such as 4:1) brings levels down more. Infinity:1 brings the sound level down to exactly match your threshold setting.

Following are three basic examples for using multipurpose dynamics compression to optimize source audio that will be streamed at low bit rates. These templates are merely starting places. As you experiment with different settings for different kinds of audio, you'll become comfortable with these terms, the processes they represent, and the results achieved by using them.

NOTE

A good combination hardware tool is a compressor/peak limiter. It enables you to compress the audio and also prevents peaks in the signal. Avoiding peaks is good in any audio scenario, not just streaming audio.

- **General purpose (mild compression)**—Set Threshold to –10dB. Set Ratio to 4:1. Set Attack Time to 100ms. Set Release Time to 100ms. Adjust the Input Level to get approximately 3dB of compression. Adjust Output Level to be about 0dB.

- **Voice only (heavy compression)**—Set Threshold to –30dB. Set Ratio to 40:1. Set Attack Time to 10ms. Set Release Time to 100ms. Adjust the Input Level to get approximately –7dB of compression. Adjust Output Level to be about 0dB.

- **Music**—Set Threshold to 0dB. (This threshold setting is for music with a narrow dynamic range. Lower the Threshold for music with a wide dynamic range.) Set Ratio to 20:1. Set attack time to .5ms. Set release time to 50. Adjust the Input Level to get approximately 5dB of compression. Adjust Output Level to be about 0dB.

FezGuys' Tip

If your listening audience tunes in from a workplace environment with a lot of ambient noise using small speakers, you'll want to use more compression to prevent quieter passages from getting lost.

Professionally mastered audio sources (such as modern pop music CDs) usually don't require too much compression optimization prior to encoding; use equalization instead (see the next section). However, compression is especially important when streaming a live signal (such as a live band or a person speaking). There's no right or wrong way to compress your audio. Let your ears be your guide.

Equalization

Equalization (mentioned briefly in Chapter 2) is a process that allows you to change the overall sound of your audio file by raising or lowering one or more frequencies anywhere along the frequency spectrum of your audio. Equalizers come in a variety of flavors, including the familiar "bass" and "treble" tone controls found on a typical consumer stereo system.

Equalization's primary purpose in the streaming audio environment is to help your audio translate more clearly after being encoded. By adjusting small amounts of boost or cut, you can change the character of the sound in a way that allows the encoder to do a more efficient job. Increased encoder efficiency generally translates into increased sonic legibility.

When encoding to low bit rates, equalization can be especially useful. The lossy perceptual encoding process functions by throwing away portions of the overall sound that a codec's engineers have decided the human ear isn't likely to miss. The lower the bit rate, the more sound that is permanently thrown out (hence the term *lossy*). The encoder analyzes the audio from a technical standpoint, so it can't make qualitative judgments based on the audio's actual content. You know more about what frequencies might be unnecessary than the encoder does. By minimizing specific frequencies before handing your source audio to the encoder, you make a decision based on a human assessment. For example, if you're encoding a classical cello suite, the lower frequencies are going to be far more important than the high end. Conversely, a voice-only interview doesn't need the low frequencies. Without optimization on your part, the encoder makes a "best guess" and discards what it thinks isn't necessary.

Think about the application of equalization as a process of taking away what you don't want (or can't use) as opposed to adding more of what you think you need.

You can perform these adjustments using the basic built-in equalization functions in your waveform editor, higher-quality software plug-ins, or a standalone hardware equalizer. Equalizer interfaces are typically one of two types. A *graphic equalizer* has individual sliders at multiple frequencies, allowing for overall shaping of the signal across the full frequency spectrum. A *parametric equalizer* allows for fine-tuning a handful of configurable areas within the frequency spectrum. Graphic equalizers are easier for beginners to use, and parametric equalizers are very effective when controlled by advanced users. A Web search on *equalizer* or *equalizer plug-ins* will detail a wide array of both hardware and software products.

A first simple step when encoding to streams less than 64Kbps is to remove both the very low (40Hz and below) and very high (15kHz and above) frequencies. Most of your low bit rate listeners are probably using inexpensive computer speakers and likely won't miss these frequencies. When encoding for 56K modem users (and below), experiment with a slight boost in mid frequencies (around 2.5kHz) to compensate. Spoken word encoding at any bit rate can especially benefit from this treatment.

For low bit rate encoded voice-only files try this starter setting: Cut everything below 100Hz and carefully boost frequencies between 1–4kHz.

Here's a reminder about high bit rate encoding: Usually little (or even no) equalization is necessary. Recent codecs do a pretty good job of translating the sound quality of source audio when encoding at high bit rates. Heavy equalization of professionally mastered audio (such as major label pop music CD releases) can easily do more damage than the encoding process.

Of course, strange things do happen in the encoding process at bit rates below 16Kbps. You might find that you need to boost certain frequencies that aren't obvious in the source audio. These results will vary on a codec to codec basis. Experiment!

Other Audio Tricks

You can do several other small tricks with your source audio to assist the encoder in doing the job more efficiently and to ensure that the listener has a positive experience.

One of the first (and mandatory) processes to perform on a digital file is to remove what is called DC offset. *DC offset* occurs as low frequency inaudible noise resulting from equipment grounding problems. If present, DC offset can skew the results of subsequent digital edits. Use your waveform editor's DC offset removal function immediately after recording a digital audio file.

When working with audio segments for on-demand previewing scenarios, use your waveform editor to place a 3–5 second fade-in and fade-out at the beginning and the end.

Use your waveform editor on your on-demand source audio files to change the number of channels (stereo to mono) or to convert (lower) the sample rate. This is another example of taking some of the decision-making process out of the hands of the encoder. Chances are good that the algorithm that performs these functions contained within your commercial waveform editor is of a higher quality (and certainly no worse) than what's used in an encoding tool. It might take some research and digging in your encoder's documentation, but you can find out the sample rate used by your encoder based on your bit rate choice. Then you can resample your source audio to that rate prior to encoding.

All-In-One Hardware Solutions

A handful of expensive hardware tools do the work of most of the processes described earlier, all in one package. These hardware boxes do the job well, but they are only appropriate to those with corporate budgets, a friend in the business, or in dire need. Both units (the Orban 6200S and the Telos Omnia 3-net) come from companies with long experience in the traditional terrestrial broadcast medium.

Using the Orban 6200S

This high-tech $5,000 1-U rackmount box is primarily a digital audio pre-processor for the audio side of digital television transmission. Orban also markets the 6200S as a Webcasting audio optimization tool. Many of the more arcane broadcast features of this unit won't be used in the typical Webcasting environment. Using the 6200S to optimize live audio for low bit rate real-time streaming requires only basic in/out processing. That processing, however, is of a high quality, providing an FM-broadcast style sheen to your stream.

NOTE

Orban also offers a more affordably priced PCI card that gives your Windows computer the functionality of the Optimod 6200S. See www.orban.com for more information.

The weighty manual includes schematics and parts lists. You can install and use the Windows-based remote control software (with a serial cable connection) to configure and maintain your 6200S from your authoring computer.

The front panel has a screen display with four *soft key* buttons below a small screen, which provide access to functions and controls. Additional flashing Next and Previous arrow buttons are used to horizontally scroll the screen and accommodate menus that cannot fit in the available display space. A large control knob makes changes to settings. Parameter settings are adjusted by holding down the appropriate soft key and simultaneously turning the control knob. A Recall button recalls any of the unit's factory or 32 user presets, and a Modify button edits those presets. A Setup button accesses the technical parameters necessary to match the 6200S with your broadcasting system. An Escape button returns you to previous menu levels.

Front panel input meters show peak input level for digital or analog inputs (referenced to "0 = digital full-scale"). An automatic gain control (AGC) meter indicates the gain reduction of the slow two-band AGC (with Orban's patented bass-coupling system) processing preceding the multiband compressor (with 25dB full-scale gain reduction). A Gate LED shows gate activity. The Gain Reduction meter shows gain reduction in the five-band multiband compressor. Limiter meters show the amount of look-ahead peak limiting in the left and right channels (with 12dB full-scale gain reduction).

This book uses the 6200S as an audio optimizer for authoring a low bit rate live stream (as described in Chapters 3–6). Make sure you have all the cabling and adapters necessary to hook up your mixer (or other audio source) to the Orban and from the Orban to your authoring computer.

Connect your live stereo audio signal into your mixer. Connect the mixer's outputs to the XLR stereo analog inputs of the 6200S. The optimized signal is sent from the analog Monitor XLR stereo outputs of the 6200S to your authoring computer. Your authoring computer will be running an encoding tool authoring a live stream for 56K dialup modems. As always, it's best to begin from factory default settings.

NOTE

The recommended configuration (for the highest quality audio) for the 6200S uses the digital AES/EBU connectors. Because this book is geared toward new streamers who probably don't have a sound card with digital inputs installed in their authoring computer, this particular Step-by-Step tutorial uses analog input and output. Regardless of whether you use analog or digital input, the Orban 6200S operates both digital and analog outputs simultaneously. Follow the instructions in the manual if you plan to use digital in/out.

STEP-BY-STEP: Using the Orban Optimod 6200S to Optimize Your Audio

1. Connect your audio source into the analog XLR input of the 6200S.

2. Connect the output of the 6200S to your authoring computer's input.

3. Press the Setup button to access the Setup Screen, and press the Next arrow button to access miscellaneous Setup parameters.

4. For MAX LPF (Low Pass Filter), leave the default of 20.0kHz.

NOTE

Advanced users who know that the sample rate of their encoded stream is lower than 44.1kHz should set MAX LPF to approximately 45% of that sample rate. This allows the Orban to do a better job optimizing its audio. Using the encoder tool to find out a stream's individual sample rate settings might require some digging. You advanced users can handle it!

5. For ST CHASSIS, leave the default of No unless you're using another automatic gain control device elsewhere in your audio pathway.

6. Leave MONO/ST (mono or stereo) at the default Stereo setting. This allows the encoder to make the choice of whether to convert to mono.

7. Press the Prev arrow button to return to the first page of Setup options, and press the soft key under I/O CALIB to calibrate your input and output levels.

8. Start your source audio.

9. Press the soft key under ANLG IN CALIB.

    1. Make sure that INPUT is set to "analog."

    2. Adjust the AI CLIP by selecting the loudest portion of your source audio so that the program peaks at approximately –10dB on the Input meters. This calibration is most important to the optimal efficiency of the 6200S. Spend the necessary time getting this level correct. Keep an eye on those meters and adjust accordingly.

    3. Adjust the AI REF VU level to approximately 10.0 on the AGC meter. Watch for a slight delay in the AGC meter adjusting after you change the value. This is because the AGC needs to listen for a moment before it decides on the appropriate level. Observe the AGC meter for a little while to make sure that AI REF VU is set correctly.

10. Press the Escape button and select the soft key under the ANLG OUT CALIB. Verify that MON OUT is set to Post Lim, and if it is not, change it.

11. Press the Escape button repeatedly to return to the top level.

12. Press the Recall button and use the big knob to scroll to TV 5B-GEN PUR W/NR. Select this preset from the preset menu. These presets are based on an anticipated format of a station.

13. To activate the preset, press the soft key button under RECALL NEXT. The preset you have just chosen is now active. The 6200S is processing your source audio and feeding it into your authoring computer's input.

14. Press the Modify button to modify the setting.

15. Press the soft key under LESS-MORE and tune between 1–10 to your preference. Increasing this setting reduces the dynamic range of the output audio by increasing the volume of the quieter sections of your source audio. Crank it to 10, listen, and back off as necessary.

16. Press the Escape button repeatedly to return to the top level. The main page now displays your preset and modif prefix for the on air (currently active) preset. Your selected preset will be displayed after the on air: label. Because you modified the preset, the text *modif* will be displayed before your preset. A SAVE PRESET option will be available for you to save your changes to a new preset.

17. Set your authoring computer's input signal appropriately and continue the encoding process as noted in Chapters 3–6.

The configuration outlined in the Step-by-Step is based on your subjective taste as a good starting point for a 56K modem stream of music in any format. If you're working with voice only, try the TV 5B-NEWS preset as a starting point. Many other customizable audio optimization settings are available within the 6200S. Advanced users can play with configuring the equalizer and FULL CONTROL settings (available by pressing the Modify button).

The manual for the 6200S includes a detailed description of what each preset does as well as extra information about the acoustic properties of this kind of industrial-strength audio processing.

NOTE

When using the 6200S to optimize high bit rate streams, you might want to use the PROTECTION presets as your starting point. Check the manual for information on these presets, designed for the highest possible fidelity.

The Orban 6200S is an audio optimization tool of choice for the big television and radio broadcast networks. It uses industrial grade materials, architecture, and software, and because of its ubiquity within the industry, the Orban 6200S is part of the reason for the current state of broadcast (TV, FM, and AM) audio quality. Tools like the Orban, increasingly efficient compression technology, and faster Internet connectivity to the home are all helping the state of streaming audio quality approach broadcast standards.

Using the Telos Omnia-3net

This unit is a digital audio preprocessor specifically designed to optimize source audio prior to streaming audio encoding. The Omnia-3net is based on the Omnia-3FM, a terrestrial broadcast preprocessor.

The 2-U rackmount box (less than $4,000) has a simple and functional design. Besides the display screen, it has two interface controls on the front panel: a push button and a jog wheel. The push button toggles the display between menus and bar graphs. These vertical bar graphs display input and output levels. Turning the jog wheel displays current gain reduction levels. The jog wheel is primarily used in the menu mode to select menu items and to change various parameter values. Pressing the jog wheel selects the highlighted menu item or accepts the current parameter value. This is a common-sense interface that's easy to operate.

On the back panel are AES/EBU digital and analog stereo XLR input and output connectors. The internal PC card holds software as well as user and factory presets. An RS-232 serial port connector is available if you want to use optional Windows software on your computer to configure the Omnia. Advanced users can use many other features, such as Daypart Automation to set and schedule program-level changes.

The manual is much more than a dry laundry list of settings. Using common English to describe technical processes, the manual provides an informed layman's grasp of relevant issues, continually reminding the reader of the larger audio/broadcast/streaming implication behind each parameter modification. The manual even includes a single-page Menu Tree with a flow chart detailing the location of every menu option. Telos is passionate about its technology, exhorting the reader to carefully take advantage of the many features of the Omnia-3net, and going so far as to recommend the amount of time to spend configuring the unit to appropriately work within a given system.

In this Step-by-Step tutorial, you'll optimize a live stereo audio signal for a low bit rate 56K live stream.

STEP-BY-STEP: Using the Telos Omnia-3net to Optimize Your Audio

1. Connect your audio source into the Omnia's input (either AES/EBU or analog XLR). This example uses the analog input.

2. Connect the Omnia's output to your authoring computer's input.

3. Start your source audio.

4. To set the Omnia to use the analog input and outputs, go to the main menu and use the jog wheel to select and enter the Input & Output menu.

   1. *To set the Omnia to use the analog input, use the jog wheel to scroll to Input Source and verify that ANALOG is chosen. If necessary, select ANALOG.*

   2. *For Mono Mode (setting the number of channels), leave the default of Stereo and allow the encoder to convert to mono, if necessary.*

   3. *For LPF Freq (Low Pass Filter), change the default values of 16kHz to 22kHz. This is necessary because some formats (such as QuickTime) use 44.1kHz even at 32Kbps.*

NOTE

The LPF Freq setting is only mentioned in documentation about the Omnia-3am (an only slightly different configuration of the Omnia than the 3net used here), so it is assumed that this is a standard low-pass filter. For that reason, the highest LPF Freq setting is chosen to allow for encoders that encode up to 44.1kHz. Choose the maximum setting of 22kHz so that the encoder has access to the full frequency range that the Omnia supports. Advanced users who know that the sample rate of their encoded stream is lower than 44.1kHz can set LPF Freq to approximately 45% of that sample rate to prevent aliasing distortion. This allows the Omnia to work more efficiently. Using the encoder tool to find out a stream's individual sample rate settings might require some digging. You advanced users can handle it!

   4. *Use the jog wheel to scroll to and enter the Input Levels menu. Because you're using an industry standard mixer to send your feed into the Omnia, you shouldn't need to adjust the Omnia's default input level settings of –10dB. Your mixer should be sending at +4dB. Tune the mixer's master level as loud as possible without clipping. If you're sending a stronger or weaker signal, adjust the*

*Omnia's left and right inputs accordingly. After you've chosen a set-
ting, check your levels by pressing the front panel button to toggle
between the bar graphs and level settings.*

NOTE

Earlier manuals for the Omnia-3net refer to an Analog Gain menu option to control the input
level. This option has been removed in recent units. If your unit has this option, then read the
manual about how the earlier process will differ from this description.

5. *Use the jog wheel to scroll to and select the backward arrow to
   return to the Input & Output menu, and then enter Output Levels.
   The system default of +4dB should be fine. Unless severe level dis-
   parities are present, it's preferable to use the default output level
   and adjust the authoring computer's input level. Use the jog wheel
   to scroll to and select the backward arrow twice to return to the
   main menu.*

5. Use the jog wheel to select and enter Audio Processing, which places you in the Preset menu.

6. To select a preset, use the jog wheel to select and enter Select Preset. For your 56K modem
   stream, choose Lo-BR-Aggr (for "low bit rate aggressive"). The Omnia is now optimizing your
   audio signal for a 56K live stream. Advanced users can enter Edit Parameters from the Preset
   menu to modify the selected preset from its default values. Numerous options allow you to
   fine-tune (or ruin) your audio, depending on your skill and patience. Also from the Preset
   menu, the Save to Card As function allows you to save the preset with any modifications to
   the internal PC card.

7. Set your authoring computer's input signal appropriately and continue the encoding process
   as noted in Chapters 3–6.

The Lo-BR-Aggr preset used in this Step-by-Step is one of five factory defaults
included with the Omnia-3net. It was selected based on the authors' subjective
listening for a 56K modem stream of music in any format. You might find
any one of the other modifiable factory presets (Lo-BR-Lite, Lo-BR-Aggr,
Hi-BR-Lite, Hi-BR-Mod, or Hi-BR-AGGR) more to your tastes.

These factory presets are based on the Omnia engineers' long experience with
coded and compressed audio. More advanced users can use them as a starting

point. Uneducated modifications of the presets can make things worse, however. Refer to the manual for details on configuring the specific components of each preset.

For more information on preprocessing audio for streaming, refer to the White Paper "Audio Processing for Digital Audio Broadcasting and the Internet" (see the Appendix for Web site URL).

Summary

A measurable portion of your listening audience will have no interest in all the work you've done to make your streaming audio sound as good as possible. But they will know whether they like the way it sounds. This is true in the terrestrial broadcast world as well. A little bit of extra work can make a big difference to the quality of your streams, especially at low bit rates. You might not win awards for the superior quality of your streaming audio, but no news can be very good news! People will continue to tune in to a better sounding stream, especially when compared to streams that haven't been optimized. Of course, there's no substitute for compelling programming.

CHAPTER 12

Advanced Authoring Techniques

This chapter covers a few advanced techniques to simplify and stabilize the authoring process of your streaming audio. Hardware encoders and batch encoding can speed up the authoring process. For those with a burning desire to learn from past mistakes, this chapter also lists many common streaming audio pitfalls to avoid.

Hardware Encoders

If you're authoring a continuous live stream, a common solution is to assemble a reliable, dedicated computer with specialized DSP cards. If you're producing a lot of live Webcasts on the road, another option is to have the aforementioned computer or a standalone hardware product contained in a solid rack-mountable road case. Using dedicated hardware can provide much-needed reliability in professional streaming environments, minimizing the common failures with computers that aren't 100% dedicated to the authoring process.

The process of creating one of these computers or standalone hardware boxes is workable but decidedly nontrivial. To that end, this chapter includes a description and explanation of an off-the-shelf product designed to encode your source audio and send it to your pre-configured streaming server. The Zephyr Xstream (Telos Systems) takes the place of a dedicated MP3 authoring computer offering a simple configuration process to streamline your work.

Using the Zephyr Xstream

Telos Systems' Zephyr Xstream (current price: $4,635.00) is a 2-U rack mount unit with no fan (so it's quiet) and no battery (so there's nothing to change). The supported codecs within the device include the most recent MPEG-2 AAC (Advanced Audio Coding), standard MPEG (Layer 2 and Layer 3), and G.722.

The following Step-by-Step uses the Xstream to create a live MP3 stream in what Telos Systems calls Netcoder mode. In Netcoder mode, the Zephyr Xstream is only used as a simple standalone MP3 hardware encoder; consequently, the only codec available is the standard MPEG Layer 3 (MP3). After encoding, the HTTP/Progressive stream is then picked up by a SHOUTcast server for redistribution to the Internet.

The Zephyr Xstream has the ability to stream audio in other codecs over ISDN phone connections to other Xstream devices elsewhere in the world. Radio stations use these devices for live broadcasts and recording studios use them for remote recording situations. A wealth of information is available in an online PDF at the Telos Web site detailing the many uses of the Zephyr Xstream.

The sophisticated design of the front panel offers a headphone output with volume control, a dialog window with numeric keypad as well as navigation, menu and preset selection keys, and input and output level meters.

The back panel includes two ISDN interface jacks (one for the U.S. and Canada, and the other for ROW [Rest of World]), a 10Base-T Ethernet jack, stereo AES/EBU in/outs, stereo analog line level in/outs (XLR and 1/4"), a "Parallel Control" (25-pin, 8 in/out, female D-sub) connector, an RS-232 (DCE configured 9-pin female D-sub for using the Xstream with a computer keyboard), and a "V.35/X.21 Interface Option" slot.

FIGURE 12.1

The audio path using an Xstream to send a live MP3 stream to a user through a SHOUTcast server.

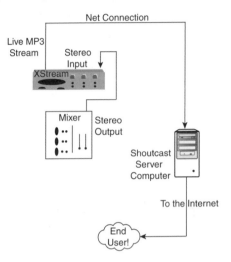

STEP-BY-STEP: Using the Zephyr Xstream to Create a Live MP3 Stream

1. Hook up your source audio through one of Xstream's available audio input connectors (AES/EBU, analog XLR, or ¼").

2. Power on the Xstream and plug in the 10BaseT Ethernet cable into your network. You'll be starting from User Default Settings that shipped with the Xstream.

3. You can configure the Xtream in three ways:

    - *Front Panel—The Front Panel has four primary configuration buttons (called Fast Action menu keys), and also has two navigation (up and down) arrow buttons, a Select button, and an alphanumeric keypad.*

    - *Serial Port—Hook up a computer to the serial port with an RS-232 cable. The default serial port settings are 19.2Kbps, 8 stop bits, 1 data bit, no parity. Your RS-232 cable must be straight through (not null modem).*

    - *Web Browser—When using a Web browser for configuring the Xstream, you must first set your network settings.*

    For the purposes of this Step-by-Step, all configuration of the Xstream will be done using the front panel interface.

4. Press the Fast Action TEL menu key to go into the TEL menu.

5. Use the arrow keys to scroll down to the Interface option and change ISDN to Ethernet. You've now enabled the Xstream's Netcoder mode. This automatically changes the available options in both the CODEC and TEL menus.

6. Press the Fast Action SYSTEM menu key to go into the SYSTEM menu.

   1. *Use the arrow keys to scroll down to IP Addr and enter the correct IP address.*

   2. *Scroll to Gateway and enter your gateway (or router) IP address.*

   3. *Scroll to DNS and enter the IP address of your DNS server.*

NOTE

If you don't already know this configuration information, get it from your System Administrator.

As soon as you complete entering your network information, the Xstream will be available on the network. At this point, as mentioned earlier, it's possible to open a Web browser and continue configuring the Xstream's encoding parameters from a remote location.

FezGuys' Tip

Although the Xstream's Web interface prompts for a username, it isn't clear how to actually set one. With the default as-shipped settings, anyone who knows the IP address of your Xstream can connect and access its configuration. The Telos Systems folks said this is a security feature that requires physical (or trusted host) access for settings changes. To modify it, you first need to connect through the Xstream's serial port or via telnet from the host you specify as "trusted" in the SYSTEM menu. Next, type "help login" for instructions on how to set a new password. When you're ready to use your Xstream in the real world, you should take a moment to change this from the default value.

NOTE

The Xstream's Web interface works well with one notable exception: On our test model the input source was reversed. This means that when we chose the Analog input, the Xstream set the input to AES/EBU and vice versa. Nonetheless, the front panel design is straightforward and functions properly, so we recommend that you continue using it over the Web interface.

7. Press the Fast Action CODEC menu key to choose the codec parameters with which to encode your stream. Because Netcoder mode handles only the MP3 codec, you don't have to choose between codecs. Netcoder mode also automatically sets your number of channels based on the bit rate you select.

8. To encode for 56K dial-up modem users, choose 32 for Bit Rate from the choices of 8, 12, 14, 16, 18, 24, 32, 40, 48, 56, 64, 80, 96, 112, or 128Kbps. The Xstream will make your stream "mono" based on this bit rate selection.

9. Press the Fast Action AUDIO menu key to select your audio input source and adjust input levels.

10. Start your source audio.

11. Use the arrow keys to scroll to Input Source and choose Analog or AES/EBU depending on which input you plugged your source audio into.

12. Use the arrow keys to scroll to Level In. You'll find the default set to Professional (+4 dBu). Depending on the quality and strength of your input source, you can leave this setting or change it to Consumer (-11dBu).

13. Adjust your input levels from your external input (typically a mixing console). Read the levels on Xstream's front panel LED meter and fine-tune through the Gain Trim setting if necessary.

14. The Xstream is now encoding a live MP3 stream.

15. Test the stream by plugging the Xstream's URL (`http://xstream.fezguys.com:8000`) into your MP3 player (preferably on another network). Enter your own host name or IP address in place of `xstream.fezguys.com`, and change the port number if you have configured something other than the default setting of 8000.

The Xstream functions as a rudimentary server that, based on your bit rate selection, supports a limited number of concurrent users. Most of the Xstream's processing power is focused on encoding (as opposed to serving). Consequently, the number of concurrent streams it can support is low enough (only two when encoding at 128Kbps) that a remote MP3 streaming server (such as SHOUTcast) is essential.

Configuring a SHOUTcast server to take its input (relay) from the Xstream is easy. Refer to Chapter 6 "Using MP3" for general SHOUTcast configuration information. Then, instead of connecting a live stream from an authoring computer to your SHOUTcast server, set the SHOUTcast RelayPort and RelayServer configuration variables to point to the Xstream. Based on this example, the RelayPort would be set to 8000 and the RelayServer to `xstream.fezguys.com`. Follow the Chapter 6 instructions to finish configuring and test the SHOUTcast redistribution of your stream.

Batch Encoding

When encoding numerous source files or encoding to multiple bit rates and formats from a single source file, you can save time by using a process called batch encoding. Now that you've fine-tuned your settings, batch encoding tools speed the process by allowing the creation of encoding templates. This makes it possible to avoid re-entering the same parameters every time you encode. Programs that do batch encoding also often include extra audio optimization features.

For example, you could take a single uncompressed digital audio file and enter all your encoding information, press OK, and walk away. Returning several hours (or maybe a day) later, you'd find all of your on-demand MP3, Windows Media, RealMedia, and QuickTime files encoded in several bit rates, ready to be uploaded to your streaming or Web server. Batch encoding many files can be time consuming, but encoding those files individually will take even longer. You could set your computer to encode everything overnight thereby freeing you to work on other tasks (or even sleep!). The time it takes to batch encode depends on your computer's processing speed, the size of the source song files, the way the files are being encoded (to what settings, formats, and so on) and, of course, the number of files you are authoring.

Using Cleaner 5

Cleaner is a multimedia encoding and authoring software program. It encodes to QuickTime, RealMedia, MP3, and Windows Media formats and includes many other features. You can author rich-media elements (interactivity, URL flips, links to sites, chapter lists, caption tracks, and so on) in your streams (depending on each format's capabilities). Cleaner also has customizable optimization filters and audio fades for the encoding process and allows you to either save files locally or upload them to a streaming server or hosting service. You can create HTML codes within Cleaner, too. Helpfully, Cleaner comes with a series of useable encoding presets. You can modify an existing preset or create and save your own presets from scratch. Presets can also be shared with other Cleaner users via e-mail.

NOTE

> Cleaner 5.1 for both Macintosh and Windows supports Windows Media v7, RealSystem 8, and the most recent QuickTime (and QDesign codecs). Cleaner also provides full support for video.

Some formats' media attributes (beyond author, title and copyright) aren't fully supported by Cleaner. Most notably, ID3 tags for MP3 on-demand files aren't supported at all. If necessary, you can always go back and edit these attributes using the format-specific application or, in some cases, override them with your metafile settings (see Chapter 7, "Serving Your Audio").

NOTE

> Another simple option for adding ID3 tags to your MP3 files is using an ID3 tag editor that supports batch encoding. Look in the list of additional tools in the Appendix, "Tools and Resources."

In the following Step-by-Step tutorial, you'll create seven on-demand files in four formats optimized for both 56K dial-up modems and 384K DSL broadband. That equals two files apiece (one low bit rate and one high) from QuickTime, Windows Media, and MP3. You only need to author one RealMedia file because you'll be using the SureStream technology (see Chapter 3, "Using RealMedia"). You'll also set the encoding parameters for each of the seven files.

STEP-BY-STEP: Using Cleaner to Batch Encode

1. Launch Cleaner 5.1 on your Macintosh or Windows computer. Add your source WAV or AIFF files by choosing File, Add File to Batch.

FezGuys' Tip

Because you're going to add your source files seven times, it'll be faster to drag and drop your files. Locate your AIFF or WAV source file. Drag your source file into the Batch Window seven times (one for each encoded file you want to create). You now have your source file named seven times in the Batch encoding window (see Figure 12.2).

FIGURE 12.2

Drag your source file seven times to Cleaner's Batch window, one for each desired encoded output file.

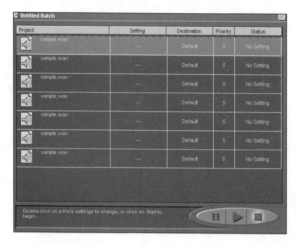

2. To choose the encoding setting for the first batch entry, click on the batch entry and select Windows, Advanced Settings (Windows: Ctrl+T, Macintosh: ⌘+T). An Advanced Settings dialog box opens with a left-hand column of available presets and a right-hand column of setting parameters.

3. To choose the encoding setting for the single RealMedia SureStream file, click on the arrow to expand the RealSystem—Streaming submenu and then choose RealAudio—Streaming. From the available choices, select RealAudio SureStream (music). The right side of the screen updates (see Figure 12.3).

FIGURE 12.3

To encode to a RealMedia SureStream file, select RealSystem — Streaming, RealAudio — Streaming, and then RealAudio SureStream (music) in Cleaner 5's Advanced Settings dialog box.

NOTE

Advanced users can play with the many settings, but leaving the default settings is perfectly okay. As you get more comfortable with the software, you'll begin to experiment.

4. Click Apply and choose the next batch entry.

5. The next two batch entries are encoded into Windows Media files (to be streamed in real-time through a Windows Media server). Set the encoding parameters to first author a 32Kbps stream for 56K dial-up modems and then author a 128Kbps stream for 384Kbps DSL broadband users.

   1. *To author the 32Kbps stream, click on the arrow to expand the Windows Media—Streaming sublevel. Choose Windows Media Audio— Streaming and then choose WMA 56K Streaming. Check the box, and the right side of the screen updates these settings (see Figure 12.4).*

FIGURE 12.4

To encode to a Windows Media file for 56Kbps modem users, select Windows Media—Streaming, Windows Media Audio—Streaming, and then WMA 56K Streaming in Cleaner 5's Advanced Settings dialog box.

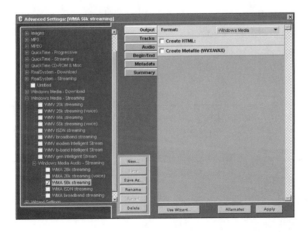

   2. *Click Apply and move on to encode the next batch entry for Windows Media for 384Kbps DSL users.*

3. *To author the 384Kbps stream, click on the arrow to expand the Windows Media — Streaming sublevel, choose Windows Media Audio — Streaming, and then choose WMA Broadband Streaming. Check the box, and the right side of the screen updates these settings.*

4. *Click Apply and choose the next batch entry.*

6. The next two batch entries will be encoded into QuickTime files (to be streamed in real-time through a QuickTime Streaming Server or Darwin Streaming Server). Set the encoding parameters to first author a 32Kbps stream for 56Kbps dial-up modems and then a 128Kbps stream for 384Kbps DSL broadband users.

FezGuys' Tip

If you happen to already have a RealServer installed, you can serve QuickTime files through it. Simply upload your QuickTime files to the content directory of your RealServer and link to them with the appropriate `rtsp://` location.

1. *To author the 32Kbps stream, click on the arrow to expand the QuickTime — Streaming sublevel. Choose QuickTime Audio — Streaming, and then choose QT 56K Audio Stream. The right side of the screen updates (see Figure 12.5).*

FIGURE 12.5

To encode to a QuickTime file for 56Kbps modem users, select QuickTime — Streaming, QuickTime Audio — Streaming, and then QT 56K Audio Stream in Cleaner 5's Advanced Settings dialog box.

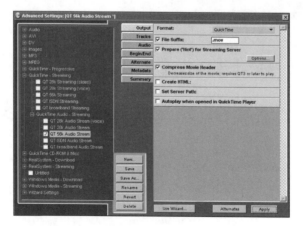

2. *Optimize the file for the efficient QuickTime Hinting protocol by clicking on the Output button of the Advanced Settings window, checking the box for Prepare ('Hint') for Streaming Server, and clicking Options within that area. A Hint Exporter Settings window pops up.*

3. *Check Optimize Hints for Server and click OK to return to the Advanced Settings window.*

4. *Leave all other QT 56K Audio Stream settings at their default values.*

5. *Click Apply and move on to encode the next batch entry for QuickTime for 384Kbps DSL users.*

6. *To author the stream for 384Kbps DSL users, click on the arrow to expand the QuickTime — Streaming sublevel, choose QuickTime Audio — Streaming, and then choose QT Broadband Audio Stream.*

7. *Optimize this file for the Hinting protocols as you did for your 56K setting.*

8. *Click Apply and choose the next batch entry.*

7. The next two batch entries will be encoded into MP3 files. Set the encoding parameters to first author a 32Kbps stream for 56Kbps dial-up modems and then a 192Kbps stream for 384Kbps DSL broadband users.

NOTE

The Cleaner default settings for MP3 encoding don't suit the particular needs of this tutorial. Instead, you're going to create your own settings templates to save and keep for later re-use. As mentioned earlier, you can create and save custom settings templates for any format.

1. *Create a new MP3 setting for 56Kbps streaming by modifying an existing template and saving it as a new one. Select MP3 Streaming Modem VBR and click Save As.*

2. *Within the Save Settings As pop-up dialog box, enter MP3 56K standard.*

3. *Save the new setting in the MP3 folder by choosing MP3 in the Save Settings in Which Folder dialog box and clicking OK (see Figure 12.6).*

FIGURE 12.6

Save your new MP3 56K standard Cleaner 5 setting template.

4. Make sure that MP3 56K standard on the left side is checked.

5. On the right side, click on the Audio tab and change the data rate from 40 to 32.

6. Uncheck Variable Bit Rate.

7. Set the sample rate to 22.050kHz.

8. Click the Save button to save the changes you've made to this preset.

9. Click Apply to accept the setting and choose the next batch entry.

10. Create a new MP3 setting for a 384Kbps streaming file by modifying the existing MP3 standard 128K template and clicking Save As.

11. Within the Save Settings As pop-up dialog box, enter MP3 192K standard.

12. Save the new setting in the MP3 folder by choosing MP3 in the Save Settings in Which Folder dialog box and clicking OK.

13. Make sure that MP3 192K standard on the left side is checked.

14. On the right side, click on the Audio tab and change the data rate from 128 to 192.

15. *Click the Save button to save the changes you've made to this preset.*

16. *Click Apply to accept the setting.*

8. To enter the metadata for each file, first double-click on the Audio icon to the left of the file-name in the Batch window. This opens a Project: yourfilename window in which you can play your source audio file and also view and edit your encoding settings. Click on the Edit button in Settings Modifiers & Metadata. This opens a Settings Modifier window.

9. Click on the Metadata tab and fill out the appropriate information.

10. Click Apply.

11. Repeat this process for each of your files as desired.

12. Go to Batch, Set Default Destination, and set the folder into which you'd like your encoded files to be placed.

NOTE

Advanced users can set individual files' custom destinations by double-clicking on the Destination box and entering the desired setting. This is usually done when you need to explicitly include special information (such as the format or bit rate) in the name of a file.

13. Select Edit, Preferences and a new window will pop up.

14. In the Streaming Server Paths section, enter your default streaming server URL paths for each file.

NOTE

Streaming Server Paths are used when Cleaner 5 is instructed to automatically create metafiles. Regardless of whether you are creating metafiles, Cleaner 5 requires you to set these values. Otherwise, you're prompted for them at the start of the encoding process. If you want to enable the creation of metafiles, open the Advanced Settings window and check the Create Metafile option in the Output tab of your preferred setting template. Cleaner only supports automatic metafile creation for the RealMedia and Windows Media formats.

15. Still in the Preferences pop-up window, check the Append Setting to Filename box. This doesn't make for a pretty filename, but it does make it clear which format and bit rate the file is.

NOTE

If you don't select the Append Setting to Filename preference when you encode a single source file into multiple templates within the same format, Cleaner 5 adds a unique number to the encoded file's name (such as "sample0001.mov") for each additional template.

If you are only encoding each source file to a single bit rate per format, you can safely leave the Append Setting to Filename preference unset. Doing so results in default names where the suffix of the source file is replaced with the corresponding format-specific suffix (such as QuickTime's .mov or RealMedia's .rm).

Another solution to filename confusion that comes from creating multiple encoded files from the same source is to use a custom destination for each encoded file. To set a custom destination, double-click on the Destination column for the file you want to alter. In the pop-up window, select your desired folder, check the Custom Filename box, and enter your desired filename. Make sure you include the appropriate file suffix (.mov, .rm, .wma, .mp3, and so forth).

FezGuys' Tip

Instead of dragging your file seven times into the batch and then applying a new setting for each file, you can drag the file in once, and then use Cleaner's Advanced Settings to create a new entry in your batch for each format you'd like to encode. After you've dragged your source file into the Batch Window, make sure it's selected by clicking on it once. Next, select Windows, Advanced Settings (Macintosh: ⌘+T, Windows: Ctrl+T) and, in the window that pops up, choose multiple settings for your file. Do this on the Macintosh by using ⌘+click, and on Windows with Ctrl+click. Click Apply to close the window and then make a new copy of your audio source for each selected setting.

NOTE

In Cleaner version 5.1 on Windows, there's a problem with Custom Filenames when encoding to a QuickTime file during the flattening process. If you need this feature, contact Discreet and check for an update that fixes the problem.

16. If you're happy with all your settings, start the encoding process by pressing the Play arrow at the bottom right of the Batch window or going to Batch, Encode (Windows: Ctrl+E, Macintosh: ⌘+E).

17. During the encoding process, Cleaner 5 displays the status of each file that is being encoded in the Batch window. Cleaner 5 pops up a dialog box telling what time the file completed. It chimes once at the end of the batch encode process.

Cleaner 5 acts differently on Macintosh and Windows during the encoding process. On a Macintosh computer, Cleaner 5 uses all the CPU available and only operates when the mouse is not moved. If you move the mouse, encoding pauses. This allows you to perform other tasks on your Macintosh during encoding but suspends the encoding process until you stop using the mouse. On a Windows computer, Cleaner 5 merely slows down if you're using other applications. Let Cleaner 5 do its thing unmolested.

You now have a directory full of files encoded in multiple formats and bit rates ready to upload to the server(s) of your choice and link into your Web site.

Using Other (Less Common) Formats

Although the formats covered in this book (RealMedia, Windows Media, QuickTime, MP3) dominate the streaming audio marketplace, there are a few other format options. This section presents a couple of other commonly used formats, explained with benefits and disadvantages.

Ogg Vorbis

This format is fairly new to the streaming media wars, but it has a major point of distinction: It's 100% free! Unlike the "free" MP3 codec, which actually requires paying licensing fees, Ogg Vorbis is completely open and patent-free with no bit stream royalties. You can easily identify Ogg Vorbis files by their filename suffix .ogg. Find out all you need to know about Ogg Vorbis at www.ogg-vorbis.com.

- **Key Benefits**—100% free! Ogg Vorbis is better quality than MP3, but roughly comparable to the other major formats. Some popular audio players, such as Winamp, now support Ogg Vorbis. Code is freely available to anyone who wants to write a player for an operating system. Players are also available for operating systems other than Macintosh and Windows.

- **Disadvantages**—As a new codec, support for Ogg Vorbis is unlikely to be preinstalled on a potential listener's computer, so if you're going to provide streaming audio in the Ogg Vorbis format, also provide another format to keep things easy. Like MP3, it will take overwhelming public popularity to reach the threshold where the industry begins to support Ogg Vorbis in their players, browsers, and streaming servers.

- **When to use**—If you are putting up streaming audio for a small audience or for personal use, Ogg Vorbis might be the solution for you. Ogg Vorbis is also a good solution if you believe in the freedom of information or you're a more technical user who likes to have access to the internal workings of your software.

Did we mention it's free?

Java Streaming

Introduced several years ago, Java quickly became a popular language for the Web. Java was used for embedding complex graphics and presentations in Web pages prior to the advent of Flash and Shockwave. Although streaming audio support was added to Java over the years, it's use was limited by poor audio quality. Recently, MPEG support has been added to Java, although its common use is now as a back-end Web page technology solution.

Several companies provide Java streaming technologies, such as www.clipstream.com and www.hellonetwork.com.

- **Key Benefits**—No additional player application download is necessary. (Only a modern Web browser is needed.) Java streaming is supported on more platforms than only Macintosh and Windows.

- **Disadvantages**—Java streaming suffers from a lack of built-in high-quality codecs to choose from, typically requiring a somewhat cumbersome installation process to use additional high-quality codecs. The additional time it takes for the Java plug-in to load in the Web browser and the requirement to use the often-unstable Web browser plug-in architecture are also big barriers, decreasing the likelihood of reliable playback.

- **When to use**—If you are planning to present streaming audio embedded in your Web page and aren't sure if your listening audience has players installed, or if you want to stream to all platforms (including Unix), use Java streaming.

Common Pitfalls to Avoid

In the early and unbelievably rapid expansion of the World Wide Web, people put up various wacky representations of their work, their interests, their music, and yes, even themselves. Some of the sites evolved into places where Web surfers returned again and again. Following is a partial list of things these people didn't do. You can learn from their experiences.

- **Ignoring your listeners**—Don't do it! Word of mouth is the best way to grow grass-roots community. Put the input of your core listener base, both positive and negative, to good use. Your listening audience will be all too happy to tell you whether your chosen format works for them, whether additional formats are wanted, and whether your encoding talents need significant improvement. Their critique is a priceless resource, and an unhappy listener can often become your biggest supporter. Remember to provide an obvious link for your listeners to send you e-mail.

- **Not testing your audio**—Many have sheepishly hung their heads in shameful sorrow when, after proudly announcing their new audio streams to the world, they got messages suggesting playback sounds like the noise under the refrigerator. Always check your encoded audio before uploading it, and spot-check a few files after uploading. The upload process can occasionally garble clean audio streams.

- **Not providing a link to a player for the format you are using**—If potential listeners want to hear your streaming audio but don't have the correct player and don't see a link from your site to get one, they'll probably give up. They might give up anyway, but why lay down now? You've come so far. Give them a link. Check these links periodically to make sure they still work—other people's sites may change without notice.

- **Streaming audio for which you have no rights**—This is a no-brainer. If you don't have the publishing and copyright permission to legally stream the audio, don't stream it—unless, of course, you want a lot of new (and rabid) legal friends. See the Appendix for online legal resources.

- **Failing to use a metafile**—Many sites still link directly to their encoded audio instead of using a metafile. As you now know, that means the audio won't stream in real time, and potential listeners must wait for the download to finish before they hear anything. Even if you don't have access to a full-featured real-time streaming server, all formats allow some capability for HTTP/Progressive streaming through a Web server (see Chapter 7 for more information).

- **Failing to include media attributes with your audio**—What was that great song you just heard? You don't know because the stream's author failed to include this information. Bad author, no donut!

- **Only offering your streaming media via embedded plug-ins**—Some people are using older browsers or new ones that simply don't support certain plug-ins. Alternatively, they might even want to listen to your audio while surfing to other pages. If you must embed your audio, offer a link to play the audio in an external player.

- **Only encoding your audio in high bit rates**—Unless you're 110% certain that your audience is on a broadband connection or an intranet LAN, always include lower bit rate streams. Broadband users often listen to lower bit rate streams anyway, using remaining bandwidth for other tasks.

- **Playing your audio automatically from your home page**—Don't do this unless you're entirely certain your listeners want sound blaring out of their speakers without warning. Many people browse at the office, and it's a potentially embarrassing situation when audio explodes suddenly out of their cubicle. If you really want to provide background audio, consider having a link to another version of the same page that includes your background audio rather than starting it the moment visitors arrive. If you simply must have audio play automatically, show good netiquette by providing a link to turn it off.

- **Serving more streams than you can handle**—Be aware of how many concurrent listeners are tuning into your streams at any given moment. Too many listeners can cause the server to dump the stream and everyone listening along with it (for more information, see Chapter 2, "Preparing Yourself").

- **Not allowing enough bandwidth to send your live stream to your streaming server** (related to the previous bullet)—Woe is the streamer who tries to send a live 128Kbps stream over a 128Kbps ISDN line across 20 network hops. It gets ugly really fast. Make sure you have plenty of network headroom when sending your live streams out for server redistribution to your listeners. Whenever possible, minimize the number of networks the stream must traverse to get to the server.

- **Failing to configure the correct MIME type**—There's nothing worse (well, maybe a few things) than preparing streaming audio only to discover that much of the audience can't listen. Why? The MIME type is set incorrectly; therefore, the audience's browser didn't launch the player application (see Chapter 7 for information on MIME types).

Summary

These advanced authoring techniques and helpful tips help to improve your knowledge base, but experience has no substitute. Experience comes with making some errors and falling on your face. Don't be afraid to mess up! Imagine yourself, beetle-browed and dragging your knuckles across the savanna, searching for dead game you can scavenge. Suddenly, you come upon a white bone and an idea hits you...

CHAPTER 13

Advanced Presentation

Your digital files have been optimized, encoded, uploaded and now are streaming happily from your server. You've already done the hard part. In the process, you've discovered that streaming audio has so many tools, standards, languages, and technologies that it can sometimes seem like an absurdly complex transit system with entirely too many ways to arrive at your destination. But you've arrived, thankfully, and you want to expand your knowledge.

This chapter talks about including your streaming audio in larger presentations, embedding your stream into a Web page, providing multiple formats, and offering playlists. It also covers some tools and techniques for mixing streaming audio with graphics, text, and video.

A couple of reminders: Remember to promote your streaming audio using e-mail, through Web sites, on business cards, on fridge magnets—the list is as long as your promotional creativity. It's also a good habit to test playback of your streams, whenever possible, from different operating systems, Web browsers, and connectivity speeds.

If you're fortunate enough to have a big audience, consider cultivating partnerships within the industry (similar to the scenarios in Part 3, "Case Studies"). One of the reasons you hold this book in your hands is because there are different and competing ways to author streaming audio. This relentless competition means that format technology providers, CDNs, ISPs, or even hardware or software manufacturers might see your streaming audio's popularity as a means to promote their own tools and technologies. You might be able to acquire free services, products, and other resources by accepting promotional partnerships.

A final general note: A Web site is an experience of the eyes and ears, so make sure your streaming audio is featured appropriately. If your site is primarily concerned with the audio, feature it prominently. However, don't distract visitors by taking up large amounts of Web page real estate if the streaming audio is only intended to be superfluous ear candy.

Multimedia Presentations with Streaming Audio

Now that your streams are running smoothly, we'd like to introduce you to presentation technologies. These toolbox goodies can expand the attraction and effectiveness of your streaming audio.

A Web page is a presentation technology in its most common form, combining different types of media in different formats all in one simple package. But Web browser technology is a broad-based, "everyman" set of tools, designed to successfully perform many tasks, actions, and processes; attempting, you might say, to please all people all the time. If you want to perform specific actions in a more effective and efficient manner, you'll need specific tools. This is where presentation technologies come in handy.

These technologies can be broken down into three areas: multimedia presentation publishing tools, presentation standards, and plug-in controls. This chapter gives an example of each as well as information on how to make an educated decision on which one (or more) to use. These tools overlap somewhat in their usefulness, and you might find new ways to put them to work.

Multimedia Presentation Publishing Tools

Multimedia presentation publishing tools are standalone applications that allow authors to create mixed media presentations for the Internet. Two of the more popular are Flash and Shockwave; both are designed and sold by software company Macromedia. Shockwave is the stripped-down version of Macromedia's Director software designed to bring some of the CD-ROM capabilities to Web pages. Flash is more geared toward animation and vector graphics (drawings and text) and is incorporated into the RealMedia and QuickTime players. Any modern computer is shipped with a browser that can view Flash presentations. Flash and Shockwave can both stream MP3 files natively. Presentations authored in either tool can also link to other media types. The RealMedia player combines Flash presentations with other media types by using SMIL (see the next section).

NOTE

Authoring Shockwave and Flash presentations is beyond the scope of this book. See the Appendix, "Tools and Resources," for online tutorial resources at Macromedia. Also see New Riders' titles *Inside Flash,* Jody Keating and Fig Leaf Software (Oct. 2001), and *Director 8.5 Shockwave Studio Interface Design,* Epic Software (March 2002).

Use multimedia presentation publishing tools to produce complex presentations that include streaming audio. For example, some music videos are produced in Flash, making it easy to use character animations and layer song lyrics on top of the video image.

Synchronized Multimedia Integration Language (SMIL): A W3C Presentation Standard

Synchronized Multimedia Integration Language (SMIL) is an official World Wide Web Consortium (W3C) authoring technology standard for interactive audio/visual presentations. It's been accurately called an "emerging standard" and, as such, it still has many implementation and compatibility issues to be worked out. The information in a SMIL file describes how to combine different media types into one linear presentation. SMIL is agnostic to streaming formats; it doesn't care how your media is encoded. SMIL can be used in many ways to alter the presentation of your streaming audio. It can be used to match up multiple clips with other streaming media sources, such as video. It can also be used to set the start and stop points from an on-demand file and integrate regular Web content (text captioning) from different servers alongside your audio. SMIL can also dynamically serve correct language or bit rate file information based on a listener's player settings.

RealMedia and QuickTime players (and some Windows technologies) support SMIL, but the different formats implement it in different (and typically incompatible) ways. Just because you author one SMIL file doesn't mean your media will play back in all players. RealNetworks was the earliest adopter of SMIL and has included the most complete SMIL support in its streaming media technology. As a result, the typical streaming media author is likely to be using the RealMedia platform when working with this particular presentation technology. The implementation of the SMIL standard by streaming companies will doubtless continue to evolve, but it needs to begin providing a consistent authoring experience across formats to survive and grow in the long term.

Similar to metafiles, SMIL files are regular text files named with the file suffix .smi or .smil (for example, sample.smil) and are usually served from a Web server.

NOTE

Although SMIL has its own MIME type application/smil, RealMedia-authored SMIL files should be delivered with the audio/x-pn-realaudio MIME type. This ensures that the Web browser passes the file to the RealPlayer. Make sure you do this to reliably have your SMIL files handled by the RealPlayer.

The actual text contents of SMIL files are similar to HTML (XML, more specifically) and include a variety of markup tags that define your presentation. SMIL files are a little less forgiving about failure to follow their strict standard, so make sure you include the relevant / or " characters.

By way of an example, pretend you're using a RealMedia SMIL implementation to link a streaming audio clip to an image of the album cover with text captions of the song lyrics (the bouncing ball effect is up to you).

This SMIL file displays a static image and scrolls lyrics while the audio streams. The lyrics and time codes of when each line begins are contained in the file mulaw.rt. This code actually works and references media on the FezGuys' Web site. Feel free to test it by using a text editor to plug the following code into a file named mulaw.smil and then opening it in your RealPlayer.

```
<smil>
  <head>
    <!--presentation with 1 audio clips, 1 image and 1 lyrics text clip-->
    <meta name="title" content="FezGuys Song With Lyrics"/>
    <layout>
      <root-layout width="550" height="145"/>
      <region id="imageregion" top="0" left="0" width="550" height="105"/>
      <region id="textregion" top="105" left="0" width="550" height="40"
        background-color="#996633" />
    </layout>
  </head>
  <body>
    <par>
```

```
            <!--play these 2 clips simultaneously-->
        <img src="http://www.fezguys.com/images/header-generic.jpg"
            fill="freeze"
            region="imageregion"/>
        <textstream src="http://www.fezguys.com/media/mulaw.rt"
            region="textregion"/>
        <audio
            src="rtsp://rtsp.fezguys.com/www.fezguys.com/media/mulaw-audio.rm"
            region="audioregion"/>
    </par>
  </body>
</smil>
```

The mulaw.rt file uses RealNetworks' RealText technology to define what text to display and at what times. Although the previous example points to a copy of this file on the FezGuys' Web site, you could create your own based on this example.

```
<window type="teleprompter" width="550" height="40" duration="1:38"
    bgcolor="#996633" wordwrap="true">
<font face="system" color="black">
<time begin="4"/>blah blah blah blah
<time begin="8"/> blah mmmwah
<time begin="8.5"/> mmmwah
<time begin="9.5"/> bwah!<br/>
<time begin="13"/>mulaw...
<time begin="16"/>is a companded compression algorithm for
<time begin="19"/> voice
<time begin="20"/> signals<br/>
<time begin="22"/>defined by the geneva recommendations g.7
<time begin="24"/>1
<time begin="25"/>1<br/>
<time begin="28"/>the g.711 recommendation
<time begin="33"/> defines mulaw<br/>
<time begin="35"/>as a method of encoding 16-bit PCM signals into a non-linear 8
-bit format<br/>
<time begin="45"/>the algorithm...
<time begin="49"/> the algorithm is commonly used in european and asian
<time begin="1:00"/>telecommunications...<br/>
<time begin="1:04"/>mulaw
<time begin="1:05"/> is
<time begin="1:06.2"/> very
<time begin="1:06.5"/> very
<time begin="1:06.8"/> very
<time begin="1:07.2"/> very
```

```
<time begin="1:08"/> similar to alaw ...
<time begin="1:11.5"/> however...<br/>
<time begin="1:12"/> each uses a slightly different encoder to encode<br/>
<time begin="1:21"/> hi-ya!
<time begin="1:22"/> babababababababa
<time begin="1:25"/> babababababababa
<time begin="1:27"/> babababababababa
<time begin="1:31"/> yaaaa!
<time begin="1:35"/> lalalaya!
</window>
```

The following table outlines some of the other commonly used SMIL clip tags supported by RealNetworks.

Other Clip Tags Supported by RealNetworks' SMIL

Tag	Used For
animation	Animation clips such as a Flash player file (.swf)
audio	Audio clips such as RealAudio (.rm)
img	JPEG (.jpg), GIF (.gif), or PNG (.png)
ref	Any clip type that is not covered by another attribute, such as a RealPix file (.rp)
text	Static text clips (.txt)
textstream	Streaming RealText clips (.rt)
video	Video or other clips that display continuous motion, such as RealVideo (.rm)

SMIL is useful if you want to synchronize multiple media types to a timeline. A simple text editor is all that's necessary to create SMIL files, although other, more organized tools are available. For more resources about SMIL and these other tools, see the Appendix, "Tools and Resources."

Web Browser Plug-In Controls

Web browser plug-in controls are software tools that control how streaming media is displayed within a Web page. Audio streams are typically accessed through basic links on your Web page to your metafiles. However, as explained in Chapter 12, "Advanced Authoring Techniques," you might instead want to embed your streaming audio using a plug-in control. Each format has its own specific plug-in control, and these controls can be specialized in conjunction with Web browser scripting languages such as JavaScript and VBScript. You can specify which playback controls or status windows are included in a Web page by choosing the appropriate control parameter.

JavaScript or VBScript also enable you to take advantage of the actions of visitors to your Web page. For example, you can create your own image to act as a Play or Stop button or adjust volume when visitors mouse over certain portions of text. In another Web browser plug-in scenario, you can create a personalized jukebox-style interface for your Web visitors to use to listen to your music. Create one frameset that lists all the songs. When visitors click on a song, have it open up in another frameset that includes your own custom Play and Stop buttons.

Web browser plug-in controls are accessed using standard HTML and, as a result, don't require the purchase of a third-party publishing tool. This makes for a quicker authoring process than using a multimedia presentation publishing tool. You can also look at the HTML source code of Web pages that embed audio in a way that appeals to you and simply copy them (respecting copyright notes, if present, and dropping the author an e-mail to make sure she doesn't mind).

Recent Web browser-based technologies such as Cascading Style Sheets (CSS) and Dynamic HTML (DHTML) allow for more advanced control over presentation through a Web page, but these other technologies (Flash, SMIL, and so forth) are more commonly used. DHTML and CSS implementation remains inconsistent among different Web browsers, and people with older browsers can still play Flash, Shockwave and SMIL through plug-ins or external players. Flash and SMIL technologies are specifically designed for this use, so you might as well consider using them.

Microsoft's ActiveX technology is used to control Microsoft's Internet Explorer (MSIE) browser. A third-party plug-in is available for the Netscape browser. Although ActiveX is capable of many other tasks, it's most common streaming audio use is as the MSIE equivalent to the Netscape plug-in architecture. Not surprisingly, ActiveX's use within streaming audio is a lot easier and more reliable when running the MSIE browser from the Windows operating system.

In Chapter 12, you saw how to use ActiveX to embed files from multiple formats into a Web page using each format's specific ActiveX control. These ActiveX controls allow a Web page author the ability to control playback parameters using custom checkboxes or buttons. A general-purpose ActiveX control "ActiveMovie" is available that allows you to integrate popular audio (MPEG, QuickTime, and so on) and video formats into a Web page. Programmers using VBScript can write their own code to interact with ActiveX controls. See the Appendix for more information and tutorials about ActiveX.

Use Web browser plug-in controls (via Microsoft's ActiveX or Netscape's plug-in architecture) if you want to provide more than just a link to a file. For example, you can design your own custom play buttons, customize what player controls are included, or modify the stream's playback based on mouseovers.

Embedding Streaming Audio in Your Web Page

You can "embed" your streaming audio so that it automatically plays from within your Web page rather than from a separately launched player. One advantage to embedding is a shorter amount of time between the moment a listener clicks on your streaming audio's link or icon and when the audio begins to play. Another advantage is design flexibility. Images and text that you design to fit with your site's visual aesthetic can surround files embedded in your Web page. You can also configure your stream to play as soon as the page loads (although a buffering delay will still be present). The embedding process is accomplished using either of these two architectures: a Netscape plug-in or Microsoft's ActiveX.

Embedding your streaming audio is not all wine, roses, and Belgian chocolate. Embedding audio in a Web page increases the time it takes for that page to load. This is because accessing your Web page now also includes loading a player application. Using browser plug-in architecture also makes that browser less stable than accessing that streaming audio from an external player. This instability typically has the browser's plug-in architecture to blame. Although a poorly programmed plug-in can crash in a perfect architecture, an unstable architecture makes it impossible to provide a perfect embedded experience. Both Microsoft's ActiveX and Netscape's plug-in architectures are widely known to be prone to problems.

More memory is also required to run a player from within a Web browser; consequently, browsers crash or the streams often don't play properly. Stability across different Web browsers (Netscape, Internet Explorer, Opera, OmniWeb, and so on) can also be difficult to maintain. In spite of all of those potential streaming horrors, embedding is useful and remains a popular tool.

Until recently, embedded files would operate in both Microsoft's Internet Explorer and Netscape's browsers using only the Netscape plug-in standard. Unfortunately, the new version of Internet Explorer for Windows requires (surprise!) using Microsoft's ActiveX method only. Because Netscape doesn't support ActiveX, the embedding process has become somewhat longer and more involved and requires more information.

NOTE

A plug-in to enable Netscape to handle ActiveX is available. Unfortunately, it's not recommended you use it because it combines two technologies of questionable stability.

RealMedia, Windows Media, and QuickTime all have their own plug-ins to embed their format into a Web page. For these formats, the necessary components are installed with the player software. MP3 can play through the plug-ins of any of the other three formats. MP3 also can be embedded using other systems such as Macromedia's Shockwave.

The examples that follow include both the Netscape plug-in <EMBED> tag as well as the ActiveX <OBJECT> tag. This ensures that your Web page will work with any browser that supports either architecture.

The bottom line on embedding streaming audio on your Web page is this: If you don't need it, don't use it! That's the best way to help guarantee that your streaming audio plays smoothly. If you do choose to embed, then consider also offering a separate link to play your streams in an external player. Those who experience problems using the embed process (or merely prefer to use an external player) will appreciate having the option.

Example: Embedding RealMedia in Your Web Page

When embedding your RealMedia encoded streaming audio, you point to a metafile (as usual), but instead of using the .ram file suffix, you use .rpm. The contents of the .rpm file are the same as the .ram file. All you're doing here is using the correct MIME type. For the correct MIME type for your Web server, see Chapter 7, "Serving Your Audio."

You have several choices regarding the information you can include in your Web page when embedding your audio stream. To start, you need to choose a size (height and width) and the controls (play buttons, status bar, and so on) to include. Advanced users can experiment until they find something that works for their needs. For now, try this simple example:

```
<OBJECT ID=RAOCX
    CLASSID="clsid:CFCDAA03-8BE4-11cf-B84B-0020AFBBCCFA"
    HEIGHT="100" WIDTH="375">
    <PARAM NAME="CONTROLS" VALUE="all">
    <PARAM NAME="AUTOSTART" Value="false">
    <PARAM NAME="SRC" VALUE="http://www.fezguys.com/samples/sample.rpm">
<EMBED
    HEIGHT="100" WIDTH="375"
    CONTROLS="all"
    SRC="http://www.fezguys.com/samples/sample.rpm"
    TYPE="audio/x-pn-realaudio-plugin"
    AUTOSTART="false">
</EMBED>
</OBJECT>
```

The preceding example links to sample.rpm, which is a metafile that contains the URL of the stream:

```
rtsp://streaming.fezguys.com/samples/sample.rm
```

For more detailed information on embedding RealMedia files, see RealNetworks' guide to extended plug-in parameters at the following URL:

```
http://service.real.com/help/library/guides/extend/embed.htm
```

Example: Embedding Windows Media in Your Web Page

When embedding Windows Media files, you point to a metafile (sample.asx) as usual.

The example that follows uses version 6.4 of the ActiveX control. This makes your Web page backward compatible to earlier versions of the Windows Media Player. ActiveX version 6.4 support is included as part of Windows Media Player 7.0. Note: As mentioned earlier, this example includes a plug-in for Netscape.

```
<OBJECT ID="MediaPlayer" WIDTH=300 HEIGHT=50
  CLASSID="CLSID:22D6f312-B0F6-11D0-94AB-0080C74C7E95"
  STANDBY="Loading Windows Media Player components..."
  TYPE="application/x-oleobject"   CODEBASE="http://activex.microsoft.com/activex/con-
trols/mplayer/en/nsmp2inf.cab#Version=6,4,7,1112">
  <PARAM name="filename" value="http://www.fezguys.com/samples/sample.asx">
  <PARAM name="autoStart" value="false">
  <EMBED TYPE="application/x-mplayer2"
    NAME="MediaPlayer"
    SRC="http://www.fezguys.com/samples/sample.asx"
    AUTOSTART="false"
    WIDTH=300 HEIGHT=50>
  </EMBED>
</OBJECT>
```

The preceding example links to a `sample.asx` metafile containing the URL to the real stream:

```
mms://streaming.fezguys.com/samples/sample.wma
```

Example: Embedding QuickTime in Your Web Page

You'll be using the same approach as in Chapter 7, except that you'll be changing the tag that caused the stream to open in an external QuickTime player to instead open within the browser's embedded plug-in. Do this by changing a parameter in both the <OBJECT> and <EMBED> tags, replacing the following:

```
TARGET="quicktimeplayer"
```

with this:

```
TARGET="myself"
```

The code from Chapter 7 would be changed to look like this:

```
<OBJECT CLASSID="clsid:02BF25D5-8C17-4B23-BC80-D3488ABDDC6B"
    WIDTH="160" HEIGHT="120"
    CODEBASE="http://www.apple.com/qtactivex/qtplugin.cab">
<PARAM NAME="SRC" VALUE="poster.mov">
```

```
<PARAM NAME="CONTROLLER" VALUE="false">
<PARAM NAME="HREF" VALUE="rtsp://streaming.fezguys.com/samples/sample.mov">
<PARAM NAME="TARGET" VALUE="myself">
<EMBED TYPE="video/quicktime"
    SRC="poster.mov"
    HREF="rtsp://streaming.fezguys.com/samples/sample.mov"
    WIDTH="160" height="120"
    CONTROLLER="false"
    TARGET="myself">
</EMBED>
</OBJECT>
```

The preceding example links to the poster movie poster.mov and includes in the HTML code the URL that actually contains the audio:

rtsp://streaming.fezguys.com/samples/sample.mov

For more detailed information on embedding QuickTime files, see Apple's guide at www.apple.com/quicktime/authoring/embed.html.

Example: Embedding MP3 in Your Web Page

As mentioned previously, you can use the plug-ins of other formats to play MP3 streams as follows:

RealMedia: Within the text of your .rpm metafile, simply change the URL (for your RealMedia stream) to the URL of your MP3 stream in the Step-by-Step, "Embedding RealMedia in Your Web Page."

Windows Media: Change the text in your .asx metafile to the URL of your MP3 stream (similar to the RealMedia Step-by-Step).

QuickTime: Change the HREF parameter to your MP3 stream's URL. The QuickTime player plug-in doesn't support playing live MP3 streams.

Shockwave: You can also use the free Shockwave plug-in that comes with the Shockwave player (information available at www.shockwave.com).

Offering Multiple Links to the Same Audio

Although the owners of each streaming format would like you to believe that their format is the best (and most popular), average home users don't care which format you use as long as it works. Listeners might or might not have any one or more players for these formats on their computer. One of the best ways to ensure that the user can easily listen to your audio is to make it available in more than one format—actually, in as many formats as possible. In some cases, this might not be realistic. At the very least, provide two formats. By providing multiple formats, you can also track what your audience prefers and even ask your listeners which format they find to be the most reliable and stable. Remember to include links to the Web sites from which your listeners can download the relevant players. Your listener might not have the most recent version of a particular player, and new players are easily downloaded and installed.

NOTE

If you are streaming audio for a small group of private users (such as a corporate intranet or a family Web site), you can get away with using a single format.

Including multiple formats on your site is a straightforward process. When authoring your on-demand files, simply author to multiple formats, upload as usual, create metafiles, and link to each. When providing multiple formats for a live stream, you need to author a separate stream for each format. This will likely require multiple authoring and serving computers. It's easy for listeners to become confused with many links to the same audio content, so spend a little extra time designing your Web page to clearly identify each format's link. Consider encouraging one format (offering the others as backups) to potentially take some of the guesswork out of a listener's experience. Listeners without knowledge of the various formats shouldn't have to decide between one and the other. You can organize your streaming files by placing the link for each format next to the information that identifies that particular file (a common practice), or you can organize your files in groups based on the format. It's important to have your page look good, of course, but it's more important that listeners be able to use it.

Playlists

To play numerous streams in a particular order, use a playlist. When the first stream in a playlist ends, the player then moves on to the next one, and so on, until the list is completely traversed. Playlist support for RealMedia, Windows Media, and MP3 is handled by the player application. QuickTime handles playlists differently, implementing this feature within the server. RealMedia, Windows Media, and MP3 use metafiles to define their playlists. QuickTime requires configuration through the QTSS or DSS server administrator program. RealMedia, Windows Media, and MP3 (but not QuickTime) make it easy for playlists to contain streams from disparate servers and also can include live streams in a playlist. Occasionally, a playlist is used when placing a brief audio clip as a station ID before a live stream begins. Playlists are most commonly used, however, for on-demand (as opposed to live) streaming audio.

Sometimes playback of a live stream may become disconnected because of temporary network congestion. Using a playlist allows you to list the same live stream multiple times so that the player will immediately attempt to reconnect to the next entry.

If you have a Web site with lots of streaming audio, you can provide a simple way for listeners to easily access a playlist or even create their own. As the Web master of your site, you can choose a predetermined, a randomly generated, or a user-selected playlist (or a combination of all three) based on any criteria you can imagine. If you're streaming files for which you don't own the rights, then provisions of the DMCA will limit you (see the Appendix).

To create playlists for RealMedia, Windows Media, and MP3, refer to the section on metafiles in Chapter 7. Follow the details to include multiple entries in a single metafile. Technically, any metafile is a playlist, whether it contains a single URL or a hundred URLs. To create playlists for QuickTime, choose Playlist Settings within the Streaming Server Administrator and follow the intuitive selection process from on-demand files you've already uploaded.

You can get creative with playlists. Following are some ideas:

- **The Author Scenario**—Your band has 10 albums but not a "best of" album. You can create a playlist of your favorite material to introduce your music to new listeners. All you need is the encoded files and the server URLs. After you've chosen your songs, simply create a playlist of those URLs in a metafile.

- **The Random Scenario**—Create a playlist containing a randomly generated list of songs (compiled from every song available) on your Web site. Your random playlist generator program creates a different random list each time a listener accesses it. For this scenario, you need to know how to program using a language that can be integrated into your Web server. You can also use JavaScript, which you include as part of your Web page. Common browsers support JavaScript. Most commonly used tools use the standard Common Gateway Interface (CGI) specification that allows Web pages to connect to locally run programs. Perl is the most commonly used language for writing CGI programs. You need to know Perl and also how to configure your Web server to allow access to your program. Remember to create playlists so that they contain only one format and are delivered with the correct MIME type. You can also limit how many (and which) songs are included.

- **The Listener Scenario**—Allow the listener to create a playlist using every song on your Web site. The difference here is that you allow a list based on the listener's own criteria. Like the prior example, you need to know how to program using a language (including JavaScript) that can be integrated into your Web server. This is a more complicated process than before, and you have to provide a Web-based form to the listener in which they can select what they want. You can get very advanced for how you allow listeners to add songs. Listeners could receive a complete list all at once, or they could add items to a playlist as they browse your site.

Summary

You can include streaming audio in a Web page in many ways. Although there's no single right way, there are varying levels of difficulty and the important issue of appropriate use. Playlists, multiple links, embedding, and presentation technologies all contribute to the creation of new art forms. People are finding original uses for the streaming medium while working within the current limitations of the technologies. The media hype continually points to the day when every home and office will have broadband and people will be streaming full-length, full-color movies with high-fidelity multi-track surround sound back and forth to each other at the click of a mouse. The reality is that it won't be happening anytime soon. But think of it as a challenge. How do you get your point across within the tight confines of available resources? Show us what you got!

APPENDIX

Tools and Resources

Streaming audio's popularity explosion is accompanied by a dizzying array of software. People looking to simplify the process, turn a quick buck, or merely monopolize the industry are leaping into the fray. This chapter contains some popular tools listed along with URLs. The lists start with free products, progress to affordable, and end with pricey. To gauge the correct product for your individual needs will require some deeper research on your part. To assist your research this Appendix also includes certain online resources that provide extensive lists of available software we don't have room to document. You can take control of the process and do the search yourself in your favorite search engine, too. Start out by searching on the software type ("rippers," "encoders," and so on).

NOTE

A good place to start is Download.com (`www.download.com`). The site has many well-organized categories for downloads of all different flavors. Some are freeware, some are share-ware, and some have a set purchase price required before use.

Waveform Editors

The waveform editors listed here handle all the basic tasks similarly, and the more expensive commercial ones often provide better quality for more complex operations such as sample rate reduction. Many provide limited demo versions you can first download and use to get a feel for whether it's worth paying for. There are decidedly fewer waveform editor downloads when compared, for instance, to players. This makes sense when you think just how much more complicated it is to create a waveform editor then a player. However, a search for "waveform editors" does bring up many interesting Web sites, and some of these sites also offer extra education and information relevant to the use (and abuse) of digital audio.

- **Audacity** — http://audacity.sourceforge.net. Linux/FreeBSD, Windows, Macintosh.
- **CoolEdit (Syntrillium Software)** — www.cooledit.com. Windows.
- **Ecawave (Kai Vehmanen)** — www.wakkanet.fi/~kaiv/ecawave. Linux.
- **GoldWave (GoldWave Inc.)** — www.goldwave.com. Windows.
- **Peak (Bias Inc.)** — www.bias-inc.com. Macintosh.
- **Sound Forge (Sonic Foundry)** — www.sonicfoundry.com. Windows.
- **SoundEdit (Macromedia)** — www.macromedia.com. Macintosh.
- **WaveForm Editor** — http://linux.davecentral.com/projects/waveformeditor/. Linux.
- **WaveLab (Steinberg)** — www.steinberg.net. Windows.
- **DMOZ Audio Editors Directory** — www.dmoz.org/Computers/Multimedia/Music_and_Audio/Software/Editors.

Rippers

Many of the tools listed here provide CD track extraction (ripping) as part of a larger set of features; therefore, these might also appear in searches on other streaming audio software categories. If you already have a waveform editor, it might handle ripping, so take a moment to check. When researching rippers, check for CDDB or FreeDB support to helpfully provide CD artist and track information when naming your extracted tracks. An online search for the phrase "CD ripper" or "CD rippers" using the Google.com search engine turns up hundreds of choices of freeware, shareware, and purchasable CD rippers.

- **AudioCatalyst(Xing/RealNetworks)** — www.xingtech.com/. Windows.
- **AudioGrabber (Jackie Franck)** — www.audiograbber.com-us.net. Also encodes to MP3. Windows.
- **Exact Audio Copy (Andre Wiethoff)** — www.exactaudiocopy.de. Good for scratched CDs, also encodes to various formats. Windows.

- **daGrab (Marcello Urbani)** — `http://linux.tucows.com/mmedia/preview/8150.html`. Linux/FreeBSD.

- **iTunes (Apple)** — `www.apple.com/itunes`. Macintosh.

- **Media Jukebox (J. River)** — `www.mediajukebox.com`. Windows.

- **RealJukebox (RealNetworks)** — `www.real.com/rjcentral`. Windows.

- **Google's Ripper Directory** — `http://directory.google.com/Top/Computers/Multimedia/Music_and_Audio/Audio_Formats/MP3/Software/Rippers/`.

Encoders

Although seemingly endless encoders are available for MP3, the most common encoders for RealMedia, Windows Media, and QuickTime are those made by the company behind each format. An online search for the word "encoder" using the Google.com search engine turns up hundreds of choices.

Each of the following handles both live and on-demand streaming for its format:

- **Windows Media Encoder (Microsoft)** — `www.microsoft.com/windows/windowsmedia`. Windows. Live and on-demand.

- **RealProducer (RealNetworks)** — `www.realnetworks.com/products/producer`. Windows, Macintosh, Linux/FreeBSD/Solaris. Live and on-demand.

QuickTime Pro handles on-demand authoring for the QuickTime format. A number of other applications provide live QuickTime streams, a few of which are listed:

- **QuickTime Pro (Apple)** — `www.apple.com/quicktime`. Macintosh, Windows. On-demand only.

- **Sorensen Broadcaster (Sorenson)** — `www.sorenson.com`. Macintosh, Windows. Live QuickTime.

- **Coolstream (Evological)** — `www.evological.com/coolstream.html`. Macintosh. Live QuickTime.

- **Live Channel (Channel Storm)** — `www.channelstorm.com`. Macintosh. Live QuickTime.

MP3 has numerous products available to handle on-demand encoding, but for live streams, the choices are considerably less. For on-demand MP3 files, the two most popular encoding engines (also called "codecs"—the part that does the actual encoding) are LAME and Fraunhofer. The company that creates the encoder usually licenses the Fraunhofer codec (it is packaged with the software). LAME usually needs to be downloaded separately (from `www.mp3dev.org`, where you can view the list of software that supports it).

Following are some common software tools to encode on-demand MP3 files:

- **AudioGrabber (Jackie Franck)** — `www.audiograbber.com-us.net`. Windows.

- **iTunes (Apple)** — `www.apple.com/itunes`. Macintosh.

- **Blade (Tord Jansson)** — `http://bladeenc.mp3.no/`. Windows/ Macintosh/FreeBSD/Linux.

The following lists some common software and hardware tools to encode a live MP3 stream:

- **Winamp SHOUTcast Plug-in (Nullsoft)** — `www.shoutcast.com/ download/broadcast.phtml`. Windows.

- **LiveIce (Icecast)** — `http://star.arm.ac.uk/%7Espm/software/liveice. html`. Linux/FreeSBD.

- **DarkIce (ákos Maróy)** — `darkice.sourceforge.net`. Linux/FreeSBD.

- **Xstream (Telos)** — `www.telos-systems.com/?/zephyr`. Dedicated hardware.

- **MaxxStream (Waves LTD)** — `www.maxxstream.com`. Dedicated hardware (running Windows).

For a considerable resource on MP3-related tools, check out `http:// software.mp3.com/software` or `http://www.mp3-encoders.com`.

Batch encoders support a wide variety of formats to easily encode a group of on-demand files. Here are two of the more popular:

- **Cleaner5 (Discreet)** — `www.discreet.com/products/cleaner/`. Macintosh, Windows.

- **Barbabatch (Audio Ease)** — `www.audioease.com/Pages/Barbabatch/ BarbaMain.html`. Macintosh.

Also, MP3 users might find the following batch ID3 tag editor handy, especially when working with batch encoders that don't support ID3 tag creation (such as Cleaner5):

- **Easy ID3 Editor (Audio Ease)** — `www.software-innovations.net/id3`. Windows.

Players

Many streaming media players can play more than one format. Most can play raw WAV and/or AIFF files, and the RealMedia, QuickTime, and Windows Media players can all play MP3 files as well.

- **RealPlayer (RealNetworks)** — `www.real.com`. Macintosh, Windows, Unix (Linux/FreeBSD/Solaris/IRIX/and so on).
- **Windows Media Player (Microsoft)** — `www.microsoft.com/windows/ windowsmedia`. Macintosh, Windows, Unix (Solaris).
- **QuickTime Player (Apple)** — `www.apple.com/quicktime/download`. Macintosh, Windows.

Because so many third-party MP3 players are available, the following presents a short list of those that can handle streaming. (Many can only handle playback of downloaded files.)

- **Audion (Panic)** — `www.panic.com/audion`. Macintosh.
- **iTunes (Apple)** — `www.apple.com/itunes`. Macintosh.
- **Macamp (Subband Software)** — `www.macamp.com`. Macintosh.
- **Media Jukebox (J. River)** — `www.mediajukebox.com`. Also acts as a ripper and encoder, with some degree of support for RealMedia, Windows Media, and QuickTime formats. Windows.
- **mxaudio (Xaudio)** — `http://download.cnet.com/downloads/ 0-10146-100-910010.html`. Linux/FreeBSD.
- **Sonique (Lycos)** — `www.sonique.com`. Windows.
- **Winamp (Nullsoft)** — `www.winamp.com`. Windows.
- **xmms** — `www.xmms.org`. Linux/FreeBSD.

Audio Processing

Although most waveform editors include basic audio-processing capabilities, more advanced users might want to go the extra step to purchase higher quality software and hardware. Following are a few useful audio-processing tools:

- **Waves** — www.kswaves.com. Macintosh, Windows.
- **Orban** — www.orban.com. Dedicated hardware.
- **Omnia 3net (Telos)** — www.omniaaudio.com. Dedicated hardware.

DJ Software

Companies and individuals looking to pick up software packages to simplify the often overwhelming task of organizing playlists and incorporating ads and even a live DJ on a microphone can check out these products. A few companies are anticipating this growth area in the streaming media market by creating DJ software.

- **OtsJuke DJ (Ots Corporation)** — www.otsjuke.com. Windows.
- **SAM — Streaming Audio Manager (Spacial*Audio Solutions)** — www.spacialaudio.com. Windows.

Legal Resources

This section contains some useful Web sites to further your knowledge of legal issues regarding online audio. These issues surrounding the online transfer and "fair use" of music have not yet been fully codified. One of the side benefits to the Internet's anarchic way of working is that you'll see many conflicting viewpoints. Nonetheless, the U.S. Copyright Office gets the last word, and new laws are hashed out on an ongoing basis.

Web Sites About Online Music Use

Following are a handful of worthy Web sites to start you on your never-ending journey toward understanding the practically incomprehensible world where the wishful orderliness of copyright law and the sentient chaos of the Internet warily cohabitate:

- **United States Copyright Office (The Library of Congress)** — http://lcweb.loc.gov/copyright. "To promote the Progress of Science and useful Arts, by securing for limited Times to Authors and Inventors the exclusive Right to their respective Writings and Discoveries" (U.S. Constitution; Article 1, Section 8). The final word.

- **Music Law Offices of Michael P. McCready** — www.music-law.com. This site contains a practical (independent) series of explanations, definitions, and how-to's.

- **ASCAP—Music and Money** —www.ascap.com/musicbiz/money-intro.html. A readable overview (in their own words) on how the whole music publishing system operates can be found here.

- **10 Big Myths about Copyright Explained** — www.templetons.com/brad/copymyths.html. This site is a somewhat passionate Q&A about online music use. Relevant subjects are covered.

- **Final Joint Version of H.R. 2281** — www.eff.org/ip/DMCA/hr2281_dmca_law_19981020_pl105-304.html. The full text of the Digital Millennium Copyright Act (DMCA) can be found here. The DMCA was the first major U.S. governmental foray into online copyright protection.

Industry Trade Groups

Here you'll find the official online presences for organizations that represent key building blocks of the music industry edifice. It's best to interpret the information on these sites with a grain of salt. They don't really know what's happening with the current climate of Internet audio any more than anyone else, although they might try to convince you otherwise. Should you be a dues-paying member of any of these organizations, make sure you make your opinions known to them. They are ostensibly representing you in their expensive lobbying efforts.

- **The Recording Industry Association of America** — www.riaa.org. The Recording Industry Association of America (RIAA) is the trade group that represents the major label music business.

- **The National Music Publishers Association** — www.nmpa.org. The National Music Publishers Association (NMPA) is a clearinghouse for acquiring the permissions (in the form of "licenses") to use other people's music online (and everywhere else).

- **The Harry Fox Agency** — www.nmpa.org/hfa.html. The Harry Fox Agency (HFA) Web page is useful for obtaining licensing. The HFA pages are housed at the National Music Publishers Association.

- **National Association of Broadcasters** — www.nab.org. The National Association of Broadcasters (NAB) is a full-service trade association that promotes and protects the interests of corporate-owned radio and television broadcasters in the United States and around the world. Their site contains a lot of information separate from the Internet, so narrow things down by using their search feature on the word "Internet."

Collection Societies

The principal purpose of collection societies is to make sure that users who play copyrighted music in public areas, such as the Internet, pay fees. These organizations offer a large online presence, and some have useful explanations about current copyright law.

- **The American Society of Composers, Authors, and Publishers (ASCAP)** — www.ascap.com. The largest music-publishing collection society. Many big-name recording stars are members.

- **Broadcast Music, Inc. (BMI)** — www.bmi.com. The second largest music-publishing collection society. Most of the rest of the big-name stars are members.

- **SESAC (formerly The Society of European Stage Authors and Composers)** — www.sesac.com. A collection society that is noteworthy for its recent decision to actually have a Web site.

- **Bug Music** — www.bugmusic.com. A scrappy independent with a long history of egalitarian royalty distribution.

MP3 Licensing and LAME

Although MP3 is an ISO standard, both Fraunhofer-Gesellschaft and Thomson multimedia own patent rights surrounding the MP3 technology. These rights enable them to collect licensing fees (see www.mp3licensing.com) from anyone who makes use of that technology.

The majority of MP3 players and encoders are packaged with the Fraunhofer or LAME encoding engine, paying the appropriate licensing for each copy distributed. However, there is an interesting legal loophole that open source advocates have taken with the LAME software.

LAME is officially distributed in source-code form only, and therefore is not subject to license fees that are attached to the actual use of the technology. Individuals are free to download and compile the source themselves, but then likely will owe MP3 license fees for any use of the technology. Other organizations provide pre-compiled versions of the LAME software on their site, with the caveat that you need to research the legal ramifications yourself.

The www.mp3licensing.com Web site states that they don't issue licenses for individual users, so if you choose to use LAME, we recommend that you contact them inquiring what the appropriate process is to pay for your single private use, and offer to send in money. A company that sells MP3 software can expect to pay between $2.50 and $5.00 for each unit, so if they do decide to grant individual licenses, the cost should be affordable.

Although Fraunhofer and Thomson multimedia are unlikely to track you down and sue you if you use an unlicensed version of LAME (or any other MP3) encoding engine, you need to be aware that you would likely be breaking the law.

Additional information is available from:

- www.mp3dev.org – This site is the official Web site for the LAME Project. In particular, www.mp3dev.org/mp3/links.html#patents and the end of www.mp3dev.org/mp3/tech-FAQ.txt contain information pertaining to the patent rights.

- www.win32lame.com – This site allows you to download pre-compiled versions of the LAME encoding engine.

- www.mp3licensing.com – MP3 and MP3PRO patent and software licensing information.

Online Authoring Resources

Okay, so we labored to provide comprehensive, easy to use, all in one tutorials on the big four streaming audio formats. And heaven knows we succeeded, right? But, of course, being the inquisitive and incredulous person you, dear reader, are, you want more. More information, more knowledge and access to more tools. Here it is. Contained in these URLs is everything you wanted to know about the RealAudio, Windows Media, QuickTime and MP3 formats (as well as some other useful info), and were not afraid to ask.

RealMedia

The following Web sites cover everything you always wanted to know about the RealNetworks format, including their proof that it's the world's most popular streaming audio format.

- `service.real.com/learnnav` – All about the site.

- `service.real.com/help/library/encoders.html` — Authoring resources.

- `service.real.com/help/library/servers.html` — Serving resources.

- `service.real.com/learnnav/rp1.html` — Web integration resources.

- `service.real.com/help/library/guides/productionguidepreview/HTML/realpgd.htm` — The RealSystem IQ production guide. Lots of information.

- `service.real.com/kb` — Searchable support database.

Windows Media

These Web sites tell the full tale of the Windows Media streaming format. It's all here, including why this is also the world's most popular streaming audio format.

- `www.microsoft.com/windows/windowsmedia/WM7/encoder/faq.asp` — Windows Media Encoder 7.1 frequently asked questions page for certain authoring resources.

- `www.microsoft.com/windows/windowsmedia/create/encode.asp` — Select the Third Party Tools link for a list of Microsoft-approved third-party tools.

- `www.microsoft.com/windows/windowsmedia/distribute.asp` — Serving resources.

- `www.microsoft.com/windows/windowsmedia/create/embed.asp` — Web integration resources.

- `msdn.microsoft.com/library/default.asp?url=/library/en-us/dnwmt/html/buildingwm.asp` — Bonus! Building a Windows Media Encoding workstation.

QuickTime

Thankfully, these excellent Web sites that cover important QuickTime information do not also tell you that theirs is the most popular streaming audio format in the world.

- `www.apple.com/quicktime/products/tutorials` — Authoring resources and QuickTime tutorials.

- `www.apple.com/quicktime/products/qtss/qtssfaq.html` — Serving resources and frequently asked questions about QTSS.

- `www.apple.com/quicktime/authoring/qtwebfaq.html` — Web integration and QuickTime for the Web FAQ.

MP3 (SHOUTcast)

A monstrously large number of tools, techniques, and Web sites have giant lists of resources for doing anything at all using MP3. Because MP3 and its proponents are a decentralized group, no single representative will hip you to the fact that this actually is the most popular streaming audio "format" on the planet. Following are some favorites:

- `www.shoutcast.com/support/docs` — Fill your brain with all things SHOUTcast! Covers authoring, serving, and linking MP3 SHOUTcast streams. It also includes links to an online forum where you can post questions and get help from SHOUTcast developers and other SHOUTcast users. If you enter the forum, make sure you read the item at the top labeled Sticky: Read Before Posting because it's a resource of links to answers of common questions.

- `www.icecast.org` — Covers all things Icecast (a compatible alternative to SHOUTcast for MP3 streaming).

- `http://software.mp3.com` — A comprehensive resource for all types of MP3 and audio software.

Other

As with any complex system, there are as many ways to get results as there are tools to make it happen. Here's a starter list. A little time spent with your favorite search engine will doubtless reveal many more.

- `www.macromedia.com/software/flash/productinfo/tutorials/gettingstarted` — Flash: The Tutorial.

- `www.macromedia.com/software/director/productinfo/tutorials` — Shockwave: The other tutorial.

- `http://msdn.microsoft.com/workshop/components/activex/tutorial.asp` — Microsoft ActiveX tutorial.

- `www.zdnet.com/devhead/stories/articles/0,4413,2193724,00.html` — Another Microsoft ActiveX tutorial.

- `www.streamingmedia.net/tutorials` — About half of these streaming media (audio and video) tutorials concern audio.

- `www.r3mix.net` — Comprehensive "not for beginners" MP3 encoding resource. Good stuff.

- `www.w3.org/AudioVideo` — Good odds predict that this online SMIL resource is the biggest.

- `smw.internet.com/smil/tools/authoring.html` — A list of SMIL authoring tools (free and pay) and some SMIL utilities.

- `www.tapeop.com` — Not necessarily about streaming audio per se, but chock-full of useful information about creative ways to record audio with inexpensive solutions (digital and analog) and all written in a real-world, no-hype style.

- `www.fezguys.com` — No online resource concerning streaming audio is complete without this useful and common sense Web site!

- `www.omniaaudio.com/techinfo/dabtech/default.htm` — The Frank Foti (Cutting Edge) white paper titled: "Audio Processing for Digital Audio Broadcasting and the Internet." A surprisingly easy-to-read document from a well-informed engineer.

- `www.digido.com/compression.html` — Useful information about compression.

- `www.webmonkey.com` — Not about streaming audio per se, but loaded with helpful information about Web development for everyone from beginners to experts.

Content Delivery Networks

Following is a short list of the most popular Content Delivery Networks out there. This book doesn't endorse any of them, and encourages you to shop around, comparing and contrasting the services of the smaller outfits that might be local to you. If you aren't streaming the Super Bowl, you can probably get away with a smaller (and cheaper) solution.

- **Activate** — www.activate.net
- **Akamai** — www.akamai.com
- **Digex, Inc.** — www.digex.com
- **Digital Island** — www.digitalisland.com
- **Digital Pipe** — www.digitalpipe.com
- **DVLabs** — www.dvlabs.com
- **EON Streams** — www.eonstreams.com
- **Globix** — www.globix.com
- **iBEAM Broadcasting** — www.ibeam.com
- **Playstream** — www.playstream.com
- **RealBroadcastNetwork** — www.realnetworks.com/products/rbn/
- **Speedera** — www.speedera.com
- **Streaming Media Corp** — www.smc.net
- **Yahoo! Broadcast Business Services** — http://business.broadcast.com

Following are some other independently compiled Content Delivery Network lists. You can also find many more by doing an online search for "Content Delivery Network" or the format of your choice (for example, "RealMedia hosting").

- **Streaming Media** — www.streamingmedia.com/streaming.
  asp?cat=223&cn=CDN. Streaming Media is primarily a publishing company (online and print) waving a flag for the streaming industry. The Web site has a serviceable list of companies that provide live streaming support to organizations and individuals.

- **WebReference.com** — www.webreference.com/internet/software/
  site_management/cdns.html. This reference site has been around a while and includes a variety of other Web resources.

GLOSSARY

Several of the terms that follow have more than one meaning in the English language. In the context of this book, they are defined by their relevance to streaming audio.

aDSL (Asynchronous Digital Subscriber Line/Loop)   An Internet connectivity technology that transfers data at different speeds depending on the direction the traffic is flowing. Typically used from home where data can be downloaded from the Internet faster than it can be served out to the Internet at large. *See also* sDSL.

AES/EBU (Audio Engineering Society/European Broadcast Union)
A digital audio data transmission standard to connect digital audio gear. Adopted by the Audio Engineering Society and the European Broadcast Union.

AIFF (Audio Interchange File Format)   A high-quality raw (uncompressed) audio format developed by Apple Computer. Most commonly used on the Macintosh operating system.

analog   A copy of audio as it exists in physical (as opposed to digital) space. Represented by continuous waveform changes and in a variety of mediums (phonograph, magnetic tape, and so on).

attributes   Aspects or indicators of an individual file's content, character, and ways in which the file is used and translated.

author (verb)   The act of creating streaming audio.

bandwidth   1.) In the realm of data transmission, the amount of information that can be sent through any digital connection. Usually used to measure the speed of a connection to the Internet. Measured in bits per second (bps). 2.) In the realm of audio equalization, a range of audio frequency, usually measured in Hertz (cycles per second). *See also* unicast, multicast.

batch   Any group of digital files.

bit (binary digit)   The smallest unit of data in a computer with a single value, either 0 or 1. Commonly abbreviated as a lowercase b. *See also* Kb, Mb.

bit rate   The rate (or speed) at which bits of data are transmitted, usually measured in bits per second (bps). Sometimes referred to as *data rate*.

broadband   A loose definition for any network with a high enough data rate (typically at or above 128kbps) to transfer audio, video, and other large files in real-time. *See also* bandwidth 1).

buffer   A temporary holding area for data. Commonly used in streaming media when data is transferred over the Internet and a reliable transmission speed is not available.

burner   A hardware device to imprint ("burn") data onto a plastic writable CD-ROM disc.

byte   A unit of data totaling 8 bits, abbreviated as a capital B. *See also* bit, KB, MB.

CDDB   A company with a large online database of information (track names, artist names, and so forth) about released CDs. Recently renamed Gracenote.

CDN (content delivery network)   The descriptive name for a company whose services mainly include streaming your source media to others through the Internet.

CGI (Common Gateway Interface)   A method of making computer programs talk to Web servers.

client   A computer that requests information or services from another computer. *See also* server.

clock-speed   A measurement of how fast a computer performs certain operations, usually measured in megahertz (millions of cycles per second). *See also* MHz.

clone   An imitation of a brand name computer that mimics design and operating system and is sold at a lower price.

co-location facility   A secure physical location where you place your server computers for high-speed network access.

codec   A COmpression/DECompression process that radically shrinks multimedia files for storage or transfer before either returning them to their normal size or reconstructing them to an approximation of their original state.

concurrent   One or more audio streams being served at the same time.

connectivity   The presence (and often speed) of a connection to the Internet or any network of computers.

DC Offset   A grounding incompatibility manifesting as added noise in a digital file.

decoder   Software or hardware that turns encoded information back into its original pre-encoded form or a close approximation. *See also* encoder.

DHTML (dynamic hypertext markup language)   A loose, unofficial standard to increase the interactivity of a Web page.

digital   The representation of information as unique units. The units are binary digits of either 1 or 0 (sometimes referred to as *on* or *off*).

DLT (Digital Linear Tape)   A magnetic tape storage medium for computer data backups.

DNS (Domain Name System)   A system to translate Internet domain names into a series of numbers. Sort of like the Yellow Pages for the Internet so that people only need to remember a recognizable name instead of a number.

download (noun)   A specific piece of software, multimedia, or other data that is transferred across a network from a server to another computer.

downloading   The act of transferring a specific piece of software, multimedia, or other data from a server computer to a user across a network.

DSL (Digital Subscriber Line)   A technology for transferring data using ordinary copper telephone wires. *See also* aDSL, sDSL.

DSP (Digital Signal Processor)   A specialized microprocessor for handling digitized audio or video.

dynamic range   In audio, the difference between the loudest and softest sections.

embed   A textual "tag" of HTML describing an object to be included as part of a Web page.

encoder   Software or hardware designed to convert raw, uncompressed audio into a highly compressed format for quick transfer over a network. *See also* decoder.

equalization   Raising or lowering a single frequency (or set of frequencies) within a piece of audio.

Ethernet   A standard protocol for connecting computers in a local area network.

fade in   A volume increase (from silence to audibility) of a sound. *See also* fade out.

fade out   A volume decrease (from audibility to silence) of a sound. *See also* fade in.

fair use   Limited legally sanctioned situations in which copyrighted material(s) can be used without permission of the copyright holder.

Flash   Multimedia publishing software/technology from Macromedia.

format (streaming audio format)   All of the pieces created by a company (or any ad hoc group) to encode, stream, decode, and play back streaming media.

frameset   Tags of HTML script to divide a Web page into subsections called *frames*.

FreeBSD   A popular open source version of the Unix operating system.

frob   A little hardware box with several kinds of input and output connectors allowing different plug ends to be used to pass audio between disparate hardware.

FTP (File Transfer Protocol)   A method for transferring files from one computer to another over a network.

G.722   A wideband speech coding standard from the CCITT (Commite' Consultatif International de Telecommunications et Telegraphy). The CCITT is an international union that makes technical recommendations about telephone and data communication.

gain   Overall audio volume.

gateway (network gateway) Software or hardware that connects two networks together, such as a LAN to the Internet.

GB (gigabyte) A measure of data storage quantity. 1024 MV, or 2^{30} bytes (approximately 1 billion bytes).

hardware A piece of computer or audio equipment with mass. A physical object.

host A single computer on a network that provides services or data to other computers on the network.

HTTP (Hypertext Transfer Protocol) The most common protocol for transferring data between Web servers and Web browsers.

ID3-tag Information within a file (most commonly MP3 files) that documents title, artist, year of release, genre, album, and so on.

IP address (Internet Protocol address) A series of numbers used to identify a computer on a network. *See also* DNS.

ISDN (Integrated Services Digital Network) Dedicated telecommunication connections for voice and data with bandwidth up to 128Kbps. The set data rate is solidly and fully available at all times whether the user is using it or not.

ISP (Internet service provider) A company that provides Internet service, typically including basic connectivity, e-mail, and other related services.

JavaScript A Netscape-based scripting language for Web pages.

Kb (kilobit) A measure of data storage quantity (also called kbit or Kbit). 1024 bits, or 2^{10} bits (approximately one thousand bits). *See also* bit, Mb.

KB (kilobyte) A measure of data storage quantity. 1024 (2^{10}) bytes. *See also* byte, MB.

kbps (kilobits per second) A measure of data throughput transfer speed. 1024 (2^{10}) bits per second.

kHz (kilohertz) A measure of audio frequency. One thousand cycles per second.

LAN (local area network) A network of computers within a limited physical area.

line input   An input that receives a line level signal.

line level   An accepted median level audio signal in a control room.

line level input   The overall volume of an incoming signal.

link   An HTML pointer that leads to a Web page (also called a *hyperlink*).

Linux   A popular open source version of the Unix operating system.

lossless   An audio compression method generally used to shape overall sound quality without inherently degrading the audio quality during the process.

lossy   An audio compression method used to highly compact a file, requiring certain data to be permanently discarded. MPEG (for audio files) and JPEG (for graphics files) compression are two examples of lossy compression.

MB (megabyte)   A measure of data storage quantity. 1024 KB, or 2^{20} bytes (approximately 1 million bytes). *See also* byte, KB.

Mb (megabit)   A measure of data storage quantity (also called mbit or Mbit). 1024 Kb, or 2^{20} bits (approximately one million bits). *See also* bit, Kb.

Mbps (megabits per second)   A measure of data throughput transfer speed. 1024 Kbps or 2^{20} (approximately one million) bits per second. *See also* bit, Kb, Mb.

metadata   Information included with a file that describes that file's contents.

metafile   A file that contains a pointer to the actual streaming content. This file is typically downloaded by a Web browser and then handed off to a player application.

MHz (megahertz)   A measure of the vibration of a tiny quartz crystal inside a computer chip. One MHz equals one million cycles per second.

MIME (Multipurpose Internet Mail Extensions) type   A descriptive string that is tied to a filename's suffix. Used to describe what format the file is, and for applications to choose how to handle those files.

mouseover   Also called a rollover, a technique using JavaScript to change a typically graphic element on a Web page when a user moves their computer's mouse to pass their cursor over the element. This is done to draw attention to the element on the page.

multicast   Communication method that describes a transfer of the same information from one server computer to multiple client computers (listeners) where the server sends just one copy of the data, regardless of the number of listeners. The server bandwidth required is the size of the data alone, regardless of how many clients are receiving the data. *See also* unicast, bandwidth.

normalize   The act of increasing the dynamic range of a digital audio file to a point just below distortion, or, making digital audio as loud as possible without distorting.

open source   1.) Any program whose source code is freely available for use or modification to anyone in any way, provided their resulting works are also open source. What's good about open source is that anyone can modify and improve on it, so the program quickly becomes more useful and a better tool, thereby benefiting everyone. 2.) A certification mark of the Open Source Initiative (OSI). Developers for freely shared and redistributed software can use an OSI trademark when they agree to the Open Source Definition. The OSI Open Source Definition: 1-The distributed software built upon the source code must be freely available to all without restriction. 2-The source code must be freely available. 3-Newer versions require a different name or number.

open system   A framework for conformance testing, certification, and promotion of international standards for computer networks. Covers everything from the transmission of the physical bits all the way up to the GUI interface of a user's application, to enable computer systems that are made by different vendors to communicate with each other.

Perl (Practical Extraction and Report Language)   A popular, free-licensed programming language. Perl scripts are commonly used for Web-related programming applications.

playlist   A list of on-demand or live streams (or previously downloaded files) for an audio player to play in a particular order.

plug-in   A third-party program to enhance the features of an application.

progressive streaming (a.k.a. HTTP streaming)   An on-demand file or live broadcast that will play in the user's player application during the download process instead of waiting until the entire file has finished downloading to play. Commonly served by a Web server via HTTP.

protocol   Strict and detailed rules, standards, or conventions of communication, transfer, and operation among computers.

RAID (Redundant Array of Independent Disks)   A redundant storage method of saving data simultaneously to multiple disks or providing increased performance by splitting data across multiple disks.

RAM (random access memory)   A computer's ephemeral working memory area that is generally composed of physical hardware circuits inside a computer and used as fast temporary data storage during processing.

real-time streaming   A two-way conversation between the streaming audio player and server that provides additional stability and features.

rich-media   A presentation that uses multiple forms of media, ostensibly to provide a better experience for the viewer.

ripping   Extracting audio tracks from a CD into digital files on a computer.

RS-232 serial   A short-range communications cabling standard that is typically used for computer terminals, modems, and other dedicated hardware.

RTSP (Real-Time Streaming Protocol)   A standard protocol for real-time streaming of multimedia on a network. *See also* real-time streaming.

sample rate   In audio, the number of times per second that a sample is taken.

SCSI (Small Computer Systems Interface)   An interface standard for connecting a computer with external devices such as hard drives and scanners. Pronounced *scuzzy*.

sDSL (Synchronous Digital Subscriber Line/Loop)   An Internet connectivity technology that transfers data at the same speed regardless of the direction that the traffic is flowing. *See also* aDSL.

server   A computer on a network that supplies information to a client computer on request. Also refers to the software that performs these functions. *See also* client.

software   Computer programs that guide computer hardware operations and control all functioning capabilities of a computer.

sound card   A circuit board in a computer that adds audio functionality.

standard   Strict and detailed compatibility specifications of use and manufacture for technologies, software, and hardware.

stereo   Two channels of sound reproduction that allow for audio source position gradations of aural perception between extreme left and right.

streaming audio   Transferring audio data between hardware devices across a network in which the audio data causes the audio to start playing on the client computer or device as the data begins to arrive at the client computer or device.

subwoofer   A speaker that is designed to reproduce only the lowest frequencies in the sound spectrum.

tag   Code within data with formatting (or other) instructions.

TCP/IP   Transmission Control Protocol (TCP) running over Internet Protocol (IP) that enables communication over disparate computers and networks.

unicast   Communication method that describes a transfer of the same information from one server computer to multiple client computers (listeners) where each client is sent a completely separate copy of the data. The server requires bandwidth for each client that is connecting, regardless of whether all clients are accessing the same data. *See also* multicast, bandwidth.

Unix   A multitasking, multiuser operating system that is available in a number of different forms, many of which are free. Unix is known for its reliability and ability to efficiently perform many tasks at once.

URL (uniform resource locator)   A standard way to describe the location of data (Web pages, streaming audio, email, and so on) on the Internet.

variable bit rate (VBR)   The process of encoding a streaming audio file at varying bit rates across the length of the audio, determined by quality, and intended primarily to improve streaming efficiency.

WAV   A high-quality audio format developed by Microsoft Corporation and the most common raw audio format used on the Windows operating system.

waveform   The graphic representation of the shape of a sound.

W3C (World Wide Web Consortium)   A group of organizations that decide standards and protocols for the World Wide Web.

Index

VOICES THAT MATTER

HOW TO CONTACT US

VISIT OUR WEB SITE

WWW.NEWRIDERS.COM

On our web site, you'll find information about our other books, authors, tables of contents, and book errata. You will also find information about book registration and how to purchase our books, both domestically and internationally.

EMAIL US

Contact us at: **nrfeedback@newriders.com**

- If you have comments or questions about this book
- To report errors that you have found in this book
- If you have a book proposal to submit or are interested in writing for New Riders
- If you are an expert in a computer topic or technology and are interested in being a technical editor who reviews manuscripts for technical accuracy

Contact us at: **nreducation@newriders.com**

- If you are an instructor from an educational institution who wants to preview New Riders books for classroom use. Email should include your name, title, school, department, address, phone number, office days/hours, text in use, and enrollment, along with your request for desk/examination copies and/or additional information.

Contact us at: **nrmedia@newriders.com**

- If you are a member of the media who is interested in reviewing copies of New Riders books. Send your name, mailing address, and email address, along with the name of the publication or web site you work for.

BULK PURCHASES/CORPORATE SALES

The publisher offers discounts on this book when ordered in quantity for bulk purchases and special sales. For sales within the U.S., please contact: Corporate and Government Sales (800) 382-3419 or **corpsales@pearsontechgroup.com**. Outside of the U.S., please contact: International Sales (317) 581-3793 or **international@pearsontechgroup.com**.

WRITE TO US

New Riders Publishing
201 W. 103rd St.
Indianapolis, IN 46290-1097

CALL/FAX US

Toll-free (800) 571-5840
If outside U.S. (317) 581-3500
Ask for New Riders
FAX: (317) 581-4663

New Riders

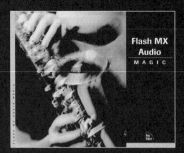

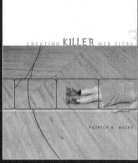

Solutions from experts you know and trust.

www.informit.com

- OPERATING SYSTEMS
- WEB DEVELOPMENT
- PROGRAMMING
- NETWORKING
- CERTIFICATION
- AND MORE...

Expert Access.
Free Content.

New Riders has partnered with **InformIT.com** to bring technical information to your desktop. Drawing on New Riders authors and reviewers to provide additional information on topics you're interested in, **InformIT.com** has free, in-depth information you won't find anywhere else.

- **Master the skills you need, when you need them**

- **Call on resources from some of the best minds in the industry**

- **Get answers when you need them, using InformIT's comprehensive library or live experts online**

- **Go above and beyond what you find in New Riders books, extending your knowledge**

As an **InformIT** partner, **New Riders** has shared the wisdom and knowledge of our authors with you online. Visit **InformIT.com** to see what you're missing.

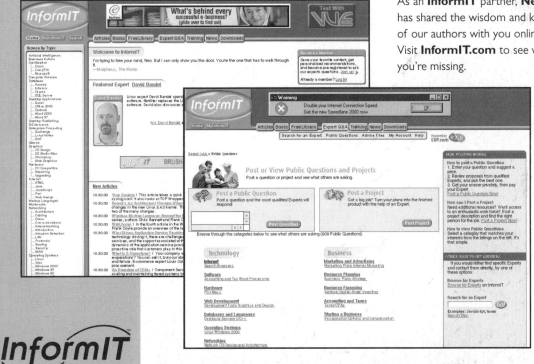

www.informit.com ▪ www.newriders.com

New Riders